IMMIGRANT
VOICES

For Ilan

CONTRIBUTORS
Emily Bruinius
Nancy Carr
Rachel Claff
Steven Craig
Louise Galpine
Allie Hirsch
Patrick Hurley
Mary Klein
Dylan Nelson
Tom Pilcher
Samantha Stankowicz
Donald H. Whitfield
Mary Williams

Cover graphic design: Gregory Borowski
Interior design: THINK Book Works

IMMIGRANT VOICES

21st CENTURY STORIES

EDITED BY

Achy Obejas and Megan Bayles

THE GREAT BOOKS FOUNDATION
A nonprofit educational organization

Published and distributed by

THE GREAT BOOKS FOUNDATION
A nonprofit educational organization

35 E. Wacker Drive, Suite 400
Chicago, IL 60601
www.greatbooks.org

First printing
9 8 7 6 5 4 3 2 1

Library of Congress Cataloging-in-Publications Data

Immigrant Voices : 21st Century Stories / selected and edited by Megan Bayles and
    Achy Obejas.
        pages cm
      ISBN 978-1-933147-65-9 (pbk. : alk. paper) — ISBN 978-1-939014-69-6 (epub) —
    ISBN 978-1-939014-70-2 (kindle) — ISBN 978-1-939014-71-9 (pdf)
        1. Short stories, American. 2. American fiction—Minority authors. 3.
    Immigrants—United States—Literary collections. 4. American fiction—
    21st century. 5. Immigration—Fiction. 6. United States—Emigration and
    immigration—Fiction. I. Bayles, Megan, editor of compilation. II. Obejas, Achy,
    1956- editor of compilation.
    PS647.E85I48 2014
    813'.010892069—dc23
                                                                    2013041068

ABOUT THE GREAT BOOKS FOUNDATION

The Great Books Foundation is an independent, nonprofit educational organization that provides opportunities for people of all ages to become more reflective, critical thinkers and readers through Shared Inquiry™ discussion of written works and ideas of enduring value.

The Great Books Foundation was established in 1947 to promote liberal education for the general public. In 1962, the Foundation extended its mission to children with the introduction of Junior Great Books.® Since its inception, the Foundation has helped thousands of people throughout the United States and in other countries to begin their own discussion groups in schools, libraries, and community centers. Today, Foundation instructors conduct hundreds of workshops each year, in which educators and parents learn to lead Shared Inquiry discussion.

ABOUT THE EDITORS

ACHY OBEJAS is the author of the critically acclaimed novels *Ruins* and *Days of Awe*, as well as three other books of fiction. Her poetry chapbook, *This Is What Happened in Our Other Life,* was both a critical favorite and a bestseller. She edited and translated into English *Havana Noir,* a collection of crime stories by Cuban writers on and off the island. She is also the translator into Spanish of Junot Díaz's *The Brief Wondrous Life of Oscar Wao/La breve y maravillosa vida de Óscar Wao* and *This Is How You Lose Her/Así es como la pierdes.* Currently, Obejas is the Distinguished Visiting Writer at Mills College in Oakland, California.

MEGAN BAYLES is a freelance editor and a doctoral candidate in Cultural Studies at the University of California, Davis, where her research focuses on museum studies and the histories and theories of bodies on display, particularly in medicalized contexts. She and Achy Obejas are Fellows of the Ellen Stone Belic Institute for the Study of Women and Gender in the Arts & Media.

Non-English words have been italicized or not according to the preference of the individual author.

CONTENTS

PREFACE

We are living in an age of unprecedented global mobility. In 2010, the United Nations Department of Economic and Social Affairs estimated that 214 million people migrated internationally. The literature produced by twenty-first-century immigrants both reflects and shapes the shifting definitions of identity—national, ethnic, political, cultural, and personal—in an age in which global communication and the increased ease and speed of travel have made the world a smaller place. *Immigrant Voices: 21st Century Stories* focuses on immigration to the United States, the country with the largest number of immigrants. The United States has historically held a particular promise of new life for immigrants—a fresh start, untold opportunities—whether or not that promise is realized.

Immigrant fiction has long had a place in American literature, especially during the twentieth century, when writers such as Isaac Bashevis Singer, Maxine Hong Kingston, and Jamaica Kincaid contributed new perspectives and insights. As the demographics of the country shifted—from the early twentieth century, with its influx of southern and eastern European immigrants, to the post-1965 era, when the passage of the Hart-Cellar Act resulted in unprecedented immigration from Latin America, Asia, and Africa—so, too, did the writing that emerged from these new communities.

Much of the literature that was produced by immigrant writers of the twentieth century chronicled American life from the viewpoint of outsiders making their way in. For many of them, the process of becoming an American was central to their narratives. Those works also frequently reflected political upheaval, with exile and displacement serving as common themes. For many twentieth-century immigrants, there was no going back. In the twenty-first century, a new kind of immigrant writing has arisen in the United States that, in many ways, breaks from the traditional themes of immigrant literature.

Twenty-first-century immigrant writers, like many of those whose works appear in this collection, frequently maintain far different relationships with their home countries than did their twentieth-century predecessors. For some of these writers, their relationship has involved physically crossing and recrossing borders; for others, it is primarily maintained through virtual channels, as they communicate via e-mail, video chat, and social networking, sharing work online or through concurrent publishing in multiple countries and languages. These writers, and many of the characters they create, see themselves as transnational, bicultural, diasporic, global. Many of them embrace, rather than struggle with, their outsider status, and they define themselves as Americans with varying degrees of fluidity and comfort.

Immigrant Voices features writers from some of the more recent waves of immigration to the United States, including those from South and Southeast Asia and the Middle East. The number of immigrants from these regions has increased significantly in the early twenty-first century, alongside immigrants with longer relationships to the United States, such as those from Latin America. The reasons people all over the world immigrate—to work; to pursue an education; to seek religious, gender, and sexual freedom; because of displacement by natural disasters, war, political conflict, and ethnic oppression—play out in a multitude of ways through the stories in this anthology, always reflecting the distinctive characteristics of an emerging global culture.

Immigrant Voices represents most of the major twenty-first-century immigrant populations in the United States. The contributors range from well-established authors to those still early in their careers. Eleven of the eighteen writers are women. Given the limitations of space, we have included only one writer from any home country, though to define many of them in terms of a single country of origin would be to seriously narrow their sense of themselves as transnational writers.

Immigrant Voices is divided into three sections. The first section, "Coming Over," includes stories that deal with the move from a home country to the United States. In the past, immigrant writers often portrayed the journey to America as a liberating trip to a promised land. In contrast, many of the twenty-first-century writers in this book portray the journey and arrival more ambivalently.

The second section, "Being Here," addresses the widest array of themes. These stories cover birth, death, family relations, work, and—always—the balancing of life before and after immigration. Here, the fine line between adaptation and assimilation, the possibility of becoming American, and the resistance to this new identity, are explored.

The final section, "Going Back," completes the cycle, telling the stories of immigrants who return to their home countries to visit or to stay.

The stories collected in *Immigrant Voices* are about daily life in a changing America, and about the kinds of relationships immigrants in the United States have with each other, with the people and places around them, and with those who remain in their home countries. Rather than seeking to be comprehensive, *Immigrant Voices* presents a cross-section of new voices and ideas about these experiences.

More than a decade into the new century, it is time for these stories to be heard, particularly as immigration plays such a large role in public discourse and in the collective political and cultural imagination of the country. The Great Books Foundation promotes critical thinking and discussion of issues in the public debate through the practice of Shared Inquiry. These outstanding stories provide a vehicle to deepen and broaden this discussion.

We are grateful to Nicole Aragi, Christina Brown, Norberto Codina and *La Gaceta de Cuba*, Jon Tribble and the *Crab Orchard Review*, and all the writers who submitted and edited stories, including those whose work does not appear here. And to Dan Born, Nancy Carr, Louise Galpine, George Schueppert, Donald Whitfield, and the rest of the Great Books Foundation team, who worked diligently and provided the gentle pushes and prods that helped produce a book that makes us all proud.

Achy Obejas and Megan Bayles

ABOUT SHARED INQUIRY

A Shared Inquiry™ discussion begins when the leader of the discussion group poses an interpretive question to participants about the meaning of a reading selection. The question is substantial enough that no single answer can resolve it. Instead, several answers—even answers that are in conflict—may be valid. In effect, the leader is telling the group: "Here is a problem of meaning that seems important. Let's try to resolve it."

From that moment on, participants are free to offer answers and opinions to the group, to request clarification of points, and to raise objections to the remarks of other participants. They also discuss specific passages in the selection that bear on the interpretive question, and compare their differing ideas about what these passages mean. The leader, meanwhile, asks additional questions, clarifying and expanding the interpretive question and helping group members arrive at more cogent answers. All participants don't have to agree with all the answers—each person can decide which answer seems most convincing. This process is called Shared Inquiry.

In Shared Inquiry discussion, three kinds of questions can be raised about a reading selection: factual questions, interpretive questions, and evaluative questions. Interpretive questions are central to a Shared Inquiry discussion, but factual questions can bring to light evidence in support of interpretations and can clear up misunderstandings. Evaluative questions, on the other hand, invite participants to consider that author's meaning in light of their own experiences and opinions in order to introduce a personal dimension into the discussion.

The following guidelines will help keep the conversation focused on the text and assure all participants a voice:

1. **Read the selection carefully before participating in the discussion.** This ensures that all participants are equally prepared to talk about the ideas in the reading.

2. **Discuss the ideas in the selection, and try to understand them fully.** Reflecting as individuals and as a group on what the selection means makes the exploration of both the selection and related issues that will come up in the discussion more rewarding.

3. **Support interpretations of what the selection means with evidence from the reading, along with insights from personal experience.** This keeps the group focused on the selection that everyone has read and builds a strong foundation for discussing related issues.

4. **Listen to other participants and respond to them directly.** Shared Inquiry is about the give and take of ideas, the willingness to listen to others and talk with them respectfully. Directing your comments and questions to other group members, not always to the leader, will make the discussion livelier and more dynamic.

5. **Expect the leader to mainly ask questions.** Effective leaders help participants develop their own ideas, with everyone gaining a new understanding in the process. When participants hang back and wait for the leader to suggest answers, discussion tends to falter.

HOW TO USE THIS BOOK

The eighteen readings in *Immigrant Voices: 21st Century Stories* were chosen for their ability to raise questions and provoke stimulating discussion about the experience of leaving one's homeland, traveling to a different country, and creating a new life. In order for discussions to be most rewarding, it is strongly recommended that a significant amount of time be spent coming to an understanding of what the author is saying by continually returning to the selection during the discussion. Doing so will provide a strong central focus for whatever personal accounts participants introduce into the conversation as they evaluate the author's ideas in light of their own experiences.

To help prompt lively discussion, each selection is preceded by a brief introduction giving some background about the author's life. At the back of *Immigrant Voices* is a section entitled "Questions for Discussion," featuring a brief set of questions for each selection to encourage exploration of the author's ideas. Most of these questions ask about something very specific in the selection, such as the meaning of a statement or the motivation of a character in a story. A few questions ask about more general issues related to the experience of immigration. Addressing both kinds of questions during a discussion will make for a more satisfying experience that not only engages with each author's distinctive voice, but also allows participants to explore the broader insights and implications of the stories.

COMING OVER

M. EVELINA GALANG

M. Evelina Galang was born in 1961 in Harrisburg, Pennsylvania, to Filipino parents. As a child, Galang and her family moved frequently—in her first ten years, the family lived in seven different cities in the United States, Canada, and the Philippines.

Her name means "respect" in Tagalog, and Galang says that her name has guided her through life. Galang has become a leader in her community; she was invited to the White House for a briefing for Filipino American leaders in the summer of 2012, and she has worked as a campaigner on Filipino women's issues. Galang teaches in and directs the creative writing program at the University of Miami.

Galang has written many books and short stories. She was the editor of *Screaming Monkeys* (2003), an anthology aiming to challenge stereotypes about Asian Americans. Her most recent novel is *Angel de la Luna and the 5th Glorious Mystery* (2013). She says that she writes so that her and others' voices can be heard. In her artistic statement she says that "it is only after I review the stories I have written that I can see this obsession of unleashing the unheard voice in my work."

Letting Go to America

The house is as dark as the new moon when Ernesto comes to her. Gently shaking her, he wakes her from a dream, tells her he is going away for good. She cannot see him lost in all that night. When the curtains blow, blue light shines on them. The smell of rotting garbage in the alley rises. She makes out the shape of his face. She smiles at him then, puts her hand on his cheek.

It's late, she tells him, undress na. Come to bed na.

Milagros, he says again. I am leaving. I am going.

She falls back into her pillows, taking his hand with her. That's not funny and it's late. He doesn't move. She tells him she was dreaming of him tonight.

I've only come to say goodbye, he says. I won't stay.

Something in his voice sounds different now. She massages his hand and with her eyes still closed, she traces the lines in his palm. She counts the ticks and the scars where years of labor have marked him. His hands so rough, the veins pop up from under his brown skin.

When his head touches the pillow, he makes her look into his eyes.

Do you hear me, he says, I'm not fooling. Aalis na ako.

She follows him for forty days. Begs him. Cries to him. Pulls at his hands. Kisses him—the lids of his eyes, his mouth, the Adam's apple she loves so well. She reasons with him.

But our love, mahal.

What about it?

And our girls.

I will always be there for them—that won't stop.

They are in a bar near Clark Air Base. The lights are red and blue and his body is hunched over a beer between sets. His drumsticks splay out like silverware waiting to be used. She swivels his stool around and puts her arms around him.

If this is what you'd rather do, play your music, sige, do it. I won't care. Just come home na, she says, Just come home.

She feels his body rise and sink as he releases a heavy sigh.

Stop driving the foreigners, she says. Go back to your music. We'll support you.

You have to move on, he tells her. You have to let go.

But why, she says. I don't understand.

The next time she finds him, he's sitting at the edge of a rice field, watching an old farmer plow the fields with his carabao. What are you doing here? she wants to know. Why have you left the city?

I was born here, he says to her. We used to have a house right here, before the fire.

The girls want you home.

You know, the house had no electricity back then.

Brownouts?

I mean no electricity. I mean darkness.

He puffs on a long thin white cigarette and she thinks it odd.

When did you start smoking again? she asks.

The city is no place for the girls. You should follow the plan.

Without you?

It'll be better there, easier for you. No brownouts. No countryside without electricity. No poor.

She looks around the land. Not far from the rice field, green kangkong peeks up out of the water.

Come home, mahal.

Finally, he holds her, the way he always has, wrapping his arms around her slight frame. He whispers in her ear and says he'll never stop loving her either. She buries her face in the crook of his neck and sniffs at skin that smells of soap. How could this be happening?

He slowly peels her off of him—finger by finger, the hand in his back pocket, the other running through his thick black hair, then her arms—the right and the left—and even her legs, he has to untangle them from his own. He wipes her face with his old handkerchief. Don't, he tells her. Don't. Where is your dignity?

* * *

4

At the house, her girls cry too. Think she has gone mad. You will understand, she thinks. When he comes home and we are all together again. When he is earning money for our passage to the States and I am a registered nurse, a healer. You girls will understand why I have to follow him.

While she is texting him, the younger one puts her arms around Milagros's waist and rests her little head on her chest.

Inay, Lila whispers. Inay, come back!

Milagros taps out the words, letter by letter, absorbed in the beep beep beep of her message, struggles out of her daughter's embrace. Doesn't even bother to answer her.

Saan ka, she writes Ernesto, I have been looking all over for you. Tell me, saan ka?

One day, she sees him sitting in his van, along the wide avenues of Makati. He's leaning back into the seat with his eyes closed and his feet thrown up against the dashboard. She assumes he's waiting for his clients. So she raps on the window. He doesn't stir. She calls his name, Ernesto, mahal ko! Wake up, she yells. Her heart fills up with a sharp current. How is this happening?

A pulis officer places his hand on her shoulder. Asks her what she's doing.

My husband, she tells him, something is wrong with him. He's not breathing. He's not answering. Ma'am, says the officer, there's nobody there.

And when she looks into the van, she sees that he is missing.

That night, when the girls are sleeping, he comes to the house and they spin around the room—first in a breath, then a sigh and then something like a storm brews.

You see, she says. You still love me.

Of course, he says. It isn't about that. I will always love you—but I have to go.

Why?

He looks at her and rolls his eyes. She knows why. He turns away from her now, searching for lost things. He's traipsing through the house, a pillowcase in hand, gathering his comb, a wallet, his Saint Christopher medallion. He's upset now, crying, bumping into the kitchen table, into free-standing lamps, footstools. He stumbles over the sleeping hen. She shakes her feathers and clucks at him. His breath is heavy and loud. He's touching everything with those hands—the metal blinds and the photos and fixtures in the wall. His footsteps thump, and a tiny earthquake rattles the statues of Mary and Jesus. Knocks Joseph off the mantle.

The girls, she says. Shh!

It's better this way, he tells her.

And then she begins. A tear running down her face, followed by another. She lets them fall without wiping them away. She lets the tears wash over her. Look what you are doing to me. She stares at him, lets her nostrils flare, lets red veins invade her brown eyes. She pulls him into the girls' bedroom. Look at your girls.

He leaves the room, calls out behind him.

You have to move on.

Not without you, she thinks. Not unless you move on too.

And then he stops. Walks right up to her and he looks into her eyes, reading her there. Things have changed. I'm moving on.

At night she cannot sleep without him in her bed. She calls him. She finds him in half dreams. She sees them as teenagers in the province, walking down dirt paths on the way to the dagat—pulling off their clothes and slipping into the cool water.

The dreams always begin this way—when they are children, getting to know each other, learning how to touch each other, how to read one another. Beautiful dreams under wide banyan trees or huddled together, riding a motor tricycle to the market in the height of rainy season. And as the night wears on, they grow older. They move to the city. They have the girls—first Angel, then Lila. Some years there is not enough money for new shoes. One year the van breaks down and they eat rice and fish sauce every night for almost six months. They grow middle-aged. They sit in the dark after two weeks of off-and-on brownouts. No fans. No aircon. Just heat. Just hot air not moving. They bathe in buckets of cold water to stay cool. They fill the house with used appliances, thinking it will save them money only to watch them surge, spark, and blow out. By two in the morning, when she should be in her deepest sleep, they have outgrown their house, their barangay, the city of Manila.

What kind of life is this? he asks her.

Our life.

We barely get by. And what about my mother?

Lola Ani?

Matanda na—getting weaker with each year.

She's stronger than any of us.

He wants to save money, to buy them plane tickets, to get them to America.

That's the life for our girls, mahal. Different than our life.

And when she doesn't buy that, he reminds her that just to make ends meet they work two jobs. Driving foreigners around the islands is lucrative, but he has to work long hard days, has to travel out of the city to other provinces.

Do you like when I am gone for weeks? he asks her. Do you think I like it?

The dream he spins moves their whole family, bit by bit, to Chicago. First you, he says, and you establish our life, Nurse Mahal. Then we save money and send Angel, tapos Lila and Lola Ani. And I will drive—ikot-ikot—and this will buy the tickets while you make us a house in a community of our people there—sa America.

In his dream he has them living in luxury. What do you think they mean by land of opportunity, mahal?

Imagine the girls going to school—good schools—college pa—and they become doctors—or engineers—or better yet movie stars in Hollywood.

She laughs and pushes him away. You have no idea what you say.

Mas ayus yan, mahal. We won't work like dogs. We'll eat meals like family—one table. We can stop dreaming. Start living.

Fool, she tells him. The dreams blur.

And when the night is darkest, she is drawn to the houses on wide streets where little white drops of frozen rain float down upon the earth. The girls will have a better life there, oo, nga. Lola Ani can rest. They will sleep in a big soft bed—she and her mahal—and never be apart.

And once she accepts the dream, she sees his face always cloaked in a kind of light—not a halo, exactly, but a sustained glow, a kind of gwapo that reaches her, makes her think that if this makes him happy now, and makes the girls and Lola happy now—what will it be like once we're there?

So the work begins—the long hours of nursing school, the nights at their tiny kitchen table with stacks of books surrounding her—even as the hen runs around the kitchen, even as the single light bulb swings low and dim over her, even as the calls of street vendors waft into the house through open windows. She studies as he drives the streets of Manila, picking up Americans, Australians, Canadians, French and Spanish businessmen, corporate hotshots, moviemakers, and, once, the head of state from some country she has never heard of. He takes them ikot-ikot around the city—Makati to Quezon City to Parañaque—and sometimes to the provinces of Luzon—to Pampanga and Illocos Sur and La Union. And in the meantime Lola Ani cooks in the convent, readies the girls for school, watches over them like Mama Mary herself.

Ito na, she thinks. We are going to make it na. We are going to America.

But the dream always ends with Ernesto driving deep into the night along the edge of the Cordillera Mountains, four moviemakers in the van, cameras and lights balanced atop stacks of suitcases. The rain starts to fall—first one drop, then another, then steady, then in sheets, then blinding like her own sorrow. A baguio. A storm. Torrential downpour. And in the dark, she sees the van tumbling down a cliff, lightning banging, fire exploding, and she sees him in that driver's seat, unable to get out. She sees him crashing into trees, the fire swallowing him up, his spirit rising from the heat of that van, and before she knows it, he is beside her, whispering goodbye, leaving her, and every time she rises out of bed and screams, No, mahal, no!

Seven weeks after the nightmare begins, Milagros walks down the long corridor, looking for her girls. The passageway is dark save the light from a window at the end of the hall. She sees a girl, bent over a bucket of soapy water, scrubbing the cement floors while church bells ring and old nuns chant, Hail Mary, full of grace; pray for us. The child's hair is tied back into a loose, low ponytail, and strands of the dark hair fall upon her face. Milagros hears her breathing in this long, cavernous hall, she hears the hiccup that comes with too many tears. The child is barefoot, crawling on hands and knees, scouring the eternally dirty floor. And this is where Milagros stops. Holds her breath. Nearly runs to her girl to take the rag out of her hands and wash the floors herself, but then, as she draws near, she sees it's not Lila after all, and it's not Angel either. It is Regina, the old maid living with the nuns. When Milagros gets to her, she sees the face, lined and worn. Stray gray hairs reach up out of her nest of black hair. She leans back on her heels, brushing the hair out of her eyes with a brown elbow.

Good morning, Ma'am, Regina says. I'm sorry for your loss.

At dawn Milagros wakes her daughters lying in their shared bed, clutching at each other, the sheets strangling them. She pulls the girls apart.

You better learn now, you can never love this much. You must learn to live independent of each other. They are crying, trying to reach out to her, to huddle their soft bodies around hers, but she shakes them off. From now on, she tells them, no more crying. Papang is gone.

She moves through the days now without expression on her face. Without the touch of affection. Desire. She cleans her body thoroughly, tells herself he has gone on before her, instead of the other way around. He is in America nesting for them. She is the one who will earn the passage. Find the way.

When she visits the U.S. embassy to inquire, the line of Filipinos wraps around the city block and back again, leans on iron gates, moves at the pace of Manila traffic. Someone tells her, If you have a parent already sa States, baka your wait is only six months. If not, forget it. A lifetime.

So, she thinks, a lifetime then. She promised Ernesto. She has to find a way to bring the girls. His mother too.

At the house, she clears out their living room and makes a shrine to her husband. Puts his portrait in a golden wooden frame. Lights a candle near his beautiful face. On the mantel, she arranges the statues of Mary and Joseph and Jesus. She puts a ceramic bowl out for donations. She pulls a rice paper screen across the room. A waiting room she makes—and on the other side of that, her examining room.

Ano yan, asks Lola Ani. What are you doing?

Mang Kula, the hilot in Parañaque, set up a stand right on the corner across from the mechanic. Foreigners come from all over the world, city dwellers too, they stand in line for six hours just to have the old drunk touch them. Heal them. They are believers. They are generous in their gratitude. Diba, I am hilot too? I have hands that move energy.

Lola Ani nods. Oo, nga, she says, I bet word will spread. You'll make the tickets in no time.

* * *

9

One day an old Filipino from the United States sits on the stool before her, his shirt off, his belly hanging low to the ground. On his back are clumps of graying hair.

Anak, he says, my American doctors give me six months to live. What do they know?

Don't tell me you came home to die?

Hindi naman! he says, shaking his head. I came home to be healed. Can you do anything?

He smiles at her then, winks at her too. A dimple creases its way along the side of the face. The teeth are big and white. So in America, she thinks, the old save their teeth, grow them big, wash them whiter than the moon.

I will try, sir. She holds her hands up to his back and feels them being drawn in circles, low to his adrenal glands. She rubs ointment there. She says prayers in Tagalog. She sings for effect.

He comes to her every day for two weeks in a row, stronger with each visit. Tells her stories about Chicago.

Chicago? She says, My husband always wanted us to live in Chicago.

And why didn't you?

Look around, old man. And besides, he died in a car crash.

Now you are free to go. Come with me.

She laughs at him, the old flirt. If only the lines at the embassy weren't so long, she says. If only the wait for the visa was not years. I'll be older than you, she says, when my turn comes along.

And this is how the old man comes to propose to her: She heals him. He flirts with her. She laughs at his audacity.

He says, Come with me. Marry me.

Beyond the house, the cock crows above the noise of traffic. Diesel trucks bump and fart along the city skyline. You are full of yourself, old man, she says.

She looks up at a photo of Ernesto and her, arm in arm, dancing at their wedding. I could never do that again, you know. Marry.

Don't be stupid, he says. I am old. I am not stupid. I'm getting stronger with each visit. And we are friends. You don't have to love me, you know. You can be my hilot sa States. You can be my companion, diba? Tapos, when you pass your boards, you can be an RN. Before you know it—the girls and your ina, and even that noisy hen, will be living in my big empty house in Chicago.

She takes the oils she has made, a mixture of coconut water, baby oil, and peppermint herbs, and runs her hands around his bald head. The old man closes his eyes, says, We can be friends. I will help you bring your family to Chicago. I will never ask you for anything more—my life is in your hands. I haven't felt this good in years. You are my hilot.

The thought of another man touching her makes her want to throw up. As far as she's concerned, Ernesto is just on the other side of the screen, hearing everything. Sometimes late at night, when the house is silent with sleep, she can hear him banging his drums, she feels his voice in the walls of the house, talking to her.

You should do it, he says. You should take this opportunity and go.

Since he has died, she has grown so angry. Ito, she says, first you die and now you push me into the arms of another man? Ano yan?

She can hear him laughing. She can see the smirk on his face.

These are difficult times, he tells her. I am not here, mahal. Even if I wanted to, I cannot touch you. Accept it na. Look out for the girls at si Mommy din.

Crazy, she says, pulling the thin cotton sheet over her head. Sira!

Move on, mahal.

You want me to marry someone else?

What is your other plan? Even if you make the money for the passage, how will you get the visa?

You want me to use him like that?

He knows the story. He knows. Didn't you hear him? You make him happy. You heal him. That's enough.

All night she talks to the dead husband. She dreams he is in bed with her, that he is holding her and kissing her awake. They fight about the old man. They dream about other ways, but nothing seems as good as this.

He will be good to you, I know.

Sira! she says into his ghost face. Loko ka!

But then she thinks of the girls, working as maids. Angel is turning into a dalaga na; her little breasts burst from her too tight T-shirts, her pants are too short. There are hips now. She takes a breath and, before you know it, she tells herself, Lila too will be a young woman. Working as maids. Then she sees Lola Ani bent before the giant pot of fish soup, crying. She feels the heat of Ernesto's memory leaving her body. The voice goes faint. The hum in the walls dies. The drums go silent. He is gone, she cries, he is gone.

And suddenly it all makes sense, this passage to America, this gift of healing. She closes up the chambers of her heart. There is no more room for unruly emotions. She has daughters to raise.

When next the old man comes to the house, she undoes the first two buttons of her blouse. She changes out of her flip-flops and slips on a pair of sandals. She invites him and his grown son to dine with them after the session. She pulls out the guitar and plays while the girls sing folk songs. And after a hearty meal of fried fish, eggplant, tomatoes, and stewed kang-kong leaves, Lola Ani serves them a sweet cassava cake.

DANIEL ALARCÓN

Born in Lima, Peru, in 1977, Daniel Alarcón immigrated to the United States at the age of three and was raised in Birmingham, Alabama. After graduating from Columbia University and teaching in Harlem for two years, Alarcón returned to Lima on a Fulbright scholarship. He taught photography to young people in San Juan de Lurigancho, a district on the eastern edge of Lima, while living in a $15-a-month room above a bodega.

Alarcón is a graduate of the Iowa Writers' Workshop, and in 2010 the *New Yorker* named him one of the top 20 Writers Under 40. His fiction, journalism, and translations have appeared in the *New Yorker*, *El País*, *McSweeney's*, *n+1*, and *Harper's*. In 2011 he cofounded *Radio Ambulante*, a Spanish-language podcast that features stories from Latin America and the United States. His new novel is *At Night We Walk in Circles* (2013).

"Absence" is taken from Alarcón's first collection, *War by Candlelight*, a finalist for the 2005 PEN/Hemingway Foundation Award. The collection was partially inspired by the effects of globalization and migration visible around him. In an interview with Loggernaut Reading Series, Alarcón said, "If I write about the neighborhoods of Lima, created through internal migration—because these are global processes at work—I am by implication writing about New York, San Jose, Atlanta, Cleveland, Madrid, London, and on and on."

Absence

On his second day in New York, Wari walked around Midtown looking halfheartedly for the airline office. He'd decided to forget everything. It was an early September day; the pleasant remains of summer made the city warm and inviting. He meandered in and out of sidewalk traffic, marveled at the hulking mass of the building, and confirmed, in his mind, that the city was the capital of the world. On the train, he'd seen break dancing and heard Andean flutes. He'd watched a Chinese man play a duet with Beethoven on a strange electronic harmonica. In Times Square, a Dominican man danced a frenetic merengue with a life-sized doll. The crowds milled about, smiling, tossing money carelessly at the dancer, laughing when his hands slipped lustily over the curve of the doll's ass.

Wari didn't arrive at the airline office that day; he didn't smile at any nameless woman across the counter, or reluctantly pay the $100 fine to have his ticket changed. Instead he wandered, passed the time in intense meditation upon the exotic, upon the city, its odors and gleaming surfaces, and found himself in front of a group of workers digging a hole in the sidewalk at the base of a skyscraper. He sat down to have lunch and watch them. With metal-clawed machines they bored expertly through concrete. Wari had made a sandwich uptown that morning, and he ate distractedly now. The people passed in steady streams, bunching at corners and swarming across intersections the instant a light changed. From a truck, the men brought a thin sapling and lowered it into their newly dug hole. They filled it with dirt. Trees to fill holes, Wari thought, amused, but they weren't done. The workers smoked cigarettes and talked loudly among themselves and then one of them brought a wheelbarrow piled high with verdant grass cut into small squares. Sod. They laid the patches of leafy carpet out around the tree. Just like that. In the time it took Wari to eat, a hole was emptied and filled, a tree planted and adorned with fresh green grass. A wound created in the earth; a wound covered, healed, beautified. It was nothing. The city moved along, unimpressed, beneath a bright, late-summer sky.

He walked a little more and stopped in front of a group of Japanese artists drawing portraits for tourists. They advertised their skill with careful renderings of famous people, but Wari could only recognize a few. There was Bill Clinton and Woody Allen, and the rest were generically handsome in a way that reminded Wari of a hundred actors and actresses. It was the kind of work he could do easily. The artists' hands moved deftly across the parchment, shading here and there in swift strokes. Crowds slowed to watch, and the portraitists seemed genuinely oblivious, glancing up at their clients every now and then to make certain they weren't making any mistakes. When the work was done, the customer always smiled and seemed surprised at finding his own likeness on the page. Wari smiled too, found it folkloric, like everything he had seen so far in the city, worth remembering, somehow special in a way he couldn't yet name.

Wari had been invited to New York for an exhibit; serendipity, an entire chain of events born of a single conversation in a bar with an American tourist named Eric, a red-haired PhD student in anthropology and committed do-gooder. He had acceptable Spanish and was a friend of a friend of Wari's who was still at the university. Eric and Wari had talked about Guayasamín and indigenous iconography, about cubism and the Paracas textile tradition of the Peruvian coast. They'd shared liter bottles of beer and laughed as their communication improved with each drink, ad hoc Spanglish and pencil drawings on napkins. Eventually Eric made an appointment to see Wari's studio. He'd taken two paintings back to New York and set up an exhibit through his department. Everything culminated in an enthusiastic e-mail and an invitation on cream-colored bond paper. Wari had mulled it over for a few weeks, then spent most of his savings on a round-trip ticket. It was the only kind they sold. Once in New York and settled in, Wari buried the return ticket in the bottom of his bag, as if it were something radioactive. He didn't know what else to do with it. That first night, when the apartment had stilled, Wari dug into the suitcase and examined it. It had an unnatural density for a simple piece of paper. He dreamed that it glowed.

Wari found Leah, his host's girlfriend, making pasta. It was still light out, and Eric wasn't home yet. Wari wanted to explain exactly what he had seen and why it had impressed him, but he didn't have the words. She didn't speak Spanish but made up for it by smiling a lot and bringing him things. A cup of tea, a slice of toast. He accepted everything because he wasn't sure how to refuse. His English embarrassed him. While the water boiled, Leah stood at the edge of the living room. "Good day?" she said. "Did you have a good day?"

Wari nodded.

"Good," she said. She brought him the remote to the television, then turned into the small kitchen. Wari sat on the sofa and flipped through the channels, not wanting to be rude. He could hear Leah humming a song to herself. Her jeans were slung low on her hips. Wari made himself watch the television. Game shows, news programs, talk shows; trying to understand gave him a headache, and so he settled on a baseball game, which he watched with the volume down. The game was languid and hard to follow and, before long, Wari was asleep.

When he awoke, there was a plate of food in front of him. Leah was at the sink, washing her dish. Eric was home. *"Buenas noches!"* he called out grandly. "Good game?" He pointed at the television. Two players chatted on the mound, their faces cupped in their gloves.

"Yes," said Wari. He rubbed the sleep from his eyes.

Eric laughed. "The Yanks gonna get it back this year," he said. "They're the white team."

"I'm sorry," was all Wari could offer.

They spoke for a while in Spanish about the details of the exhibit, which was opening in two days. Wari's canvases stood against the wall, still wrapped in brown paper and marked FRAGILE. They would hang them tomorrow. "Did you want to work while you were here?" Eric asked. "I mean, paint? At my department, they said they could offer you a studio for a few weeks."

That had everything to do with the radioactive ticket interred at the bottom of his suitcase. Wari felt a tingling in his hands. He'd brought no brushes or paints or pencils or anything. He had no money for art supplies. He guessed it would be years before he would again. What would it be like *not* to paint?

"No, thank you," Wari said in English. He curled his fingers into a fist.

"Taking a vacation, huh? That's good. Good for you, man. Enjoy the city."

Wari asked about phone cards, and Eric said you could get them anywhere and cheap. Any bodega, corner store, pharmacy, newsstand. "We're connected," he said, and laughed. "Sell them right next to the lotto tickets. You haven't called home?"

Wari shook his head. Did they miss him yet?

"You should." Eric settled into the couch. Leah had disappeared into the bedroom.

His host spoke to the flickering television while Wari ate.

The American embassy sits hunched against a barren mountain in a well-to-do suburb of Lima. It is an immense bunker with the tiled exterior of a fancy bathroom, its perimeter gate so far from the actual building that it would take a serious throw to hit even its lowest floor with a rock. A line gathers out front each morning before dawn, looping around the block, a hopeful procession of Peruvians with their sights on Miami or Los Angeles or New Jersey or anywhere. Since the previous September, after the attacks, the embassy had forced the line even farther out, beyond blue barricades, to the very edge of the wide sidewalk. Then there'd been a car bomb in March to welcome the visiting American president. Ten Peruvians had died, including a thirteen-year-old boy unlucky enough to be skateboarding near the embassy at exactly the wrong moment. His skull had been pierced by shrapnel. Now the avenue was closed to all but official traffic. The line was still there, every morning except Sundays, in the middle of the empty street.

Before his trip Wari presented his letter and his fees and his paperwork. Statements of property, financials, university records, a list of exhibitions and gallery openings, certificates of birth, and legal documents regarding a premature marriage and redemptive divorce. The entirety of his twenty-seven years, on paper. The centerpiece, of course, was Eric's invitation on letterhead from his university. Eric had let him know that this wasn't any old university. Wari gathered that he should say the name of the institution with reverence and all would know its reputation. Eric had assured him it would open doors.

Instead the woman said: We don't give ninety-day visas anymore.

Through the plastic window, Wari tried pointing at the invitation, at its gold letters and elegant watermark, but she wasn't interested. Come back in two weeks, she'd said.

He did. In his passport, Wari found a one-month tourist visa.

At the airport in Miami, Wari presented his paperwork once more, his passport and, separately, the invitation in its gilded envelope. To his surprise, the agent sent him straightaway to an interview room, without even glancing at his documents. Wari waited in the blank room, recalling how a friend had joked: "Remember to shave or they'll think you're Arab." Wari's friend had celebrated the remark by shattering a glass against the cement floor of the bar. Everyone had applauded. Wari could feel the sweat gathering in the pores on his face. He wondered how bad he looked, how tired and disheveled. How dangerous. The stale, recycled air from the plane compartment was heavy in his lungs. He could feel his skin darkening beneath the fluorescent lights.

An agent came in, shooting questions in English. Wari did his best. "An artist, eh?" the agent said, examining the paperwork.

Wari folded his fingers around an imaginary brush and painted circles in the air.

The agent waved Wari's gesture away. He looked through the papers, his eyes settling finally on the bank statement. He frowned.

"You're going to New York?" he asked. "For a month?"

"In Lima, they give to me one month," Wari said carefully.

The agent shook his head. "You don't have the money for that kind of stay." He looked at the invitation and then pointed to the paltry figure at the bottom of the bank statement. He showed it to Wari, who muffled a nervous laugh. "Two weeks. And don't get any ideas," the agent said. "That's generous. Get your ticket changed when you get to New York."

He stamped Wari's burgundy passport with a new visa and sent him on his way.

At baggage claim, Wari found his paintings in a stack next to an empty carousel. He made his way through customs, answering more questions before being let through. He waited patiently while they searched his suitcase, rifling through his clothes. His paintings were inspected with great care, and here the golden letter finally served a purpose. Customs let him through. Wari felt dizzy, the shuffling noise of the airport suddenly narcotic, sleep calling him to its protective embrace. Ninety days is a humane length of time, he thought. Enough time to come to a decision and find its cracks. To look for work and organize contingencies. To begin imagining the permanence of goodbyes. It wasn't as if Wari had nothing to lose. He had parents, a brother, good friends, a career just beginning in Lima, an ex-wife. If he left it behind? Even a month spent in meditation—ambling about a new city, working out the kinks of a foreign language—might be space enough to decide. But two weeks? Wari thought it cruel. He counted the days on his fingers: twenty-four hours after his paintings came down, he would be illegal. Wari had imagined that the right decision would appear obvious to him, if not right away, then certainly before three months had passed. But there was no chance of clarity in fourteen days. Wari walked through the Miami airport as if he'd been punched in the face. His feet dragged. He made his flight to La Guardia just as the doors were closing, and was stopped again at the Jetway, his shoes examined by a plastic-gloved woman who refused to return his weak smiles. On the plane, Wari slept with his face flush against the oval window. There was nothing to see anyway. It was an overcast day in South Florida, no horizon, no turquoise skies worthy of postcards, nothing except the gray expanse of a wing and its contrails, blooming at the end like slivers of smoke.

Leah woke him with apologies. "I have to work," she said softly. "You couldn't have slept through it anyway." She smiled. Her hair was pulled back in a ponytail. She smelled clean. Leah made jewelry, and his bedroom, which was actually the living room, was also her workshop.

"Is okay," Wari said, sitting up on the couch, taking care to hide his morning erection.

Leah grinned as Wari fumbled awkwardly with the sheet. "I've seen plenty of that, trust me," she said. "I wake up with Eric every morning."

Wari felt his face turn red. "Is lucky," he said.

She laughed.

"Where is? Eric?" he asked, cringing at his pronunciation.

"Studying. Work. He teaches undergrads. *Young students*," she said, translating young, in gestures, as small.

Wari pictured Eric, with his wide, pale face and red hair, teaching miniature people, tiny humans who looked up to him for knowledge. He liked that Leah had tried. He understood much more than he could say, but how could she know that?

He watched her for a while, filing metal and twisting bands of silver into circles. He liked the precision of her work, and she didn't seem to mind him. Leah burnished a piece, filed and sanded, bent metal with tools that seemed too brusque for her delicate hands. She held a hammer with authority, she was a woman with purpose. It was a powerful display. "I'm finishing up," she said finally, "and then you can come with me. I know a Peruvian you can talk to."

He showered and ate a bowl of cold cereal before they left for downtown. The Peruvian she knew was named Fredy. She didn't know where he was from exactly, though she was sure he'd told her. Fredy worked a street fair on Canal. Leah had won him over with a smile a few years before, and now he let her sell her jewelry on consignment. Every couple of weeks, she went down with new stuff, listened as Fredy catalogued what had sold and what hadn't, and to his opinionated take on why. He lived in New Jersey now, Leah said, and had married a Chinese woman. "They speak to each other in broken English. Isn't that amazing?"

Wari agreed.

"It must say something about the nature of love, don't you think?" Leah asked. "They have to trust each other so completely. That window of each other that they know in English is so small compared to everything they are in their own language."

Wari wondered. The train rattled on its way downtown. But it's always like that, he wanted to say, you can never know anyone completely. Instead he was silent.

"Do you understand me when I speak?" Leah asked. "If I speak slowly?"

"Of course," Wari said, and he did, but felt helpless to say much more. He noted the descending numbered streets at every stop, and followed their subterranean progress on the map. A sticker covered the southern end of the island. They got off before they reached that veiled area. On Canal, only a few blocks was enough to remind Wari of Lima: that density, that noise, that circus. The air was swollen with foreign tongues. He felt comfortable in a way, but didn't mind at all when Leah took his arm and led him swiftly through the crowds of people. He bumped shoulders with the city, like walking against a driving rain.

Fredy turned out to be Ecuadorian, and Leah couldn't hide her embarrassment. She turned a rose color that reminded Wari of the dying light at dusk. Wari and Fredy both reassured her it was nothing.

"We're brother countries," Fredy said.

"We share border and history," said Wari.

The Ecuadorian was all obsequious smiles, spoke of the peace treaty that was signed only a few years before. Wari played along, shook Fredy's hand vigorously until Leah seemed at ease with her mistake. Then she and Fredy talked business, haggling in a teasing way that seemed more like flirting, and of course Leah won. When this was finished, she excused herself, and drifted away to the other stands, leaving Wari and Fredy alone.

When she was out of earshot, Fredy turned to Wari. "Don't ask me for work, *compadre*," he said, frowning. "It's hard enough for me."

Wari was taken aback. "Who asked you for work? I've got work, *cholo*."

"Sure you do."

Wari ignored him, inspected the table laid out with small olive forks bent into ridiculous earrings. At the other end, there were black-and-white photos of Andean peaks, silvery and snowcapped, and others of ruined fortresses of stone and colonial churches. The scenes were devoid of people: landscapes or buildings or scattered rocks carved by Incas, unified by their uninhabited emptiness. "There's no people," Wari said.

"They emigrated," sneered Fredy.

"This shit sells?"

"Good enough."

"That's my girl, you know," Wari said all of a sudden, and he liked the tone of the lie, the snap of it, the way the Ecuadorian looked up, surprised.

"The gringa?"

"Yeah."

"I bet she is," said Fredy.

Then two customers appeared, a young woman with her boyfriend. Fredy switched to English, heavily accented but quite acceptable, and pointed to various objects, suggesting earrings that matched the woman's skin tone. She tried on a pair, Fredy dutifully held the mirror up for her, her distracted boyfriend checking out the photos. Wari wondered where Leah had gone off to. The woman turned to him. "What do you think?" she asked, looking back and forth between Wari and Fredy.

"Is very nice," Wari said.

"Like a million bucks," said Fredy.

"Where's this from?" she asked, fingering the lapis lazuli stone.

"Peru," said Wari.

Fredy shot him a frown. "From the Andes," he said.

"Trev," she called to her boyfriend. "It's from Peru! Isn't it nice?"

She pulled out a twenty and Fredy made change. He wrapped the earrings in tissue paper and handed her a card. The couple walked away, chatting. Wari and Fredy didn't speak.

Leah reappeared and Wari made sure to touch her, thoughtlessly, as if it meant nothing at all. He could feel Fredy watching them, studying each of their movements. "Did you tell Fredy about your opening?" she asked Wari.

He shook his head. "So modest," Leah said and filled in the details and, to his delight, exaggerated its importance and weight. Wari felt like a visiting dignitary, someone famous.

Wari put his arm around Leah. She didn't stop him. Fredy said it would be difficult to make it.

"Okay, but maybe?" she asked.

"Please come," added Wari, not worrying about his pronunciation.

Leaving is no problem. It's exciting actually; in fact, it's a drug. It's the staying gone that will kill you. This is the handed-down wisdom of the immigrant. You hear it from the people who wander home, after a decade away. You hear about the euphoria that passes quickly; the new things that lose their newness and, soon after, their capacity to amuse you. Language is bewildering. You tire of exploring. Then the list of things you miss multiplies beyond all reason, nostalgia clouding everything: in memory, your country is clean and uncorrupt, the streets are safe, the people universally warm, and the food consistently delicious. The sacred details of your former life appear and reappear in strange iterations, in a hundred waking dreams. Your pockets fill with money, but your heart feels sick and empty.

Wari was prepared for all this.

In Lima, he rounded up a few friends and said his goodbyes. Tentative, equivocal goodbyes. Goodbyes over drinks, presented as jokes, gentle laughter before the *poof* and the vanishing—that Third World magic. I may be back, he told everyone, or I may not. He moved two boxes of assorted possessions into the back room of his parents' house. He took a few posters off the walls, covered the little holes with Wite-Out. He encouraged his mother to rent out his room for extra money if he didn't come home in a month. She cried, but just a little. His brother wished him luck. Wari offered a toast to family at Sunday dinner and promised to come home one day soon. He embraced his father and accepted the crisp $100 bill the old man slipped into his hand. And in the last days before leaving, Wari and Eric exchanged feverish e-mails, ironing out the fine points of the exhibit: the exact size of the canvases, the translated bio, the press release. All the formalities of a real opening, but for Wari, it was so much noise and chatter. The only solid things for him were the ticket and the runway and the plane and the obligatory window seat for a last, fading view of Lima. The desert purgatory, the approaching northern lights.

I'm ready, he thought.

And if no one questioned him, it's because the logic was self-evident. What would he do there? How long could he live at home? A divorced painter, sometime teacher—what does an artist do in a place like that? In America, you can sweep floors and make money, if you're willing to work—you are willing to work, aren't you, Wari?

Yes, I am.

At anything? Outdoor work? Lifting, carting, cleaning?

Anything.

And that was it. What other questions were there? He'd be fine.

Only his mother gave voice to any concerns. "What about Elie?" she asked a few days before he traveled. Wari had been expecting this question. Elie, his ex-wife, whom he loved and whom he hated. At least there were no children to grow up hating him. Wari was relieved it was over, believed she must be as well.

"No, Ma," he said. "It has nothing to do with her."

So his mother smiled and smiled and smiled.

In Eric's apartment, Wari daydreamed. He dressed up the lie about Leah. He lay on the couch, composing e-mails about her to his friends back home, describing the shape of her body, the colors of her skin. The solution to his fourteen-day quandary: marry her and stay, marry her and go. Marry her and it would be all the same. He imagined falling in love in monosyllables, in nods and smiles and meaningful gestures. Telling Leah the story of his life in pictograms: His modest family home. The drab, charcoal colors of his native city. His once-happy marriage and its dissolving foundations, crumbling from the inside into a perfect parody of love. It was early afternoon and Leah readied herself for a waitressing job. The shower ran. Through the thin walls he could hear the sound of the water against her body. Her light brown hair went dark when it was wet. He closed his eyes and pictured her naked body. Then Elie's. Wari turned on the television, let its noise fill the living room. Almost a year from the attacks, and the inevitable replays had begun. He changed the channel, his mind wandered: Fredy on a train home to his Chinese wife, wondering if what Wari had boasted of was true. Elie, somewhere in Lima, not even aware he was gone. Leah, in the shower, not thinking of him. On every channel, buildings collapsed in clouds of dust, and Wari watched on mute, listening hopefully to Leah's water music.

Wari rapped on the wooden door. This was years ago. "*Chola*," he called to the woman who would be his wife. "*Chola*, are you there?"

But Elie wasn't there. She'd left the music on loud to discourage burglars. She lived in Magdalena, a crumbling district by the sea, in a neighborhood of stereos playing loudly in empty apartments. Fourteen-year-old kids cupped joints in their palms and kept a lookout for cops. They played soccer in the streets and tossed pebbles at the moto-taxis. Wari knocked again. "She ain't home," someone called from the street. Wari knew she wasn't, but he wanted to see her. He wanted to kiss her and hold her and tell her his good news.

He was a younger, happier version of himself.

My good news, baby: his first exhibit in a gallery in Miraflores. A real opening with wine, a catalogue, and they'd promised him press, maybe even half a column interview in one of the Sunday magazines. This is what he wanted to tell her.

Wari knocked some more. He hummed along to the melody that played in her apartment. He pulled pen and paper from his bag and composed a note for her, in English. They were both studying it at an institute, Elie with much less enthusiasm. English is tacky, she'd say. She mourned the passing of Spanish, the faddish use of gringo talk. It was everywhere: on television, in print, on the radio. In cafés, their peers spoke like this: "*Sí, pero asi es la gente nice. No tienen ese* feeling." Why are you learning that language, *acomplejado*, my dear Wari, you just paint and you'll be fine. She made him laugh and that was why he loved her. On a piece of paper torn from a notebook, he wrote:

I come see you, but instead meet your absence.

It's perfect, he thought. He put a *W* in the corner, just because—as if anyone else would come to her home and leave a note like this. He tacked it to the door and walked down to the street, music serenading the walls of empty apartments. Music that slipped out into the street. He had nothing to do but wait for her. A kid on the corner scowled at him, but Wari smiled back. It was late afternoon, the last dying light of day.

The show went up, but the reception was sparsely attended. "It's a bad time," said Eric, with Leah on his arm. "The anniversary has everyone on edge."

"On edge," Wari asked, "is like scared?"

"Just like that," Leah said.

Wari didn't care. He was scared too. And not because the world could explode, or because Manhattan could sink into the sea. Real fears. His paintings were glowing beneath the bright lights. A handful of people filtered in and out, sipping champagne from plastic cups. Already there was something foreign about his paintings, as if they were the work of someone else, a man he used to know, an acquaintance from a distant episode in his life. There was nothing special about them, he decided. They exist, as I exist, and that is all.

The grandiose illusion of the exile is that they are all back home, your enemies and your friends, voyeurs all, watching you. Everything has gained importance because you are away. Back home, your routines were only that. Here, they are portentous, significant. They have the weight of discovery. Can they see me? In this city, this cathedral? In this New York gallery? Never mind that it was nearly empty, and a hundred blocks from the neighborhoods where art was sold. Not for himself, but for their benefit, Wari would manufacture the appropriate amount of excitement. Make them all happy. I'm doing it, Ma, he'd say over the static. It's a bad connection, but I know now everything will be all right.

Afterward, Eric and Leah took Wari out for drinks with some friends. He could tell they felt bad, as if they had let him down. Eric complained about student apathy. Lack of engagement, he called it. His department was in disarray, he said, they hadn't done a very good job of advertising. Leah nodded in solemn agreement. It was all words. Nothing Wari said could convince his host that he really didn't care. *I used you*, he wanted to say. *I'm not a painter anymore.* But that seemed so cruel, so ungrateful, and still untrue.

"Is no problem," he repeated over and over. "We have a good time."

"Yes, yes, but still . . . I feel *bad.*"

Americans always feel bad. They wander the globe carrying this opulent burden. They take digital photographs and buy folk art, feeling a dull disappointment in themselves, and in the world. They bulldoze forests with tears in their eyes. Wari smiled. He wanted to say he understood, that none of it was Eric's fault. It's what had to happen. He took Eric's hand. "Thank you," Wari said, and squeezed.

The bar was warm and lively. The televisions broadcasted baseball games from a dozen cities. Eric's friends congratulated Wari, clapped him on the back. *"Muy bien!"* they shouted gregariously. They wouldn't let him spend a single dollar. They bought round after round until the lights from the beer signs were blurred neon arabesques. Wari felt it nearly impossible to understand a single word of their shouted conversations. There was a girl, a woman who kept making eyes at him. She was slight and had a fragile goodness to her. Wari watched her whisper with Leah, and they looked his way and smiled. He smiled back.

"I liked your paintings very much," she said later. The night was winding down. Already a few people had left. Leah and Eric had separated from the group. They kissed each other and laughed and, by the way they looked into each other's eyes, Wari could tell they were in love. It made him feel silly.

He was ignoring the woman in front of him. "Thank you," he said.

"They're so violent."

"I do not intend that."

"It's what I saw."

"Is good you see this. Violence sometime happen."

"I'm Ellen," she said.

"Is nice name. My ex-wife name Elie."

"You're Wari."

"I am."

"How long will you stay?"

"I have ten more days on the visa," Wari said.

"Oh."

"But I do not know."

There were more drinks and more intimate shouting over the cacophony of the bar. Ellen had a sweet smile and lips he could see himself kissing. His hand had fallen effortlessly on her knee. In the corner of the bar, Leah and Eric kissed again and again. *How long will you stay I do not know. HowlongwillyoustayIdonotknow.* Wari wanted to drop his glass on the floor, but he was afraid it wouldn't shatter. He was afraid no one would applaud, no one would understand the beauty of that sound. The days were vanishing. Then he was in the street and Ellen was teaching him how to hail a cab. You have to be aggressive, she said. Does she think we don't have cabs? he wondered, shocked. Does she think we ride mules? Just as quickly, he didn't care. She meant nothing by it. He could feel the planet expanding, its details effaced. Who is this woman? What city is this? The evening was warm, and the sky, if you looked straight up, was a deep indigo. They were downtown. His head was swimming in drink. I should call my mother, he thought, and tell her I'm alive. I should call Elie and tell her I'm dead.

They stood on the street corner. Cab after yellow cab rolled past Wari's outstretched arm. He was no good at it. Wari turned to find Ellen in a daze, gazing down the avenue.

"They were there, you know. Just right there," Ellen said. She reached for his hand.

They were quiet. She pointed with two fingers in the direction of the southern horizon, toward the near end of the island. Wari stared at the yawning space in the sky, a wide and hollow nothing.

POROCHISTA KHAKPOUR

Porochista Khakpour is an Iranian American writer born in Tehran in 1978 but raised in the Los Angeles area. When she was three years old, her family immigrated to the United States to flee post-revolutionary Iran. Khakpour's U.S. citizenship was finalized shortly after 9/11, and in a 2010 *New York Times* article, she discussed her complex feelings about the citizenship process and "the hyphen that would from now on gracefully declare and demarcate [her] two worlds: Middle-Eastern-American."

Khakpour's debut novel *Sons and Other Flammable Objects* (2007) won a California Book Award for fiction. In 2012, she was awarded a National Endowment for the Arts Literature Fellowship in Creative Writing (Prose).

Khakpour's writings have also appeared in the *New York Times*, the *Los Angeles Times*, the *Daily Beast*, the *Village Voice*, the *Chicago Reader*, and the *Paris Review Daily*. She recently began teaching at Columbia University and Fordham University in New York.

Mother the Big

There was a tiger, a rabbit, a bear, a pig, a donkey, and a kangaroo mom and child—but this is about the tiger and the rabbit, I had begun, my voice cracking and crushing itself underneath the weight of her eyes. *The tiger was very enthusiastic and it caused problems, his enthusiasm. One day, he ran over the rabbit in his garden and ruined all the vegetables. The rabbit was angry*—she looked like she was about to interrupt, so I sped up—*so the rabbit called a meeting with the bear and the pig, and the bear fell asleep through much of the meeting but the rabbit decided they would take the tiger out into the woods and lose him maybe forever*—was I tearing up? I could not let her see me tearing up, so I decided to go even faster—*and so they did just that, but in the process they themselves got lost and it was the tiger who ended up saving them, and saving especially the rabbit who had had a nightmarish time in the woods all alone.* I paused; she looked glazed, like maybe she thought there was more. *The thing about the story is, nothing really changed after all that and everyone still got annoyed at the tiger. He was not a hero. As hard as he worked, as useful as he was, he could never be more than what he was.* In my head, a better, brighter, American TV version of me jazz-handed "*The End!*" but the me I was stuck with just swallowed too hard and tumbled into a coughing fit.

They couldn't get rid of the tiger, my grandmother said through clenched teeth. *He would not die. That's the whole point.*

I nodded. *Yes, that too.*

My grandmother looked as she often did in those days: madly unamused. *A terrible story. I don't know why you'd tell me such a terrible story.*

It didn't hurt my feelings because I had been through it before with her. She had very high standards for stories, her own opaque and angled and more terrifying than anyone could imagine, certainly too striking for a young boy of my age back then. *Well, it's the story I learned in school today.*

31

But I was the one who had it wrong. *I didn't ask what story you learned. I asked what you learned. American class and its terrible stories don't count.*

Even at that age I wanted her to know she was not always right: *English. English class.*

What difference was it to her? She ignored me, and got to the point of points, the reason why back then she'd make me tell the details of school and even English class so thoroughly: *Do you see why it's better here?*

Here. For only a little while longer *here* would mean Iran. I decided, with the wild abandon of a man at a cliff's edge, to go for honest: *No.*

That was incorrect, of course. Again, with raised voice: *Do you see why it's better here?*

Tiptoe, retreat, lie: *Sure, yes.*

Those were the only moments when I'd see her smile, that breaking of her face that at least looked like a dry and cracked smile, like it hurt to attempt. One time, her lip had bled when she smiled. This time the smile flickered on and off hesitantly, like a dying light bulb. *When you really learn that, we'll be ready to go.*

But we were just weeks from moving to the United States. *We have to go anyway,* I argued.

We don't have to do anything.

Then why are we going? I was younger than my years would indicate—a single-digit soul in ill-fitting newish double digits—and so these decisions were never clear to me, even when an aura of desirability surrounded them. Just the year before, I had teared up at a friend's house when he told me that at the end of a movie I had never seen, the young girl left a very magical green city with flying monkeys and talking animals and things like that and returned home to a dismal rural place named Kansas. *But why?* I asked. My friend shrugged. *Why? Why?* I kept asking . . .

Because we've lost it.

Our minds? Was I joking? I was likely not joking.

No. Our lives.

Will we find it? Or will it find us? This is how I know I was not joking. Back in those days, I felt suffocated by all the things that they complained we could never find again, in season after season of loss and more loss.

It'll do something.

And that was that.

It stayed with me, this second-to-last memory of us before we came to this country. The first memory: years before that, the time she had taken a meat tenderizing mallet that had been sitting in the oven for an hour—the hour after I had said my first profanity, a term for dog waste—and placed it on my dry, quivering tongue.

If it hadn't been for her, my feelings about my new life would have been good. I had heard all sorts of things about America: basketball courts in every yard, restaurants where you could eat endlessly for a one-time fee, child entertainers who made ten times what the president did.

But when it turned out Mother and Father were not coming and neither was my older brother Ali, and that it would be just my grandmother and me, I felt drenched in sudden worry.

This will not end well, I said to them all. It was a line I had heard in an Iranian movie about a woman who is a spy who falls in love with a man who is a clown; the spy woman had said it to the clown man, and she had been right.

When I said it, my parents—always somewhere else, always a bit distant—until they really were somewhere else, really were distant—just smiled brothily and pretended I was joking, I suppose.

And on that final early summer day, at the airport, my father—son of my grandmother—tried to console me with a final whisper. *She's old, yes, but on our side of the family everyone is practically invincible. She will be with you for a long time.*

There are so many American stories for what we do, the most American stories of all. In American school, we learned about people who looked all sorts of ways, getting on ships and coming to America to "start over." Men with buckles on their hats, men who ate potatoes, men who ate spaghetti, men who ate fortune cookies. Men who had nothing in common but their coming here. What we had done made sense here, this is what I learned.

Though I was probably the only child who had a "guardian" instead of a parent. The teachers seemed so curious and so enchanted, as if I was a mystery novel, and so soon I memorized a sentence true and yet twinkling: *My grandmother and I have been sent by my parents, who could not afford to leave their business behind, to start a new life.* The teachers would sigh and sigh. *Why your grandmother, of all people?* they would sometimes go on to wonder. I could never get that to sound too romantic: *My parents thought my grandmother, so old, could use the good doctors here, while I could use the good schools.* Still: sighs and sighs. *They want me to take care of her, as she takes care of me, my guardian, my grandmother.* Sighs, sighs, sighs.

I didn't tell them there was not too much care on either end.

Who needed to know that, who could face that reality? Forgive me, You-who-still-may-or-may-not-loom, I never loved you the way American kids loved their grandmothers; I never loved my grandmother the way Iranian kids did. I called her the same thing—"grandmother," which in Farsi is "Madarbozorg" and which literally translates to "Mother the Big"—but she did not feel like the grandmother people talked about when talking about grandmothers.

One time she told me to watch out for ugly people because their ugliness came from being ugly inside. I quickly dropped my eyes lest she think I was mocking her by staring—of course, she was not beautiful. She was indeed the Big, a very overweight woman. I equated her body with a very big brown paper bag, her skin loose and yet dry. She wore dark, shapeless velvet caftans that made her look even more impossibly big. And she was also the only balding woman I had ever seen, though I was reminded of the condition only when her headscarf slipped off during those long naps on the couch. The big brown spotted head with its light dusting of white hair was like a dirty harvest moon before a storm, its awful glory something more terrible than simply *ugly*, I suppose.

Madarbozorg had decided long before we arrived that America was no good, that we had to be there because there was no other choice, and that before I'd hit adulthood, we'd be back to Iran. Never mind what Tehran had turned into. Overnight new cries scored the city: prayers and curses, men on rooftops shrieking or singing, hard to tell which; my mother and my female cousins and all my schoolmate girls draped in black like they were wearing crow costumes. One time, we went to our favorite shopping center and there suddenly was no shopping center, but a government building. Another time I went to see my friend on Prosperity Street and it had turned into Allah's Promise Drive. Another time my parents had tried to take me to the playground by the house, but it was filled with the crow women and double the number of men all screaming and shouting with fists in the air, while police with large guns braided through the masses like unfazed snakes.

How could America be worse? I had asked her over and over, but she'd shake her head and tell me I'd see.

How is this worse? I asked over and over in our first month there, but still she'd insist I'd see.

For one thing, she hated our apartment in America, in a part of town that was supposed to be okay but evidently was not good enough for her. A distant relative of ours, a man named Moe, had put a well-worn plaid couch in the living room with two simple white plastic chairs on either side. Two identical mattresses, lying bare on the ground like shameless dead bodies, were the only items in the other room—the room we were to share.

(*The room we were to share. The room we were to share. The room we were to share.* I begged my body and mind to stay strong, as something in me knew this was just the beginning, that her premonition of all the worseness coming was likely right.)

Moe came every few days with armfuls of supplies: toilet paper, sheets, cleaning supplies, bread, and tea. He was a single man, about as old as my father, but had no interest in taking over, he often wanted me to know.

We got to teach you to drive, so you can start helping Madarbozorg yourself, he'd say.

Are twelve-year-olds allowed to drive here? I'd ask.

He would pound my back and say, *Everything is possible here.*

Other times, Moe would talk about how he was the happiest man in the world, but always without a smile. *I have it all*, he'd say, but it was hard to see what. He was very thin, with a pelt of mustache that took over most of his pock-marked face. He drove a pickup truck that was very old and rusted. He worked as a plumber, but he told me I should make sure to familiarize myself with basic household repairs, so I could start helping Madarbozorg myself. *Americans find me expensive*, he'd remind me often with a pride I found both inspiring and sad.

He did give me one bit of advice that really made me: *Change your name.* I asked him what was wrong with my name, why didn't he like it, and he shook his head and said, *Try to imagine an American pronouncing it. What a mess!* I didn't understand: *But what is a mess?* I wondered. *Your name which equals you!* he snapped and told me his name was Mohammed

35

and he had shortened it to the American name Moe. It had jump-started great luck, turning him into the happiest man in the world. *I have it all*, he said, hugging the air.

I thought about it. What would be my American name? Moe had brought us a television (much smaller than the one we had in Iran), and he told me that it would be the best English teacher in the world. I watched hours and hours. It was from a crime show that I got my name, the name of an actor I was sure was Middle Eastern at least: *Michael Nouri.* It had a nice sound and it was apparently a name Middle Easterners could pull off in this country.

By the time it was September and time to go to school, I knew myself as Michael, and so would everyone else.

Moe approved. *Michael Jackson! A lucky name! Everyone loves Michael Jackson!* he said. I did not mention Nouri; instead, I embraced my name even more.

The only person who did not know—and wouldn't hear it anyway—was Madarbozorg.

Once a week, Moe came to our house for dinner. Madarbozorg was always cooking. She made elaborate, complicated feasts out of the limited grocery lists she'd send off to Moe. But when Moe actually sat down to dinner, you could always see that he was tense, tenser than when he was with just me. Always, just after the initial silence of us three mismatched relatives chewing, Madarbozorg would begin her usual questioning.

What about my cousin Mansoor? Lovely girl, keeps a very clean house.

Moe would nod and grunt every time. They were always in Iran, so he didn't have to worry about it.

Eventually, she'd get frustrated. *You need a wife*, she'd demand. *It's meaningless being all alone out here in a fake place like this.*

Once in a while he'd defend himself with a simple, *I have everything I need.* And rarely would he finish his food.

Eat more, she'd always say, and one time in a rare self-doubting moment, she added, *You don't like it?*

It's very good, he said, *but I'm not used to Iranian food. I usually eat dinner out, McDonald's or Pizza Hut, you know.*

At that point I had only had Tehran pizza and only heard of McDonald's. I started to doubt Moe's happiest-man-in-the-world status less.

* * *

Mother the Big, as I liked to call her more and more each day as I became more and more absorbed into the big body of the English language, had certain obsessions. In the first few months after our arrival, she constantly spoke in warnings, warnings about two things mainly: American women and earthquakes. One or both would get me, she seemed to think, and it was my duty to keep myself safe from them.

But don't they have earthquakes in Iran? I asked.

Yes, but our houses were strong there. Look at this cheap place. It wouldn't survive a kitten chase on its roof.

She asked Moe to get helmets for us and he brought back basic bicycle helmets, which she inspected with pleased grunts. He didn't ask any questions. I didn't either, because I knew it was going to be bad, whatever it was that was coming.

That night, she demanded we wear them to bed. She was convinced earthquakes would only come at night. And because we shared a room there was no way out. The first night, I couldn't get five minutes of sleep with my cheek uncomfortably wedged inside the round cage. I noticed Mother the Big was tossing and turning, too. But by the second night she was asleep—I could hear her snores—while I tossed.

I complained after a few days and she snapped, *Is it better to be dead or have some bad sleep? You haven't suffered!*

There was no way out.

Eventually I got used to bad sleep. But I thought of the other me in a parallel universe, sneaking the helmet under the bed when she was deep in snores. That me would be defeated, of course; the story would not end well, said a spy to a clown, but where was the story that would end better?

After all, what did it mean to stand up to Mother the Big? How could I *not* dream of that once in a while, O Madarbozorg-please-forgive-me?

In Iran, I was said to possess the seeds of insolence—I remember my parents telling everyone this, as if the more people knew, the more they'd be safe from it. But in America, it rarely broke the surface, happening less and less as time went by. And for good reason: insolence meant being subject to *behaviors*. It meant roars and wails. It meant slaps. It meant claws. It meant your tongue carrying a burning hot tenderizer, while she sang, as if it was a nursery rhyme, *You did it once, now you won't do it twice.*

It was not a good idea to disobey her.

So I endured the helmet. And I didn't worry about her second obsession, American women, assuming that was for Moe, not the preteen me, to worry about, at least for a while.

But they start young here, she warned me. *So don't trust the little girls either. Or the lady teachers—only do enough to get a good grade but don't linger.*

One time, a combination of bored and annoyed, I asked her what she thought American women did exactly.

They will bring you and your family more bad luck than you can imagine.

In some ways, her description thrilled me. What a strange new set of monsters these women were. In other ways, it terrified me. I caught myself looking the other way, cutting conversation short, even eyeing the women of the television with superstitious caution. I worried about Moe when he was over watching sports while Mother the Big cooked. When the cheerleaders came to do a dance, I told Moe it was better to cover the eyes.

Why?

They bring bad luck.

Who?

Women.

Women?

American women.

Moe shook his head; he knew where I got it from. Another time, I again warned Moe, after I saw him chatting enthusiastically with a drugstore-cashier-American-woman, and he said, both too firmly and a bit strangely, *You don't need to worry about me and that problem.*

There were secrets, myths and truths, rumor and history, all forbiddens that glittered for me, since what else did I have in my life but school and her? One time I was alone after school with Moe while Mother the Big went to the doctor (Moe was both her ride and my babysitter, though it would be the last of those days, as Moe declared I was old enough to take care of myself soon afterward), and Moe told me the biggest secret about her.

He told me Mother the Big's first husband, whom she'd only been married to briefly, before all her children, was a man known as the Butcher. He was a war general who had reportedly ordered brutal massacres of entire villages, Moe said. He always killed women and children first and then hung dozens of leaders of tribes in gallows for days. He poured hot lead on the heads of men 'til their eyes popped out and delivered the eyes to the king. The children in those southern villages were always warned, *Be careful, the Butcher will get you.*

I was not entirely surprised, of course, but that didn't stop me from being even more careful. At night I learned to see the helmet as a good thing, protection from tactics that were certainly in Mother the Big's blood, in something like her past-life muscle memory perhaps, the hot mallet suddenly seeming like nothing. Sometimes I'd wake up with a start convinced there was a burning at the back of my head, certain my eyes felt just a bit loose, and I'd look over and see the rise and fall of Mother the Big at rest, and I'd realize I was intact, at least for now.

How could it be possible that a single person could have no good features, like a scary Halloween mask, all entirely menace? I used to try to mentally argue for the things she did do that were good. I first thought of the meals, but I grew to dread them more and more. Soon I was dipping into her jar of laundry money for cafeteria food, which meant her packed lunches were getting tossed and sometimes even with a complete lack of remorse, O-Madarbozorg-forgive-me.

There was, of course, what came *after* dinner: the telling of stories.

Unlike my stories that were filled with cartoon animals and greeting-card morals, hers were just memories of Iran really, all true and almost cinematic in their realness. The more the American landscape became my reality, the more she seemed to flood me with the other stories, like documentaries of a foreign land that she was trying to program into my head before it was too late.

One time she did include an animal, a sheep she called Sepideh, an old pet of hers. Have you ever known boredom to be soothing? For me, boredom was the greatest gift, and I treasured her boring stories for interrupting our hard life together—what bad could ever come of things that didn't exist? And so as it often went, Sepideh's tale was long and flat, and I drifted in and out as she rattled away about how *Sepideh mewed not unlike a cat* and *Sepideh cried not unlike a child* and I thought about all my homework and why I couldn't get a B in Language Arts, if only I could get a B in Language Arts *and she was the best friend of your father who had no friends in the world but his sisters* and why was it so important to Ms. Norman that we run those eight laps around the ring and how on earth did she know when we did just seven *but when you live off the land like we did, really live off it in a way you can't imagine, there are sacrifices though he was too young to understand* and what would happen if I suddenly told the teacher I lost my grasp of English overnight, please could I get allowances like the ESL kids, could I be forgiven for being slow on tests and allowed to linger between classes, when suddenly *Do you hear me? If you're not going to take notes you have to listen—this is a man's job, what I'm telling you here* and I was snapped back by a certain harshness in her voice that told me that this was going somewhere else entirely: *First you kill the lamb by restraining it and then cutting into its neck with a special knife made for such things (that you have probably never seen) and then you cut through to take off the head and legs and then drain out the blood by hanging them upside down in a bucket and then you leave them to soak in cold water overnight and then the next day you take the head and legs with all the guts and veins still in them and put them in a pot of boiling water and boil it until all the wool comes off and if the wool doesn't all come off you burn the rest of the fur over a fire and then have a new boiling pot ready for the meat you clean and while it's all cooking, you add two large onions and four cloves garlic and turmeric and salt and pepper and then you cut the other parts of the body to eat later—you waste nothing—and once the head and legs are done (this is many hours, eight hours at least) you cut out tongue, eyes, and brain and serve them separately or add them as a topping to the stew with a bit of lemon and vinegar. Serve with bread and that's the end of that.*

I dared only blink after that story. It seemed too dangerous for an audible breath even. I had only one thought in my head.

She nodded at me, as if reading my mind. *This is the food that made me. One day.*

He always killed women and children first, the Butcher.

Sometimes the madness would break me.

One day, Mother the Big woke me up with a hard couple knocks on my helmet and said, *Look what Moe bought me.* I slowly pried my eyes open and saw her waving a tube of something that looked like toothpaste. *Dumb boy, don't you know what this is?*

I read the label. *Super Glue*, I said out loud.

She told me it was a miracle glue, the world's strongest glue. It could glue any two things in the world together and they would be one forever.

I wanted to go back to sleep so badly, but she pulled me out of bed, and handed me a tube, letting me know Moe bought two for us. Her instructions were simple: glue everything in the house to its foundation—books to bookshelves, lamps to tables, etc. The only exceptions were foods and toilet paper and objects too big to lift.

I dared ask. *Why?*

She looked so triumphant. Of course why. *Because it's coming, the big earthquake, I can feel it.*

I helped her glue things and in my head I prayed—and not in the way you would have it, O Madarbozorg-how-sorry-I-am-today—but I prayed terribly, prayed acidly, and prayed most jaggedly, for all the bad in the world, all of it and then It too, for It to come and knock us both off the planet to orbit in space, a nothing-place where no one belonged to no where, where she could still be in my vision but couldn't actually get me, where the care we were supposed to take of each other could happen at something greater than a god's arm's length, oh grandmotherfucker! As I glued, I realized I was badly breaking down but, like Americans put it, I was breaking like a tree that falls in the woods that no one witnesses, but with a slight twist: one person did witness the tree falling, saw everything and took it all in, and still she insisted there was no falling, and maybe no tree even.

I thought it would be the other way around but as I grew older I thought it may not be so—that the earthquakes she could maybe control, but the American women, perhaps not. Suddenly I had a vision of something else, the thing that would save me, a dream of dreams. I dreamt of another *her*, the only *her*, this girl who would be mine. In my dreams she had hair as yellow as Scooby's Daphne and eyes as blue as the Frosted Flakes box. And she had freckles, like all American girls, and she was thin, maybe with braces. In my dreams, we'd be holding hands as we floated in revolutions among fog and neon lights, to the tune of pop songs. The third time I dreamt this, I realized we were roller-skating, something I had never done of course, but something I suspected would be a delight to master, a perfect pastime for me and my dream girl.

Where was this girl? She was everywhere, in every class of mine since then, from elementary to junior high to high school; she was the mother of other students, the girlfriend, the sales clerk, the actress on TV—

She was, I knew, Mother the Big's greatest fear in the world for me. I knew and yet—

—she was the pageant queen and the murder victim and the milk-carton-missing and the punk rocker and the cartoon of an early settler in the history book. She was dancing alone to Madonna in her bedroom; she was in a skirt, with one leg up a tree, tying her shoelaces; she was laughing so hard milk was coming out of her nose at lunch; she was buried behind shopping bags at the mall; she was the first girl who called me *sandnigger* with a flick of her shimmering pink-nail-polished middle finger . . .

And yet! Why would I—*I*—have ever looked for her? I was invisible here. I was the weird kid, so odd that I did not register. I watched girls giggle about boys and pass notes over and over and over my desk; I saw couples form like magic at all the afterschool dances I never went to but lingered to watch before the dreary walk home; one lunch break, I even saw two of my classmates kiss just like movie stars. It was all around me, but the rules were clear—it was not for me, fake Michael, that Michael of all the hidden syllables and sounds of my other life.

But with time, it seemed, I was wrong about that too, like many things out here. In high school, a girl who had been in many of my classes for years, a girl named Amy, slipped me a note between classes one day. She did it with a strange, beautifully brace-faced sort of smile and ran off quickly afterwards. I opened it, the note folded in an origami bird of some sort, and read the pink-penned cursive that I could have sworn left a smell of berries.

It said, *Michael you are so great this is so weird I know whatever but I like you just thought I'd let you know see you around Amy.* Under her name she had made a happy face.

I did what they called "died," over and over, as I reread that somehow real note. Here she was, and not just any girl, but a girl with golden hair and blue eyes (I was pretty sure they were blue) and freckles and braces. My American dream girl liked me.

Amy became my girlfriend in a matter of weeks. We secretly held hands between classes and started sitting next to each other more and more until everyone knew. Soon we were "going around." And for the first time, Madarbozorg-forgive-me, I was not alone.

Are your parents strict? she wondered one day when I clumsily dodged her movie invite.

My guardian—my grandmother, I corrected, explaining the scenario.
Is she strict? she asked again.

I shrugged, not because I didn't know if she was, not because the word didn't do it justice. You could say I shrugged to change the subject, and she complied. This exchange happened over and over again: I was somewhere else, always somewhere else to be at that point, maybe somewhere along the axis to whatever planet my distant parents parented from. I thought over all the hard questions about the who and what and how of me, and commercial breaks would insert themselves, carrying on about the selling of something with a cheerful, mindless jingle—or perhaps, best of all, just the Lego colors and the relentless drone of the Emergency Broadcasting System and its this-is-only-a-test promise.

When it came time for her to come home with me, of course I snuck her in—that, we always knew, was how the story would go. In our TV shows you always saw kids sneaking in through each other's windows. But, since some basic testing revealed that the windows were too high and the screens too loud to pop open, and because those days Mother the Big went to sleep quite early, we took an even simpler route. It was ingenious, we thought, for its boneheaded simplicity: Amy would come to the door at an hour late enough for Mother the Big to be sleeping and I would simply *let her in.* By then, Mother the Big was used to me getting up in the night, wandering, often sneaking to the living room to watch TV.

A risk, but a risk worth taking, we loosely calculated.

(And who knows, maybe I felt there was nothing to do but to get caught to rid myself of you, O forgive-me-Madarbozorg.)

By that point Amy and I had done it all: tried beer (I liked the buzz and pretended to love the taste, and she loved it all, or maybe she was pretending, too), and shared a cigarette (all we did was cough through it, both hating it). Our lips had even met one day at lunch period when she pulled me into a girl's bathroom stall—a perfect first kiss, as the fear of being caught in the girl's stall eclipsed the more rational lifetime fear I had of kissing a girl, and of all girls, *this* girl, my dream girl! I went with it, this dream life, and all its twists.

For the first half of that sleepover night at least, we were in top form; we behaved like experts. Tiptoes that were almost levitation they were

43

so light, whispers that were just a wisp more substantial than mouthed words, and then all the things that did not require a sound: nudges and brushes and nuzzles and bites and embraces and kisses. How we didn't worry about Amy's exit or how it would end or everything being over, I don't know. We just stayed in every one of those precious moments like they were bonus frames added to the movie of our lives, and we just took and it gave and we took and it gave, and the world suspended itself for us, dream lovers drunk on the rhythm of our luck.

But maybe, O Madarbozorg, that's precisely the tragedy: the folly of teenagers. Maybe you knew this, maybe even in your sleep you sensed it. Many stories in Persian legend speak of heroes that fall only when they get too comfortable with things and maybe that was my problem too. Suddenly you entered my thoughts and I resented that intrusion even for a second, O Madarbozorg-certainly-you'd-be-unable-to-forgive-me, and I began cursing you in my head like I'd never cursed you before, over and over, I said it all, nothing unsaid, and I said it all and added some even to that, and I said it all and took the whole universe down.

Or maybe *you* did. O Madarbozorg, why didn't I know just how big, just how larger than life you were then, when all around us the world began to tremble into itself, with a rattling the likes of which I had never heard, and then a rumbling, the sensation of every inch of foundation on this very earth shuddering, the whole miserable universe so awfully alive.

And we grabbed our clothes and put them half-on and ducked under the table as they'd too many times drilled us in school and we wordlessly watched the spectacle of some sort of undoing. All I remember is that at first I prayed—to my parents, to comic book gods, to the inventor of Super Glue (indeed as much as we shook, only the biggest objects teetered since everything else was glued in place). And how we shook and how we shook even more when suddenly your wail, followed by your person, helmet in place, missiled towards us.

And that was when the one bookshelf in the living room, perfectly intact with the books all glued in place, collapsed right on top of Mother the Big like a mugger perfectly toppling his choice bystander. It took her over and she disappeared almost silently, though it was hard to make out one sound from another between Amy's cries, my whimpers, and the gasps and stammers of everything rattling in its place.

When the shaking stopped, Amy and I went over to the bookshelf and propped it up to uncover what we believed would be a terrible scene underneath.

But there was no blood, no guts, no nothing. Just a groaning, dusty, scratched Mother the Big getting up on her feet. For a second her eyes looked lunatically confused, like an animal plucked from the wild and dropped amidst city streets. But then her look went back to its ugly normal. *Next time, we glue even the big things to the ground*, she growled straight at me.

As if on cue, the earth began shaking again, and again we were under the table, this time all three of us. The earth fiercely shook and timidly shook and stopped and then reluctantly shook and defiantly shook, and in one of these brief stops she pointed at Amy and turned to me and said, *What is this? I will tell you what it is. It's what's caused the world to end on us* . . . I was amazed it had taken her so long to say even that and then I was less amazed at what followed: curses that matched and then topped mine, her hands clawing at the trembling air.

Amy, frightened by it all, began to cry and I held her—not just to comfort her, but to hold her away from Mother the Big. Finally when the shaking stopped she whispered a single question, what had my grandmother said about it, all of it—stupid girl, she wanted to be spared nothing.

Maybe that was the beginning of a sort of end for us, I don't know, but I gave into exhaustion and just blurted the truth: *She said she wished she had actually died instead of witnessing that girl—you know, you*, but at least that was where I stopped, since it was the least offensive of everything she had said.

Amy nodded and cried again and I hurried her out to rush her home, where her parents were no doubt angry on top of worried. At the door, her bloodshot eyes looked hard into my bloodshot eyes, and finally she uttered, *How did that not kill her? Not even hurt her?*

I shrugged it off, but I was thinking the same thing. Still, I was surprised at the calm I felt—everything bad that could have happened did, it was all over—until I worried it was just the incubation period for all my worries to turn into one much bigger worry.

I'll never forget the slowness and care with which I closed the door on my dream girl, to prolong the second before I had to turn and meet the eyes of my nightmare woman, my maker's maker, that unfathomably big

Mother the Big. But I wasn't sure what she could have in store that was worse than what had come to be anyway: everything she feared for me was slowly coming true.

Nothing had changed; everything was changing. It all seemed to revolve around a main problem: the thought, that very thought we did not know what to do with, that she wasn't supposed to have lived through the earthquake. But what surprised me the most was that Mother the Big must have shared this thought with us. Over the next weeks, just as aftershocks checked in here and there like clingy reminders of where we'd been and how far we still had to go, her behavior seemed frozen in that one moment.

It was harder to watch than I would have imagined, this phase in which Mother the Big repeatedly tried to kill herself.

I don't know what she was thinking. Were we her theater audience? Did she see us watching it all? Did she care? Maybe she was too busy surviving the kitchen knives slicing at her wrist only to produce no blood; vomiting the laundry detergent that did little more than cause a burp marathon; outliving the noose that refused to tighten, left like a necklace around her neck as she did household chores. And what did she think we were thinking? If Mother the Big had been anywhere near as invested as I had imagined in wanting to terrify us into submission, this would have been the ultimate. But during this phase she just seemed dazed, resigning herself to it perhaps, the bad we had all brought on ourselves.

We felt a silent *we* in it all, for once.

Amy, maybe starting to crack from guilt, decided Mother the Big had been a ghost from day one. *It's the only logical thing*, she'd say again and again, *It's the only thing that's somewhat human sounding. I mean, we have a reference point for that. Whoever heard of someone being indestructible?*

It happens in comic books, I'd retort.

And they're not real, she'd snap.

Just saying—that's a reference point.

It was hard to know which was worse—going through it or being witness to it. But Amy and I were definitely having trouble surviving it. She started coming around less and less, which honestly relieved me.

And yet being alone with you, O Madarbozorg, how it chilled me. Maybe the worst element of all was the mere visual spectacle, so impossible to forget. One day, after a panic attack brought on by seeing her gouge screwdrivers into her eyeballs to no result, I finally got the courage to tell Moe. *Moe, there is something I have to tell you that you can't tell anyone. It's very important.*

Anything, lips sealed. He sounded so casual.

I wondered if he could be trusted and decided probably not entirely. *I'll tell you this thing in exchange for something. So my secret for one of yours, okay?* It seemed like a proper tough guy transaction.

Moe had chuckled. When I told him the chuckling stopped.

Are you okay, Michael? he said over and over.

I am okay, I told him. *I'm the one who is okay.*

I'm coming over, he said. *We're in a car now nearby, we'll be right over.*

Your secret, please, I demanded, the sibilance a snake's hiss.

Moe sighed. *I'm coming over with my* boyfriend. *Good enough?*

I pocketed the revelation without a further thought. Normally, that idea would have been like a cartoon cliff drop, a dead-in-my-tracks, half-way-off-the-mountain sort of deal. But in the context of everything, it barely hit me.

I went to find Mother the Big by the window, a flicker of something in her eyes, no doubt conjuring another suicidal scheme as was her pastime in those days.

Madarbozorg, I said in that tone of voice I had begun talking to her in, the tone of a good Iranian grandson, I hoped. And then I said the craziest thing of all: *Everything will be all right.*

Her look went from daze to suspicion, the most she had for me during those weeks, it seemed.

I scanned the outside with her silently. Never had the idea of Moe been so relieving.

Mother the Big's eyes narrowed. *If you're looking for the girl to come here, I will burn this whole place down.*

I'm not, I said, and made a mental note to make sure Amy never came again. *It's just Moe who is coming over.*

That did it: her eyes flickered, a candle in a dust storm. Possessed, she rushed to the door and stood in the driveway and then in the middle of the street. I tried to call her back in, figuring out what she was up to, but soon I was out and taking in yet another hideous action scene: Mother the Big charging the maroon Chevy with Moe in the passenger seat.

The driver, Moe's boyfriend—all I registered then was a big blonde man—turned off the engine and ran out yelling. Moe calmly gave me a pat on the back hello and then we both kneeled down, trying to pull out Mother the Big's body from halfway underneath the car.

See what I mean? I said to Moe.

Mother the Big was out and standing soon enough. She coughed a few times, straightened her dress, which was lined with tire tracks, and went inside, cursing under her breath.

The minute she was out of sight I collapsed into Moe's arms and cried and cried; his boyfriend, also crying and crying, completed the sandwich, our sad weeping man sandwich, while we all imagined the eyes of her on us: all disapproval, all disdain, all divine wrath.

We talked for hours and hours that night at Moe's house about how to get rid of her. Report her? Imprison her? Institutionalize her? But a person incapable of death was basically god, who were we kidding.

While we thought of ways to get rid of her, apparently she was trying to think of ways to rid herself of us, though not in the ways we imagined. When we got back there, she was gone, her stuff and her one rolling suitcase from Iran. Like a normal runaway human, simply gone.

We weren't sure what it meant—living on the streets? Excursion to other undead folk? But we were relieved we had over- and underestimated her. The whole time we wanted her gone, why did we imagine she'd want anything else herself?

For too many months to count everything was as it should have been: Amy and I in each other's lives constantly, McDonald's and sleepovers, beer and a few more tries at cigarettes, and eventually the thing that comes after the American proverbial third base, should O-Madarbozorg-disapprove-of-a-more-descriptive-word. Amy and I were alone, so blissfully alone to enjoy each other, that we even began jokingly calling each other *husband* and *wife*.

One night, we drank too much and I began going on with my stories— *did you know the tiger was in love with the little pig, oh yes he was, and without the rabbit, the tiger could cause a ruckus to entertain the pig and the pig, afraid of everything but him in the world, cheered him on and on*—and suddenly Amy got serious and asked about the future.

What will happen? She wondered. *We're not kids. I don't even know what I want to be.*

I laughed, inappropriately. *Just stick with me! I know it all! I'm going to be a star!*

Sometimes, when drunk especially, I entertained notions of becoming the first big Middle Eastern entertainer, bigger than Nouri, Jackson, any other Michael out there.

The conversation was full of these twists and turns—Amy's anxiety and my deflection of it with jokes and nonsense and lofty declarations and stumbles back into storytelling. At some point we must have passed out. When I woke it was barely dawn, the world the very pure, fragile blue of liquid ballpoint pen scribble-scapes, the light shy in breaking through, the day clinging to night. I looked at her, in her own dreams then, still my dream girl, and I thought everything was perfect. And then when bits of the night before came to me like torn scraps of notebook paper scattering in the wind, I knew what to do.

We were not kids. We were teenagers, older teenagers. Once young for my age, I was now too old. We had been through things now. We were all potential and future and finally, we were just about allowed to choose it all ourselves. We were on the cusp of all that everything.

And so I woke her up with a kiss and watched her eyes flutter open and close and open like a baby farm animal resisting the crass fluorescence of the real world. And I said to her immediately, *I know what will happen, wife. Just that: you will be my wife.*

And she blinked at me some more, this time very much awake.

And I rephrased: *What I mean is, will you be my wife?*

And when we kissed it was a kiss unlike any kiss we had committed at that point—forget our setting, that teenage den of pizza boxes and DVD cases and sleeping bags and dirty clothes—it was the kiss of hotel lobbies and skyscraper rooftops, the kiss of movie stars, of grown beautiful people on top of the world, a kiss meant to be watched by millions with tissues in their hands, a kiss made for standing ovations and awards, the kiss before the credits, the kiss before the cut, the kiss just as the sun rose behind us and announced, *this is the beginning of your life.*

In that moment as they—storytellers or sages or cliché-makers or some combination of them—always said, all my troubles indeed seemed far away and my worries melted. Even the worry behind all my worries, that worry that would not let go of me, was gone. For that moment.

And just that moment. Because when she pulled away from me, blinking more quickly, as if suddenly everything was different. I knew it was true and everything had changed, more than I had even anticipated. Something else was happening, and I found myself blinking too, the room suddenly white with a blinding brightness, daylight screaming at us, an angry imposing sun absorbing and claiming all the potential we had in that moment.

In my head I heard the voice of a woman hiss to a man, *This will not end well*.

Out loud I heard a voice I knew too well, O worry of worry, O Madarbozorg-in-the-flesh-forgive-me: *What did I tell you? They will bring you and your family more bad luck than you can imagine.*

She was back, but was she ever gone? I had nothing in me but a wave: I waved hello, I waved goodbye.

At first we spent every spare hour of school trying to conspire. But how could we do anything? We were wasting away. I watched Amy grow thinner by the day—her blonde and her blue eyes all somehow looking more gray. I was also thinning, finding little interest in burgers and pizza and beer and the precious few illicit things that had become fixtures in our American life.

I began dreaming of Iran more and more, and thinking of Amy and America less and less.

I had declarations, like mantras: *We're stuck with her.* I had resolutions, like resignations: *That's what we get.*

Then one day we walked together to my home and opened the door to an apartment full of helmets. The entire living room was like a bombed bowling alley with helmets of all shapes and sizes, at least several dozen, clustered in various chaotic displays. Mother the Big was sitting by the TV, watching a game show in her own new helmet, a Halloween Viking one with horns and braids that would have looked comical was it not so frightening on her.

Amy and I gasped—she of plain horror, I guessed; me of horror and logistics. How did she manage to conjure all those helmets?

Don't be afraid, American girl—she looked at her, but said to me in Farsi—*from now on everyone who sleeps in this house sleeps in helmets. I feel another one coming! But this time we will be prepared!*

My translation came out in rasps and croaks. Amy lost it suddenly. She turned to her and said in English she must have known she couldn't understand, *Why won't you*—and I knew what Amy was going to say, three reckless words no one I could ever love would dare utter, of course—*leave us alone?*

Mother the Big began laughing in a way I had never heard, high-pitched cackles, long and sharp and manic and almost extraterrestrial in their resonance. American girl, of course, had really done it now.

And somehow she had understood. *Tell her I'm not going anywhere. I'm quite happy here in hell, Michael.*

It was the first time she had called me by my chosen name. I nodded and told Amy.

Amy went over to a plastic chair, gently removed the two helmets that were claiming that space, and sat and wept silently—I knew the expression well—as Mother the Big went on to speak of how for weeks and weeks on end she had walked, hoping to drain her own battery, of course, but no exhaustion had come, just more and more and more hunger. *I'm now so very hungry I'm making a dinner of dinners to welcome me home.*

My American girl—sometimes in those days *American girl* to me too, I had to confess—excused herself to the bathroom and stayed there for a very long time. Soon I was going to lose her; that I knew. She was easily lost, unlike that forever woman, maker of makers, Mother the Big.

But for that night, we were together. We politely picked out our helmets and sat at the dinner table in them, looking glumly at the settings. She tended to the very strong-smelling pot of something, humming a particularly somber Persian dirge as she stirred, the Viking helmet making her look all the more mad. Amy and I would sneak looks at each other, looks that for me at least were not meant to project anything really.

I tried to escape to other places, like trigonometry homework and the SATs and how little was left of it all and wondering if my credits could transfer to school in Iran—but inevitably my eyes rested on that Viking dome of horns and braids and the spirit underneath it stirring furiously. The pot was not unlike a cauldron, all of it a sort of Halloween confusion.

Amy's eyes just rested shut in waiting, which made me feel like I needed to open mine up all the more—we were still connected but like a rope and its two ends, in opposite directions, freed of potential, no forced ties—and I watched the thing boil and boil, and it let out a stench that went from odd to otherworldly, only understanding her fervor when for a second I got a flash of what was to come, what deserved to come, I suppose, our last meal together as three: the eye of a long-gone animal—some being's beloved, some being's sacrifice—rolling helplessly in the cradle of its own limb.

ALEKSANDAR HEMON

Aleksandar Hemon was born in Sarajevo, Yugoslavia (now Bosnia and Herzegovina), in 1964. He was visiting the United States in 1992 when war broke out across Yugoslavia and Sarajevo was besieged. Unable to return, Hemon settled in Chicago to work and study English.

Hemon has since published many works in English, including *The Lazarus Project* (2008), a finalist for both the 2008 National Book Award and the National Book Critics Circle Award. He also published three story collections and, most recently, a nonfiction work called *The Book of My Lives* (2013). Hemon received a Guggenheim Fellowship in 2003 and a MacArthur Foundation Fellowship in 2004.

"The Bees, Part 1" comes from his 2009 collection of stories, *Love and Obstacles*. In a 2009 interview with *Bookforum* about the book, Hemon discussed his split life between the former Yugoslavia and the United States. "There was a time, and this is in itself a symptom of trauma, when I thought about the previous life and this life—the discontinuity, the rupture. Whatever happened in the previous life was inaccessible and unavailable. . . . But then, I closed that gap, and it's now all part of one life because writing has provided me with a context where the previous life and the present life could be reconciled and engaged with each other. Still, there is a sense that something is irretrievably lost, but I've learned to live with that."

The Bees, Part 1

This Is Not Real

Many years ago my sister and I went to see a movie with our parents. The movie was about a handsome lad on a treasure hunt in Africa, in the course of which he meets a beautiful young lady he seems to get along with. Mother passed out instantly—moving pictures regularly put her to sleep. Father snorted derisively a few times, whispering into my ear: "This is stupid." He started turning to people around him, touching them as if to make them snap out of their dreams, imploring them: "People, don't believe this! Comrades! This is not real!" The audience, deeply invested in the trials and tribulations of the hero, who was presently dangling topsy-turvy over a pit of ravenous crocodiles, did not respond well to my father's prodding. An usher came by and tried, in vain, to silence him. My sister and I pretended to be focused on the screen, while our mother was woken by the ruckus only to find herself in the middle of an embarrassment. In the end, Father stormed out furiously, dragging my sister and me, Mother apologizing to the peevish audience in our wake. We took a departing look at the screen, as distant as a sunset: the hero and the disheveled (yet fair) damsel, deep in the jungle teeming with invisible villains, riding a pair of comically trotting mules.

The Nightmare in Installments

My father developed his hatred of the unreal back when he was at university. One morning in his dorm room he emerged from his slumber with a clearly remembered nightmare. He immediately described it to his two roommates, the experience still disturbingly fresh in his mind. The dream involved danger, pain, and mystery, although there was also an encounter with a woman. His roommates were transfixed listening to him, while he led them down the steep, untrodden paths of his subconscious. But a moment before the face of the woman was to be revealed and the dream resolved, my father came to.

The following night, the nightmare resumed just where it had ended—the woman was beautiful and held my father's head in her lap while he wept. Then he wandered and roamed in absurdly changing landscapes; he came across talking animals, including a dog from his childhood whom his father had killed with an ax blow to the head; there were more women, including his dead mother. Then he held a watermelon with the distorted face of someone he knew but could not recognize, and when it broke open, he found a letter addressed to him. He was just about to read it when he woke up.

My father's roommates, who skipped their morning classes to hear the new developments in his troubling dreams, were sorely disappointed not to find out what was in the letter. In their afternoon classes, recounting Father's nightmare to their fellow students, they kept speculating—titillated by the fact that it all meant something they could not grasp—what could have been in the letter, and whether the beautiful woman would ever return.

When my father woke up the following morning, the room was full of people sitting in silence, patiently waiting, their breathing slow and deep. Many eyes stared at him, as if trying to read the denouement from his face. Whatever dream my father might have had evaporated the instant his roommates asked him what was in the letter. Father did not dare disappoint them, so he opened the letter and made up the content—there was a woman who was kept in a dark dungeon by an evil man. Thence my father spun an epic narrative, obviously influenced by the archetypal picaresque stories he had read and the horror movies he had seen at the university cinema hall. Yet, even making it up, he didn't know how to end his nightmare narrative. He reached the point of confronting the evil man, but could not think of what to say, so he insisted he had to hurry to his international relations class.

And so it went on: my father would wake up to face an audience simultaneously demanding the resolution and hating the prospect thereof. But he got entangled in all his subplots and minor narratives and kept evading the conclusion, hoping it would come to him eventually. His audiences dwindled, until one of his roommates (Raf, who was to become a manic-depressive flight controller) accused him of lying. It hurt my father, for he was an honest man, but he knew that he could not say that Raf was not right. He was trapped by his own imagination, my father; he slid down the slippery slope of unreality and could not crawl back up. That was when he learned his lesson, he said. That's when he became committed to the real.

My Life

One day Father came back from work with a Super 8 camera, which he had borrowed from one of his coworkers (Božo A., who had a black belt in karate and a budding brain tumor—he died before my father could return the camera). The camera was smaller than I had imagined, possessing a kind of technological seriousness that suggested only important things could be recorded with it. He announced his desire to make a film that would not lie. When my mother asked what the movie would be about, he dismissed the question as immature. "The truth," he said. "Obviously."

Nevertheless, Father wrote the script for his film in a week, at the end of which he declared that it would be the story of his life. I was cast to play the young him, and my sister to play his sister (he didn't say which one—he had five), and my mother would be his assistant. She instantly resigned from her assistant director position, as she wanted to spend her vacation reading, but the shooting was scheduled for the middle of June 1986, when we were supposed to go to the country to visit my grandparents—we would shoot, as they say, on location.

My father refused to show us the script, uninterested in the fact that the actors normally get to see scripts: he wanted life itself to be our inspiration, for, he reminded us, this film was to be *real*. Nevertheless, during our regular inspection of his desk (my sister and I went through our parents' documents and personal things to keep apprised of their development), we found the script. I'm able to reproduce it pretty accurately, since my sister and I read it to each other a few times, with a mixture of awe and hilarity. Here it is:

My Life

1. *I am born.*
2. *I walk.*
3. *I watch over cows.*
4. *I leave home to go to school.*
5. *I come back home. Everybody's happy.*
6. *I leave home to go to university.*
7. *I'm in class. I study at night.*
8. *I go out for a stroll. I see a pretty girl.*
9. *My parents meet the pretty girl.*
10. *I marry the pretty girl.*
11. *I work.*
12. *I have a son.*
13. *I'm happy.*
14. *I keep bees.*
15. *I have a daughter.*
16. *I'm happy.*
17. *I work.*
18. *We are by the seaside, then in the mountains.*
19. *We are happy.*
20. *My children kiss me.*
21. *I kiss them.*
22. *My wife kisses me.*
23. *I kiss her.*
24. *I work.*
25. *The End*

Farewell

The first scene we were supposed to shoot (and the only one that was ever shot) was Scene 4. The location was the slope of the hill on top of which my grandparents' house was perched. I, in the role of my father at the age of sixteen, was supposed to walk away from the camera with a bundle hanging from a stick on my shoulder, whistling a plaintive melody. I was to turn around and look past the camera, as if looking at the home I was leaving—and then I would wave, bidding farewell. My father would pan to my grandparents' house, though, strictly speaking, that house was not the home he'd left.

The first take failed because I didn't wave with enough emotion. My hand, my father said, looked like a limp plucked chicken. He needed more emotion from me—I was leaving my home never to return.

The second take was interrupted as my father decided to zoom in on a bee that just happened to land on a flower nearby.

My two aunts suddenly appeared in the third take, as my father was panning from my poignant goodbye to the house. They stood grinning, paralyzed by the lens for a moment, then casually waved at the camera.

Each time, I had to walk uphill to my starting position, so I could walk away downhill in the next take. My legs hurt, I was thirsty and hungry, and I could not help questioning my father's directorial wisdom: Why wasn't he/I taking a bus? Didn't he/I need more stuff than what could fit in a bundle? Didn't he/I need some food for the road?

During the fifth take, the camera ran out of film.

The sixth take was almost perfect: I walked away from home, my shoulders slouching with sorrow, my pace aptly hesitant, the bundle dangling poignantly from the convincingly crooked stick. I turned around, completely in character, and looked at the home and life I was about to leave for good: the house was white with a red roof; the sun was setting behind it. Tears welled up in my eyes as I waved at the loving past, before heading toward an unknowable future, my hand like a metronome counting the beats of the saddest adagio. Then I heard a bee buzzing right around the nape of my neck. My metronome hand switched to allegro as I flaunted it around my head trying to defend myself. The bee would not go away, revving furiously its little engine, and the sting was imminent. I dropped the stick and started running, first uphill, toward the camera, then downhill, until my heels were kicking my butt, my arms flailing, all semblance of rhythm abandoned. The bee pursued me relentlessly and unflinchingly, and I was more terrified by its determination than the forthcoming pain: it would not quit even as I was hollering, throwing in the air all the arms I could muster, lunging at incredible speed, a manic mass of discordant movements. And the more I ran, the farther I was from any help and comfort. It was in the moment before I tripped and tumbled head over heels that I realized the bee was entangled in my hair—the attempt to escape was meaningless. I felt the sting as I was rolling downhill, toward the bottom I would never reach. I was stopped by a thornbush, where the sting became indistinguishable from many a thorn.

Need I say that my father kept filming it all? There I am, verily flapping my arms, as if trying to take off, a clueless Icarus leaping downhill farther from the skies, while a cow watches me, masticating with a sublime absence of interest, suggesting that God and his innocent creatures would never give a flying fuck about the fall of man. Then I tumble and hit the bush of thorns, and my father, with a cold presence of his directorial mind, my father fades me out.

Other Works

To my father's creative biography I should add his carpentry, which frequently reached poetic heights: more than once we witnessed him caressing or kissing a piece of wood he was about to transform into a shelf, a stool, or a beehive frame; not infrequently, he forced me to touch and then smell a "perfect" piece of wood; he demanded that I appreciate the smooth knotlessness, its natural scent. For Father, a perfect world consisted of objects you could hold in your hand.

He built all kinds of things: structures to hold my mother's plants, toolboxes, beds and chairs, beehives, et cetera, but his carpenterial masterpiece was a nailless kitchen table he spent a month building. He paid a price: one afternoon he emerged from his workshop, his palm sliced open with a chisel, the blood gushing and bubbling from its center, as from a well—a detail worthy of a biblical miracle. He drove himself to the hospital, and afterward the car looked like a crime scene.

He also liked to sing anything that allowed his unsophisticated baritone to convey elaborate emotional upheavals. I remember the evening I found him sitting in front of the TV, with a notebook and an impeccably sharpened pencil, waiting for the musical show that was sure to feature his favorite song at the time: "Kani Suzo, Izdajice"—"Drop, You Traitor Tear." He wrote down the words, and in the days that followed he sang "Kani Suzo, Izdajice" from the depths of his throat, humming through the lyrics he couldn't recall, getting ready for future performances. He sang at parties and family gatherings, sometimes grabbing a mistuned guitar from someone's hand, providing accompaniment that comprised the same three chords (Am, C, D7) regardless of the song. He seemed to believe that even a severely mistuned guitar provided "atmosphere," while the harmonic simplification enhanced the emotional impact of any given song. There was something to be said for that: it was hard to deny the power of his baritone against the background of the discordant noise worthy of Sonic Youth, a tear glimmering in the corner of his eye, on the verge of committing betrayal.

His photography merits a mention, even if its main function was to record the merciless passing of time. Most of his photos are structurally identical despite the change of clothes and background: my mother, my sister, and I facing the camera, the flow of time measured by the increasing amounts of my mother's wrinkles and gray hair, the width of my sister's beaming smile, and the thickness of the smirking and squinting on my face.

One more thing: He once bought a notebook, and on the first page wrote: *This notebook is for expressing the deepest thoughts and feelings of the members of our family.* It seemed he intended to use those feelings and thoughts as material for a future book, but few were expressed. I, for one, certainly wasn't going to let my parents or my sister (ever eager to tease me to tears) in on the tumultuous events in my adolescent soul. Thus there were only two entries: a cryptic note from my mother, who probably just grabbed the notebook while on the phone and wrote:

> *Friday*
> *Healthy children*
> *Thyme*

and a line from my sister, in her careful and precise prepubescent handwriting:

> *I am really sad, because the summer is almost over.*

The Real Book

Whatever conveyed reality earned my father's unqualified appreciation. He was suspicious of broadcast news, relentlessly listing the daily triumphs of socialism, but was addicted to the weather forecast. He read the papers, but found only the obituaries trustworthy. He loved nature shows, because the existence and the meaning of nature were self-evident—there was no denying a python swallowing a rat, or a cheetah leaping on the back of an exhausted, terrified monkey.

My father, I say, was deeply and personally offended by anything he deemed unreal. And nothing insulted him more than literature; the whole concept was a scam. Not only that words—whose reality is precarious at best—were what it was all made from, but those words were used to render *what never happened*. This dislike of literature and its spurious nature may have been worsened by my intense interest in books (for which he blamed my mother) and my consequent attempts to get him interested. For his forty-fifth birthday I unwisely gave him a book called *The Liar*—he read nothing of it but the title. Once I read him a passage from a García Márquez story in which an angel falls from the skies and ends up in a chicken coop. After this my father was seriously concerned about my mental capacities. There were other, similar incidents, all of them appalling enough for him to start casually mentioning his plan to write a *real* book.

He didn't seem to think that writing such a book was a particularly trying task—all one needed to do was not get carried away by indulgent fantasies, stick to what really happened, hold on to its unquestionable firmness. He could do that, no problem; the only thing he needed was a few weeks off. But he could never find a time: there was his job, and bees, and things to be built, and the necessary replenishing naps. Only once did he approach writing anything—one afternoon I found him snoring on the couch with his notebook on his chest and a pencil with a broken tip on the floor, the only words written: *Many years ago.*

The Writer's Retreat

My father began writing in Canada, in the winter of 1994. They had just landed, after a couple of years of exile and refugee roaming, the years I spent working low-wage jobs and pursuing a green card in Chicago. They had left Sarajevo the day the siege began and went to my deceased grandparents' house in the countryside, ostensibly to escape the trouble. The real reason was that it was time for the spring works in my father's apiary, which he kept at the family estate. They spent a year there, on a hill called Vučijak, living off the food they grew in the garden, watching trucks of Serbian soldiers going to the front. My father occasionally sold them honey, and toward the end of that summer started selling mead, although the soldiers much preferred getting drunk on slivovitz. My parents secretly listened to the radio broadcast from the besieged Sarajevo and feared a knock at the door in the middle of the night. Then my mother had a gallbladder infection and nearly died, so they went to Novi Sad, where my sister was attempting to complete her university degree. They applied for a Canadian immigration visa, got it, and arrived in Hamilton, Ontario, in December 1993.

From the window of the fifteenth-floor unfurnished apartment they moved into they could see piles of snow, the smokestacks of the Hamilton steel mills, and a vacant parking lot. It was all black and white and bleak and gray, like an existentialist European movie (which my father found unreal without exception, and morbidly boring on top of it). He started despairing as soon as he set foot on Canadian soil: he didn't know where they had landed, how they were going to live and pay for food and furniture; he didn't know what would happen to them if one of them got terribly sick. And it was perfectly clear to him that he would never learn the English language.

My mother, on the other hand, let her stoic self take over—partly to counterbalance my father's darkest fears, partly because she felt so defeated that it didn't matter anymore. It was okay now to give herself to the tragic flow of things and let happen whatever was going to happen. My mind stores an image of her patiently and unfalteringly turning a Rubik's Cube in her hands, while a report on a Sarajevo massacre is on TV, completely unfazed by the fact that she is not, and never would be, anywhere close to the solution.

Soon enough, my mother set up the apartment with the used furniture her English teacher had given them. The place still looked hollow, devoid of all those crumbles of a lived life that lead you back home: the heavy green malachite ashtray Father brought back from Zaire; a picture of me and my sister as kids, sitting in a cherry tree, smiling, my sister's cheek pressing against my arm, me holding on to a branch with both of my hands like a chimpanzee (I fell off the tree and broke my arm the instant after the picture was taken); a spider brooch my mother kept in a heavy crystal ashtray; a moisture stain on a bathroom pipe that looked like an unshaven, long-haired Lenin; honey jars with labels that had little bees flying out of the corners toward the center, where the words "Real Honey" stood out in boldface—none of those things was there, now slowly fading into mere memories.

My father dropped out of his English class, furious at the language that randomly distributed meaningless articles and insisted on having a subject in every stupid sentence. He made cold calls to Canadian companies and in unintelligible English described his life, which included being a diplomat in the world's greatest cities, to perplexed receptionists who would simply put him on indefinite hold. He nearly got sucked into a venture set up by a shady Ukrainian who convinced him there was money in smuggling Ukrainian goose down and selling it to the Canadian bedding industry.

Sometimes I'd call from Chicago and my father would pick up the phone.

"So what are you doing?" I'd ask.

"Waiting," he'd say.

"For what?"

"Waiting to die."

"Let me talk to Mom."

And then, one day, when his woe became so overwhelming that his soul physically hurt, like a stubbed toe or a swollen testicle, he decided to write. He wouldn't show his writing to my mother or sister, but they knew he was writing about bees. Indeed, one day in the early spring of 1994, I received a manila envelope with another envelope inside, on which was written, in a dramatic cursive, *The Bees, Part 1*. I have to confess that my hands trembled as flipped through it, as if I were unrolling a sacred scroll, uncovered after a thousand years of sleep. The sense of sanctity, however, was diminished by a huge, sticky honey stain on page six.

The Bees, Part I

There is something faithfully connecting our family and bees, my father starts his narrative. *Like a member of the family, the bees have always come back.*

He then proudly informs the reader that it was his grandfather Teodor (the reader's great-grandfather) who brought civilized beekeeping to

Bosnia, where the natives still kept bees in straw-and-mud hives and killed them with sulfur, *all of them*, to get the honey. He remembers seeing straw-and-mud hives in the neighbors' backyards, and they looked strange to him, a relic from the dark ages of beekeeping. He recounts the story of the few hives that arrived with the family from the hinterlands of Ukraine to the promised land of Bosnia—the only thing promised was plenty of wood, which enabled them to survive the winters. The few hives multiplied quickly, the development of beekeeping in northwestern Bosnia unimpeded by World War One. My grandfather Ivan, who was twelve when he arrived in Bosnia (in 1912), became the first president of the Beekeeping Society in Prnjavor. My father describes a photograph of the Society's founding picnic: Grandfather Ivan stands in the center of a large group of nicely dressed peasants with a then fashionable long mustache and dandily cocked hat. Some of the peasants proudly exhibit faces swollen with bee stings.

Sometimes there were interesting mischiefs with bees, my father writes, failing to mention any *mischiefs*. The sudden sentence is one of his many stylistic idiosyncrasies: his voice wavers from establishment of the historical context with a weighty, ominous phrase like *War was looming across that dirt road* or *Gods of destruction pointed their irate fingers at our honey jars* to the highly technical explanations of the revolutionary architecture of his father's hives; from the discussion of the fact that bees die a horrible death when they sting (and the philosophical implications thereof) to the poetical descriptions of hawthorn in bloom and the piping of the queen bee the night before the swarm is to leave the hive.

Father devotes nearly a page to the moment he first recognized a queen bee. *A hive contains about 50,000 bees*, he writes, *and only one queen*. She's noticeably bigger than other bees, who dance around her, swirl and move in *peculiar, perhaps even worshipful ways*. His father pointed at the queen bee on a frame heavy with bees and honey, and, my father writes, *it was like reaching the center of the universe*—the vastness and the beauty of the world were revealed to him, *the logic behind it all*.

In an abrupt transition, he asserts that *the most successful period of our beekeeping ended in 1942, during World War Two, when we for the first time lost our bees*. It is clear that was a major catastrophe for the family, but my father keeps everything in perspective, probably because of what was going on in the besieged Sarajevo at the time of his writing. *There are worse things that can happen to you. A whole family, for example, can perish without a trace*, he writes. *We didn't perish, which is excellent.*

He then draws a little map at the center of which is the hill of Vučijak, near the town of Prnjavor, whose name appears at the fringe of the page. He draws a straight line from Prnjavor to Vučijak (*6 kilometers*, he writes along the line), ignoring the creeks, the forests, and the hills in between (including the hill I tumbled down). He places little stars around the page, which seem to represent different villages and people in that area. *It was a truly multinational place,* he says, wistfully. *Germans, Hungarians, Czechs, Poles, Ukrainians, Slovaks, Italians, Serbs, Muslims, Croats, and all the mixed ones.* He calculates that there were seventeen different nationalities—there was even a tailor in Prnjavor who was Japanese. Nobody knew how he got there, but when he died, there were only sixteen nationalities left. (Now, I have to say that I've inquired about the Japanese tailor, and no one else remembers him or has heard about him.) In 1942, lawlessness was rampant, and there were roaming gangs of Serbs and Croatian fascists and Tito's partisans too. All those *others*, who had no units of their own, save the Germans, were suspect and vulnerable. One day, two *semi-soldiers* showed up at the door of the family's house. They were their neighbors, ordinary peasants, except for their rickety rifles and caps with the partisan red star in the front and the Chetnik insignia (an ugly eagle spreading its mighty wings) in the back—they switched according to need. There was going to be a great battle, the peasants said, the mother of all battles. *They said we should be well advised to leave.* The peasants said they would padlock everything, and *they showed us a huge key, for which obviously no padlock existed.* They suggested, touching the knives at their belts as if inadvertently, that *we take only what we could carry. Father begged them to let us take a cow; my mother, five sisters, and two brothers wept. Winter was around the corner.* Perhaps it was the weeping that made these neighbors take pity and let my father's family bring a cow, although it was the sick one—her shrunken udder would not provide any milk or solace. *And we left thirty beehives behind.*

My father's handwriting changes at the beginning of the next paragraph; the thick letters thin out; his cursive becomes unstable; there are a couple of crossed-out sentences. Under the shroud of fierce scratching I can make out several words and discontinuous phrases: *urine . . . aspirin . . . belonging to . . . and skin . . . scythe.*

I was six years old, he continues after the interruption, *and I was carrying a meat grinder*. His mother was carrying his youngest brother—*he hung to her chest like a little monkey*. His brother was sobbing and clutching a picture of two children crossing a bridge over troubled water, *a chubby angel hovering over them*.

Only after a few months did *all the details of the pillaging and pilfering done by the neighbors* come to light, but my father doesn't list the details. After they had emptied the house and the attic and the barn, they finally got to the bees. All they wanted was honey, even if there was not much, just enough to help the bees survive the winter. They opened the hives and shook the bees off the frames. The bees were helpless: this was late October, it was cold, and they couldn't fly or sting. They dropped to the ground in absolute silence: *no buzz, no life; they all died that night.* When the family returned home, my father saw a mushy pile of rotting bees. *Before they died, they crawled closer together to keep warm.*

A few hives were stolen by Tedo, a neighbor, who also was a beekeeper. Grandfather Ivan knew that Tedo had some of our bees, but he never asked for them. Tedo came by one day and, unable to look Grandfather Ivan in the eye, claimed that he was only taking care of the bees while the family was away. He offered to give them back. *I remember going with my father to retrieve our hives. We went on a sleigh and we had to be careful not to shake our two hives, lest the bees unfurl their winter coils, which kept them warm.* My father sat between the hives, holding them, on their way back. It was a cold night, *with stars glittering like ice shards.* If they were careful and patient, his father told him, these two hives would breed many more. The following year they had six hives, and then twice as many, and in a few years they had twenty-five.

The Conditions of Production

I ought to respect my father's desire—indeed, his need—to produce a real book. Hence I must spend a few paragraphs on the conditions of his truth production. Of course, I wasn't there at the time, so I have to use the accounts of reliable witnesses (my mother, mainly). Thus: He wrote mainly in the afternoon, with a pencil, on filler paper, in a diplomat's slanted cursive. He sharpened his pencil with a Swiss Army knife (his duty-free present to himself from years before), littering the bedroom floor with shavings, sitting on the bed with the nightstand between his legs. The pencils, bought in a dollar store, broke their tips frequently, and he snapped them, infuriated. Over the phone, I had to listen to elaborate laments and retroactive appreciation of "our" pencils, which would last and which you could trust. Sometimes he'd just sit there staring at the smokestacks of Hamilton or hissing at the pigeons on the balcony, attracted by the bread crumbs my mother had left for them. He'd often interrupt his inspiration-gathering time by getting himself a slice of bread with butter and honey. Eventually he would start writing, and would sometimes keep at it for as long as forty-five minutes—an eternity for someone who had a heart rate perpetually above normal, someone as impatient and miserable as my father.

I'm holding his manuscript in my hand right now, and I can see the ebb and flow of his concentration; I can decode his back pain increasing and decreasing: smooth, steady handwriting at the top of, say, page ten, which then meanders on page eleven; random words written in the margins (*dwarf . . . horsemen . . . watermelon . . . slaughter*); complete sentences pierced by the straight lance of the writer's discontent (*Beekeeping was an attractive summer activity*); adjectives keeping company with lonely, arid nouns (*stinky* wafting around *feet*; *classic* accompanying *theft*; *golden* melting over *honey*). Toward page thirteen, one can sense longer breaks between sentences, the thickly penciled words thinning out after a sharpening session. There are mid-sentence breaks, with syntactical discrepancies between independent and dependent clauses, suggesting his thought splitting, the splinters flying off in different directions. Sometimes the sentence simply ceases: *We know*, then nothing; *It must be said*, but it is impossible to know what must be said.

And something troubling and strange happens around page seventeen. My father is in the middle of conveying a humorous story about Branko, a neighbor, yet again a victim of a bee attack. At this point in the narrative, Grandfather Ivan is in charge of a socialist-collective apiary, because all his hives have been taken away by the co-op. He is in charge of about two hundred hives—far too many to keep in one place, *but an order is an order*. My father, thirteen at the time, is helping him. *The day is gorgeous; the birds are atwitter; there is an apple tree in the center of the apiary, its branches breaking with fruit.* They work in complete, profound silence, interrupted only by the occasional thud of a ripe apple falling to the ground. A swarm of bees is hanging from one of the branches, and they need to get the bees into a hive. Grandpa Ivan will shake the branch, while my father holds the hive under it, and when the swarm hits the hive, it'll just settle in, following the queen. *But I might be too weak to hold the hive, and if the swarm misses it, they might just fall on me. Now, they don't sting when they're swarming, but if they fall down with their stings first, they might still hurt me. What's more, we would have to wait for them to gather again. My father is contemplating the situation.* Here comes Branko, clearly up to no good. He hates bees, because he's been stung so many times, but he offers his help. He probably hopes he'll be able to steal something, or spy on Grandpa Ivan, who accepts his help. So Branko stands under the swarm, fretfully looking up at the bees, trotting around in a small circle, trying to center the hive. As he's still moving, Grandpa Ivan shakes the branch with a long, crooked stick, and the swarm falls directly on Branko. Before a single sting breaks his skin, Branko is screaming and shaking his head and shoulders and sides as if possessed by a host of demons.

The paragraph breaks off as Branko stampedes out of the apiary, then crashes through a hedge and throws himself into a mud puddle, while a humongous sow, the mud-puddle proprietress, looks at him, lethargically perplexed. My father is rolling on the ground with laughter, while a twitch that could be a smile surfaces on Grandpa Ivan's face, then quickly vanishes.

In the next paragraph, in cursive so tense and weak that it seems evanescent, my father talks about an epidemic that attacked the co-op hives, rapidly spreading, as they were much too bunched up, and decimating the bee population. He describes the harrowing image of *a thick layer of dead bees glimmering in the grass.* Grandpa Ivan is squatting despondently, leaning on a tree, surrounded by rotting apples that beckon hysterical flies. *This is life,* my father concludes, *struggle after struggle, loss after loss, endless torment.*

Fathers and Daughters

It took me a while to find out what had happened between the paragraphs. My source confirmed that the break was one month long, at the beginning of which time my father received a call from Nada, his first cousin Slavko's daughter, who had emigrated, alone, from Vrbas, Yugoslavia, and ended up in Lincoln, Nebraska. She had gone to college there, majoring in library science and minoring in theology. Slavko grew up with my father—they were the same age—and had recently died as an accomplished alcoholic. Nada called my father, because, she said, her father had told her childhood stories: the games, the adventures, the poverty—their childhood, he'd said, was golden. My father was delighted, told her to call anytime, for "family is family." There followed a few phone calls, but they were too expensive, for both Nada and my father, so they started exchanging letters. Instead of writing *The Bees*, my father reminisced in letters to Nada, fondly recalling his and Slavko's childhood *mischiefs*, implicitly listing his losses. My mother said that if Nada hadn't been his family and thirty or so years younger, she would've thought that my father was in love. There was now someone he could paint his life for, practically from the first scratch, someone to whom he could tell the true story. I've never seen Nada's letters, but my mother says they were often ranting, bemoaning the fact that, despite the golden childhood, her father ended up a weak, bitter man. And her mother was overly receptive to the attention of other men. And her brother was not very smart and she never had anything in common with him. She also hated America and Americans, their provincialism, their stupid, rootless culture of cheeseburgers and cheap entertainment. She was clearly wretched, my mother said, but my father was by and large oblivious of that. His letters were rife with apples of indescribable taste (unlike the apples you got in Canada, which tasted as if they had been dry-cleaned) and family get-togethers where everybody sang and hugged and licked honey from the tips of their fingers.

Then, after a break in correspondence and many unreturned messages my father left on her voicemail, Nada faxed an unfinished sixty-five-page letter in the middle of the night—my parents were woken by an avalanche of paper slithering out of their fax machine. In the fax, her father was upgraded to a child molester, her mother to a cheap prostitute, her brother to a compulsive, shameless masturbator. America had evolved into a filthy inferno of idiocy and nothingness run by the Jews and the CIA. Her roommate (a Latina whore) was trying to kill her; her professors discussed her with her classmates when she was not around, showing secretly taken

pictures of her naked body, before which frat boys frantically mastur-
bated. Her physician tried to rape her; they refused to sell her milk in the
supermarket; in the INS office, where she went to apply for her green card,
the woman who interviewed her was touching herself under the desk and
had hooves instead of feet; and somebody was changing the words in the
books she was studying from—every day, the books were full of new *lies,
lies, lies.* She had first believed that she was persecuted by jealous people,
who hated her because she was virginally pure, but now she believed that
God had become evil and begun purging the innocent. *The only hope I
have is you,* she wrote on page sixty. *Could you come and take me from this
pit of hell?* Then, in the last few pages, before the fax abruptly ended, she
warned my father about me, reminded him of the Oedipus myth and the
fact that I lived in the United States, which meant that I was corrupt and
untrustworthy. *Keep in mind,* she wrote, *that God preferred sons to fathers
and daughters.*

I had never met Nada or her father. At the peril of being maudlin, or
appearing malicious, let me note that her name translates as "hope." I
have since seen this fax from hell: its hysterical letters and exclamation
points are faded, because of fax toner shortage and the passing of time.

A Different Story

My father kept calling Nada, receiving no answer, until her meretricious
roommate, one Madrigal, picked up the phone and told my father that
Nada had been "institutionalized." He did not understand the word, and
could not pronounce it for me to translate it, so I called Madrigal. "She
just went nuts," Madrigal told me. "In the library. She heard voices coming
from the books, spreading hateful rumors about her."

My father was devastated. He called someone at the University of
Nebraska and in his Tarzan English asked this person to visit Nada at the
institution and tell her that he had called. "We don't do that," the anony-
mous Nebraskan said. Father sat at his nightstand, frantically sharpening
his pencil, but not writing, until it was reduced to a stump he could barely
hold between his fingers. He called every member of the family he could
reach, as if they could pool their mental waves and send a telepathic rem-
edy to Nada. He called me almost every day and then demanded that I

immediately call him back, as they could not afford those calls. He gave me reports of his futile attempts to reach Nada, and finally asked me to go to Lincoln and track her down, but I couldn't do it. "You've become American," he said disconsolately. But that's a different story.

The Message

After the break, his story trickles away with unmentioned sorrow. My father flies through an incident in which Grandpa Ivan was stung by hundreds of bees, and consequently spent a few days in what by all accounts must have been a coma. *But he never again felt the back pain that had tortured him for years.*

He devotes a paragraph to beekeeping in the sixties and seventies, *which could be considered the second golden age of family beekeeping, even if Father was going completely blind.* When Grandpa Ivan eventually lost his sight, the bees slowly died off, and shortly before his death there were only three hives left. My father couldn't help with the beekeeping. *Traveling and working around the world, mainly in the Middle East and Africa, I could barely manage to see my parents three times a year, and there was no way I could devote any of my time to the bees.*

There is a presence of regret in the space between the previous sentence and the next (and last) one:

Shortly before his death, Father summoned me and my brothers for a meeting on the family beekeeping tradition. His message

And there *The Bees, Part 1* ends, no message ever delivered, though it is easy to imagine what it might have been. My grandfather died, my grandmother too, my father, along with his brothers, kept the bees. They (the bees) survived a varroa epidemic, a drought, and the beginning of the war in Bosnia. When the family emigrated to Canada, they left behind twenty-five hives. Shortly after their departure, a horde of their neighbors, all drunken volunteers in the Serbian army, came at night and kicked the hives off their stands, and when the bees feebly tried to escape (it was night, cold again, they crept on the ground), the neighbors threw a couple of hand grenades and laughed at the dead bees flying around as though alive. The neighbors then stole the heavy frames, and left a trail of dripping honey in their wake.

The Well

My father found a job in a Hamilton steel mill, filling wagons with scrap metal. The mill was hot in the summer, cold in the winter, and when he worked night shifts, he would sometimes fall asleep waiting for a green light at the wheel of a used, decrepit Lincoln Town Car. He'd say that his Lincoln brought him home while he was sleeping, like a faithful horse. He hated the job, but had no choice.

One day, surveying the ads in the papers, pursuing a perfect garage sale, he found an ad selling honey. He called the number and told the man outright that he had no money to buy the honey, but that he would love to see his bees. Because there is such a thing as beekeepers' solidarity, the man invited him over. He was a Hungarian, a retired carpenter. He let my father help him with the bees, gave him old copies of *Canadian Beekeeping*, which my father tried to read with insufficient help from my mother's dictionary. After a while, the Hungarian gave him a swarm and an old hive to start his own apiary. He admonished my father for refusing to wear beekeeping overalls and hat, even gloves, but my father contended that stings were good for all kinds of pain. I still can't figure out what language they might have been speaking to each other, but it almost certainly wasn't English.

My father has twenty-three beehives now and collects a few hundred pounds of honey a year, which he cannot sell. "Canadians don't appreciate honey," he says. "They don't understand it." He wants me to help him expand into the American market, but I assure him that Americans understand honey even less than Canadians do.

He has recently decided to write another true book. He already has the title: *The Well*. There was a well near their home when he was a boy. Everybody went there to get water. *The Well* would be a story about people from the village and their cattle, their intersecting destinies. Sometimes there were "interesting incidents." Once, he remembers, somebody's mule escaped and came to the well, sensing water. But its head was tied to its leg—that's how people forced the mules to graze. The mule got away, found water, but then was unable to drink. It lingered around the well, furiously banging its head against the trough, dying of thirst, the water inches away. And it brayed, in horrible pain. *It brayed all day*, my father says. *All day and all of the night.*

MEENA ALEXANDER

Born in Allahabad, India, in 1951, Meena Alexander moved with her family to Sudan when she was five years old. She studied at Khartoum University and in England before returning to India to teach in Delhi. Alexander currently lives in New York and is a professor of English at Hunter College and the Graduate Center of the City University of New York.

Alexander has published seven poetry collections, including *Illiterate Heart* (2002), winner of the PEN Open Book Award. The most recent is *Birthplace with Buried Stones* (2013). Her memoir is called *Fault Lines* (1993; 2003). She regularly reads at international poetry gatherings and is the recipient of fellowships from many foundations, including the John Simon Guggenheim Foundation, the Fulbright Foundation, the Rockefeller Foundation, and the Arts Council of England.

Alexander's special interest in transnational poetry, migration, gender, and memory reflects a central aspect of her identity. In her autobiography she writes, "That's all I am, a woman cracked by multiple migrations. Uprooted so many times she can connect nothing with nothing." And writer Maxine Hong Kingston has said that "Meena Alexander sings of countries, foreign and familiar, places where the heart and spirit live, and places for which one needs a passport and visas. Her voice guides us far away and back home."

Grandmother's Garden

1

The branches are crusted with snow blossoms. Puffs of crystal cling to the branches. I am back in New York City.

As you know, our family house has been sold.

Cord of dark blood, unseen umbilicus, all that tethered me there. Perhaps now I can start to speak of it.

Going, going, gone. Someone banged the gavel down.

Grandmother's house gone. The house of Amma's childhood, the house of my childhood. One by one the flowering trees cut, the house emptied of all that belonged to it.

Amma has moved far away to Chennai, which feels like another country, to live in a small modern house next door to my youngest sister. I like to think she is happier there.

I am back at my writing table set in an overfull apartment. Back to what I call my life, as if something so creased, so oddly colored, shadowed, and stained could be called that.

Now this.

Nothing good will come of this, I think, by which I mean this writing project will be a failure in the way in which so much else I have tried to do has come to naught.

A little silence, a little patience, that is all you need, I tell myself.

I seem to hear your voice.

The music of failure, that is the title of something I might write.

A story about my grandmother, a woman I never knew.

2

Ever since I learned to speak I had two words—*amma* (mother) and *vide* (house). When I wanted to say "mother's house," referring to the Tiruvella house, I would say *ammede vide*.

But the word I have now is different. It has heft—old silk rubbed against the palm, scent of fresh frangipani, burnt grass. That's how it is with language you are estranged from: its flows in dreams, and from time to time you step into a pool of words utterly old and unutterably new.

Ammavide.

The Malayalam word means mother-house, ancestral house, mother's house.

House of childhood, house with red-tiled roof and sandy courtyard where Grandmother's mulberry tree blooms.

House with whitewashed walls and high teak ceilings, long cool front veranda, parapet, and pillars.

House that holds firm when the first monsoon storms break, when the green frogs croak in the well, when dragon flies swarm in the love-apple tree.

Avede, evida, vide evida, avide, vide avide.
There, where, where is the house? There, the house is there.

3

A garden encircles the ammavide.

Grandmother's death hangs over it like a pall of smoke.

Wild grasses are burnt at dusk at the edge of the mango grove and wild nettles turn their blistered leaves into the rays of the setting sun.

At dawn in the bamboo grove, water rats crawl.

Green snakes curl under the stones at the foot of the mango tree.

Nothing remains of the children who used to play there, tossing balls made of threads of raw rubber.

Aoui, aoui, the children cried when wild nettles stung them.

They rubbed their knees and elbows and ran to the well to dash cold water on the hurt.

4

Shadows of the palm leaves turn crisp black organza, the kind used to make mourning veils. Shadows become umbrellas that go whirr-whirr-whirr in the wind. Sun cuts rippling knife patterns on the sand, and on the ornamental stones under the trees.

On rainy days ladies in saris sit sipping tea on the front veranda; men with mustaches, dressed in muslin dhotis, talk politics in loud voices; children skip on the tiles of the veranda playing hopscotch; sparrows peck dirt on the parapet and by the gravel path where rainwater falls.

In between the palm trees, at the front of the house, there is a wire that comes down from a lightning rod. The lightning rod stands at the very tip of the red-tiled roof, a roof shaped like the prow of a ship.

Amma said, We have the long wire from the tip of the roof so that if lightning strikes it will go down into the ground. She didn't add, So no one will get hurt.

Why did Grandmother have to die, I wanted to ask, but I bit my tongue. I gulped hard. A funny sound came from my throat.

I felt I had swallowed a bird that couldn't fly.

5

Amma was sixteen when her mother died. They sent a telegram to the Women's Christian College telling her to come back. There was only a servant woman with her on the long train ride south. By the time the train passed through the Palghat Pass with its blue crags, Amma was exhausted by her own prayers.

Dear Lord Jesus, let her live. Dear Lord Jesus, don't let my mother die.

She stepped in through the stone gates. Then they told her.

The gulmohar trees my grandmother had planted stood on either side of the gates. Red blossoms littered the ground; stick insects clamored in the crevices of the earth. A terrible emotion she could not name filled Amma.

I refuse to set foot in the house. Why should I come into a house where my mother has died? I'll never enter this house, ever again!

When I heard this, I thought it sounded unlikely. My own mother screaming like that. Beating her fists against Ayah's back.

Grandmother had gone away without giving anyone notice, and Amma could have stuck up for her.

Why did Grandmother have to die? I finally asked this.

Amma made a face as if she had sucked on a sour love-apple. She could have said, Look, it wasn't her fault that English doctor with the name Churchwarden—imagine a doctor with a name like that—pumped her full of gold injection. Her skin turned blue. She was dead in a day.

She could have said, Your beautiful grandmother, gone like that.

She could have shoved me with the flat of her hand, saying, Awful child, cruel awful child, why bring up that sorrow?

Instead she just stood there. The folds of her sari clapped shut, brown petals wilting in the heat. Her two feet in the leather chappals stuck out. The sun was fixed behind a mango branch. Smoke came out of the mango branch. There was smoke in the folds of Amma's sari.

Then the wind started blowing, and with it came Great-Aunt Chinna, double chins cackling. She used her ivory walking stick to poke me away.

Get out of the way, child. Standing in the sun like that, you'll get all black. What would your mother say?

I puffed out my cheeks like a puffer fish at my great-aunt but kept quiet. All I wanted was the story. I wanted to know if someone had deliberately killed my grandmother.

I wanted to know if Grandmother Eli had run away and tripped on a monsoon cloud, dark as the grave and as bare.

6

Beautiful things summon ruin.

My grandmother was dark and beautiful—the photographs attest to this. She died one month short of fifty.

There is a photo, slightly torn at the edges: Grandmother stands next to a palmyra tree. She is wearing puffy leg-of-mutton sleeves, chic at the time. Her sari is folded about her waist and fans out in tiny flutes that must have taken so very long to fashion. There are pearls about the dusky curve of her neck.

Gold around her wrists. Droplets of gold and ruby in her earlobes.

It comforts me to think that she cared little for these tokens of grace. Something else drew her on. Pale fire that death sucked out of her.

Would it be true to say that through her death our family drew close, feeding off that bleak sustenance?

We have to help your grandfather, Amma whispered to me. He is so lonely. He has lived alone for so long.

Once I saw Grandmother's pearls lying unstrung, the thread broken, scattered in velvet, droplets of milk. The velvet was indigo, the color of the sky when the monsoon breaks. The droplets of milk lay against that.

I had gone with Amma to the bank vault. The manager led us into a crooked corridor and drew a curtain over the entrance. He used his key to open a long metal drawer, and Amma, out of her faded leather purse, drew out another. When the man had stepped away, Amma raised herself as high as she could go on her tiny toes and pulled out a carved wooden box in which the pearls lay.

How had this happened? It was intact when she put it in, she was sure of this. Her voice broke. I helped her sit down for a minute, the rosewood box held in her lap. She sat there utterly silent.

I myself thought the pearls looked lovelier, tossed and scattered against the velvet, though of course there was no way with the string broken that they could have adorned a delicate throat or finely turned wrist.

Lying on the dark velvet they were just what they were, shining droplets in and of themselves.

7

She traveled hard, my Grandmother Eli.

There are letters from her about seeing the Great Wall of China, buying silks in Shanghai.

There are letters about traveling in the cities in the north of India and seeing rickshaws with huge wheels and painted sides and men crying out in Urdu and Hindi, languages she tried to understand.

There are letters written from Ceylon where she describes the great rock where people prayed, the paddy fields of Kandy so like those of home.

There are letters she wrote from Madras to Grandfather before they married. He had gone to Trinity College in Hartford, Connecticut, to study theology. Perhaps it was in that letter that she writes: "My dearest, I do not understand this life. I do not know what will become of me."

I do not know what made her write those lines. Sometimes I think that is a line I myself have composed.

Perhaps it was an excess of travel that led Grandmother to conceive of a quiet garden, a garden with golden grasses, fan-shaped palmyra trees, a bamboo grove where the monsoon wind whistled, a knot of sweet mango trees and, close to the front veranda of the great house with its red-tiled roof, clusters of laburnum and sweet-scented jasmine to draw the tiny sun birds she loved.

On my shelf in New York, in an acid-free box, I have letters she wrote about the garden, the flowering trees she planted by the stone gates, the silver birch her English friend Sabrina carried in a paper bag from Ooty, those high hills native to that tree.

Then there are letters she wrote to her mother Anna, who was dying in a huge house with mosaic floors, not too far away from the ever-evolving garden.

The garden as flesh, as mother space, was that what it was?

But it was also a place to work. Her friends and family stared hard as she dug into the earth with a stick and bare hands, and kept company with the male gardeners she had hired. One was a man who sported a conical hat made of banana *coomb*.

I do not know how to translate that word into English—the hard curved-out cusp of the banana plant that is sometimes molded into hats for peasants in the field or into vessels for newborn babies. How does it work?

A woman sets the tiny baby into the coomb, and the infant's limbs squirm and shine in sunlight. Oil trickles down from the woman's palm onto chest and dimpled thigh.

You loved your first massage, Amma tells me. It happened in a corner of Grandmother's garden, under the shade of the passion fruit vine—which is where your ayah decided the sun wouldn't hurt you. I kept the coomb they used, but now I think its all moldered away. As she spoke she kept moving her slender brown hands in sunlight.

8

I am in another country. On a morning of clear sunlight, I walk into a garden thousands of miles from where Grandmother lived and died. I speak of the Heather Garden at the mouth of Fort Tryon Park in Upper Manhattan, a stone's throw from my apartment.

I stroll on the curved path past a lilac tree with its gnarled trunk. I stoop to touch purple fuzz of heather, I try to avoid earthworms twisted at the roots. In between the stalks of heather I see tiny snails. Their shells are the color of laterite soil in the garden of my childhood, a reddish hue with shades of indigo from the minerals buried in the earth.

Close by a baby gurgles, its limbs held tight to the mother's chest in a pouch made of cloth, its tiny head bobbing. A dragonfly on iridescent wings glides by the mother and child. Overhead clouds shift and pass.

Later, by stone steps that lead down to a grassy knoll, I see a child.

He wears clothing at least two sizes too large for him and on his feet are sneakers of a dull green color with frayed laces he has bound to his ankles. He is standing on tiptoes, rooting in the trash bin.

He picks out a half eaten sandwich and clutches it tight. Then he brings it to his lips.

I stand very still. I do not want to scare him, and I watch as he runs hard, a brown streak of light, past the lilac tree, out of the park.

9

How old was I? Six. My cousins and I were in the rose garden, playing catch-the-dragonfly. Catch a dragonfly, tie a stone to its tail and watch it fly. A small stone, not one so huge that the creature couldn't rise in the air.

I want to see it fly with a stone stuck to its tail, Cousin Koshi yelled.

I shut my eyes. I couldn't bear to see a body, that slender shimmering thing knocking at the tail.

Don't shut your eyes like that, Sophie yelled.

They'll shut your eyes when you're dead. Someone else will. Aunty hid her eyes in church, she couldn't bear to see her mother dead. You look just like her, Meena. When someone dies, their child has to cover their face in church.

What did you say?

I had to be sure—sometimes Sophie made things up. Like Gandhi having four wives like a Muslim might. Or Queen Elizabeth eating raw swan. I don't know where she got these things.

No, it's not in church, said Cousin Koshi pushing forward.

He had a boat in his hand the size it would be if it were made of a square of folded paper. But this was made of tin, painted green and blue, fit to slide into the lotus pond in the middle of our garden.

When the dragonfly game was over, Cousin Koshi would move onto another amusement.

Where, then? I asked.

In the grave, silly. Just before they put the body in and close the coffin, the child has to come forward and cover the face.

Which child?

The oldest child of the person who dies. Your mother was the only child, so she had to do it.

I started trembling. I could feel the tremble start in my hand. I bent over and picked up a stone. Cousin Koshi looked surprised.

I'm trying to hit a dragonfly, I said.

I tossed the stone up into the air right under the branch of the white blossoming incense tree where a horde of dragonflies buzzed away, scratching the clear air with their wings.

The stone, the size of my fingernail, surprised one dragonfly. It had green-blue wings and it scuttled off into the sunlight, the transparent air.

They buried Grandmother deep in the soil. Amma covered Grandmother's face with a piece of muslin.

So the soul, looking back at the body, already starting to putrefy, wouldn't take umbrage and fly away and leave the body knocking at its tail, drawing it down into purgatory.

10

For Dante, purgatory was a mountain filled with fire. Virgil, his guide, explains that the poet will suffer deeply, but he will not die.

You will not die, not even the hem of your robe will be burnt when you enter into that fire, he tells Dante.

> Just as . . .
> the sun shed its first rays, and Ebro lay
> beneath high Libra, and the ninth hour's rays
> were scorching Ganges's waves; so here, the sun
> stood at the point of day's departure when
> God's angel–happy–showed himself to us.

What does the angel say? He says the poet can't move on unless the fire stings him. He will suffer, but he will not die. He adds: When you enter the flames, keep your ears open. Don't be deaf to song.

11

Soon after I first arrived in Manhattan I thought I felt the sting of fire. You and I were walking down a canyon of buildings, not too far from the pier.

You gripped my arm and drew me to the side. Look!

I stared down Thirty-Fourth Street, a thin rivulet between blackened walls. I saw a ball of fire. It was spinning on an unseen axle. A reddish light poured out of the Hudson and bathed our bodies.

This happens once in how many years, I don't know: the setting sun aligns itself to the city streets. So it was that we saw the great orb about to vanish into darkness that filled the other side of New Jersey, the other side of where we were.

My feet and legs were on fire. What would become of me if I kept walking the streets of this city?

Behind me I heard a tight knot of people on the sidewalk, squabbling. They sounded like parrots from Grandmother's garden. It's Three Card Monte, you said. I tried to make sense of your explanation.

A woman dressed in a spotted garment was holding up a card in her hand.

It's mine, its mine, it's mine, she cried. Her hand was bathed in a reddish glow and on the card a landscape split in half by a fierce streak of lightning.

12

Squabbling songs, that's what they made; the wild parrots clustered in the mango trees, and we could see them from the veranda. They made such a ruckus that I had to get Amma to help me to put on the gramophone very loudly to shut out their cries.

The gramophone was on loan from Cousin Koshi. I was allowed to keep it for a few weeks while Koshi was away in riding camp. He was learning to ride horses in the hills so he could become one of the leaders of the new nation. Uncle Itty told me this.

The riding requirement for the Indian Administrative Service has been abolished, Appa argued. But Uncle Itty didn't believe him. He felt that knowing how to ride would help matters. It certainly had in the British days.

When it worked, the music from the gramophone played loud and clear.

> *Blu, blu*
> *I love you*

Cousin Koshi crooned, back home now. He danced as the gramaphone sat in the shade cast by a bamboo screen of a pale green color, tiny slats of bamboo that kept the bright sunlight out. The gramophone had a horn attached to it, and sounds came deep-throated from the innards of the machine.

Cousin Koshi got the record from a relative, Auntie Amachi, a lady doctor in Ceylon who shipped him the latest hits she found on the black market. They arrived wrapped in layers of white cloth Auntie Amachi had cut with her surgical scissors. Black discs filled with music I was too scared to touch in case I scratched them. Sometimes the needle on the bone arm of the machine rattled and spun and a gargling noise came out of the horn. It sounded like a lorry coughing too close. Or Uncle's horse having a bad night in its stable.

As music swarmed out pure gold, Cousin Koshi and I danced, twirling our hips on the veranda, and all the servants rushed out to look at us. Earlier when I tried to put on the gramophone without help, the needle slipped out of the right groove, and made an ugh-ugh sound, the turntable started creaking, and all the fixing I tried to do with the loose leg of the rosewood table didn't help.

Peering under the table, I could see the initials E K gleaming in the moist dark. They were cut in there, Amma told me, so that if the British came to arrest grandfather for his nationalist work, at least the furniture, marked with Grandmother's name, would remain in the house. It would not belong to him, but rather to her.

I ran my fingers over the incised letters, then stood up, dusted off my skirts and looked around. The gramophone was my main concern. Often there would be someone to help me with the gramophone, but this afternoon the grownups were engaged in sipping tea and picking up the sweetmeats made of crushed almonds and honey, popping them into their mouths.

No one noticed me. Cousin Koshi was out of earshot on the other side of the incense tree practicing the jumping jacks he would have to do in riding camp in the hills.

Suddenly Grandfather walked in, clapping his hands. The parrots rose in a flock shaking the arms of the tree. The conversation swirled around him. Uncle asked Grandfather's opinion about the new local elections and the plans to develop the tourism industry in the outlying islands. Aunt Omana showed off her new string of pearls. Do you like it? she whispered.

Amma was bent over her embroidery, pretending not to listen, and Appa was shuffling his sandals around with his toes. I knew that Appa was just waiting to stroll out into the jamun trees to smoke one of his Camel cigarettes. He would never dare do that in Grandfather's presence.

Something tugged inside of me like a kite on a string blown from a rooftop, struggling to be free. I was waiting for Grandfather; he was the only one I could trust would notice me. Perhaps he would help me with the gramophone. But Grandfather had other things on his mind. Unlike my other grandfather, who chewed endless rounds of tobacco and played kabbadi well into his old age, my mother's father was a lover of paper and books.

13

Grandfather pulled down a book from a shelf in his library. He dusted it off and one or two silver fish fell out, delicate creatures that eat the spines and pages of bound books. The brown covers gleamed, soft silk in the lining and even the glue that held the spine together was visible, crystalline in the afternoon light.

We must read *Dak Ghar—The Post Office*, he said, pointing to me. Then turned to Cousin Koshi, who had suddenly appeared. You too, young sir. Tagore's play will live on into eternity.

I thought it was strange that Grandfather would say something like that, particularly because the copy of the play he was holding had belonged to my grandmother, who bought it in 1914, the very year it was translated into English. How could he speak of a book she owned living on, when she was dead and buried? In those days I thought of eternity as a tablet, molten, covered in gold, immeasurably heavy.

Grandfather stood on the veranda. The wind puffed out his white dhoti, turning it into a sail. Aunt Omana stopped fidgeting with the silver jug filled with milk the maid had just brought in for tea.

I want to see everything, everything there is to see. Those faraway hills, for instance, that I can see from my window: I would love to cross over them!

There was something in his voice as he spoke Tagore's lines that made me think that Grandfather knew his traveling days were behind him.

Come on, child, he said to Cousin Koshi. I want you to read out Amal's lines. It's a boy's part. Go on, son, go on. They're lines by our Nobel laureate, son. This was Uncle butting in. Don't you want to say that part?

In reply, Cousin Koshi knocked over a wicker chair and turned it into a horse, jumped over it and over the parapet into wild grass. Hey, he yelled at me, let's go catch butterflies. I shook my head. I couldn't let Grandfather down. I followed him to the library and sat close as he read all the parts except two in the play about a child's death.

I had to be Amal, the boy who falls asleep, still waiting for a letter from the king, and I had to be Sudha, the girl who comes with flowers in her hand, to keep him company.

It was a sad play, and I hated being alone with Grandfather and having to read both those parts. It struck me that I was just like the girl with two heads. I had seen her in the circus by the riverbank, a poor grotesque thing, never knowing which way to look.

Outside the window Cousin Koshi sauntered through the tapioca bushes, mewing like a wild cat. He belted out lines from the latest film song, giving little whoop-whoops in between.

Cries of parrots hung in the air. Cousin Koshi had his face pressed to the bars of the library window listening hard, then all of a sudden he pulled away. The mango tree outside the library window shook like a banshee.

Grandfather didn't notice. He read out lines in his booming voice, as if he were doing the liturgy in church. Lines about an island filled with parrots who live in hills the color of green feathers. He set his hand on my shoulder. I could feel the heat in his bones pressing down on me. When you grow up, you'll travel far away. You'll come back and go away. Over and over you'll go and come. That will be your life. Grandfather's voice fell.

Somewhere in the ocean there is an island filled with talking birds. You must write down their stories.

Then it was as if he were repeating words he had heard someone use, words that did not belong to him: The isle is filled with shadows.

Isle? Island, silly, Cousin Koshi yelled through the window, and I saw his head bob upside down from the tree. Come here! I cried, but if he heard me, my cousin gave no sign; he vanished into a quivering bowl of leaves.

Words flew out of my mouth, and I have no idea why: Where is she, where is my grandmother?

When I looked at Grandfather's face it was as if he had swallowed bitter gourd with chili and didn't have enough water to wash it off his tongue. He turned and looked at me with a strange light in his eyes.

I was utterly quiet—I wanted to curl up in darkness, like the chrysalis of a cabbage butterfly. I saw Grandfather grip the window frame. It took a long time for the quiver in his fingers and face to subside. Then he started to breathe deeply, rhythmically, as if he were in a yogic asana, and slowly, ever so slowly, using all the strength in his arms, he lowered himself down into his chair.

Come here. Come here, he whispered.

I went close to him and, with my outstretched hand, I touched his white head. Under my hand I could feel his scalp trembling.

14

In *The Post Office*, the boy Amal lies in his bed, waiting for a letter from the king. He sees shadows cross his wall, the shadow of a cloud, then the shadow of a parrot that flies out of the banyan tree. Then the shadow of the flower girl.

Sudha leaves but returns. She has flowers in her hand. Blue flowers, the kind that grow by the well. Amal is dying, though she doesn't know this. His bed is at the edge of a dark doorway.

She says to the old physician, Can you say something to him, whisper it in his ear? The old man nods.

Tell him Sudha says I will never forget you.

15

I wonder if you know this.

Tagore's play, *The Post Office* had a powerful afterlife.

It was performed in wartime London. It was broadcast on French radio the night before Paris fell to the Nazis. It was performed on July 18, 1942, in the Warsaw ghetto, in an orphanage run by Janusz Korczak.

Three weeks later, together with the children of the orphanage, he was taken to a death camp.

After the performance Korczak said he had chosen the play because it tells us something we need to learn. "We must all learn to face the angel of death."

And he had this to say of his young troupe: "The play is more than a text, it is a mood, it conveys more than emotions, it is an experience . . . and the actors are more than actors, they are children."

16

One December in Upper Manhattan, with winter light pouring in through the window, on the shelf where Grandmother's letters are stored, I find a poem. I wrote it in ballpoint pen in a cheap lined notebook. When I wrote it, I'm not sure. Normally I like to write with a fountain pen, but this was another texture entirely. Gluey. Shiny in an unattractive way. I imagined I was forced to use the ballpoint pen because ink from a fountain pen would have run on cheap paper. These are the lines I made:

In the Indian Ocean is an island with talking birds
And grasses made of beaten gold.

Floating seeds turn into pearls.
Things that are not, become shadows.
One shadow with two heads = the living can never rest.

17

Sometimes I feel I am a shadow with two heads. One head in Manhattan, the other in a childhood place that exists inside me.

Grandmother's garden is gone, and where an orchard blossomed they are building a ten-story apartment building.

It's the tale of the new India. The builder drives around our small town in a white BMW. Twenty years ago all we had were the stolid Ambassador cars and, of course, buses and bullock carts.

Now all manner of exotic plumage where cars are concerned. Soon, if I am not mistaken, they will have a Louis Vuitton store in town—only a matter of time.

I am older than Grandmother was when she died. I think of the child trying to draw a secret veil over one part of her life. I think of the adult writing it all down. What does she know? What must she invent in order to tell the truth?

18

In New York City, the passage of days and night crosses things out.

You enter JFK along with a string of others—brown people, black people, people of all tints, all ages, voices breaking with eagerness, sore voices.

Your throat hurts with all the words. You think you know the language but the words sound so different.

A few years later, in that bleak courthouse on Center Street, you put up your right hand. You are there with women from Latvia, men from Kashmir, mothers from Mesopotamia, fathers from Sri Lanka.

You swear to belong. You fear you will never fully belong. But who could have guessed how fierce it is, the longing to belong.

You become hostage to that bright bloody thing inside the migrant's soul that says, here, here, this is where you belong. Now no one can cast you out.

You hear a voice say this to you in a dream. You do not believe the voice.

You know you are on Manhattan Island, not the island of birds.

Where else could you be?

BEING HERE

JUNOT DÍAZ

Junot Díaz was born in Santo Domingo, Dominican Republic, in 1968. When he was six, his family moved to New Jersey to join his father, who worked as a forklift operator.

After receiving his MFA from Cornell University, Díaz published the story collection *Drown* (1996) and, more than a decade later, the novel *The Brief Wondrous Life of Oscar Wao* (2007), winner of the 2008 Pulitzer Prize for Fiction. Díaz's stories have appeared in the *New Yorker* and the *Paris Review*. His latest collection of stories, *This Is How You Lose Her*, from which "Otravida, Otravez" is taken, was published in 2012—shortly before he received a MacArthur Foundation Fellowship.

Díaz has said that the challenges and opportunities of immigration shaped his passion for reading and writing from a young age. He told National Public Radio that "the solitude of being an immigrant, the solitude of having to learn a language in a culture from scratch, the need for some sort of explanation, the need for answers, the need for something that would somehow shelter me led me to books."

Otravida, Otravez

He sits on the mattress, the fat spread of his ass popping my fitted sheets from their corners. His clothes are stiff from the cold, and the splatter of dried paint on his pants has frozen into rivets. He smells of bread. He's been talking about the house he wants to buy, how hard it is to find one when you're Latino. When I ask him to stand up so I can fix the bed, he walks over to the window. So much snow, he says. I nod and wish he would be quiet. Ana Iris is trying to sleep on the other side of the room. She has spent half the night praying for her children back in Samaná, and I know that in the morning she has to work at the fábrica. She moves uneasily, buried beneath comforters, her head beneath a pillow. Even here in the States she drapes mosquito netting over her bed.

There's a truck trying to turn the corner, he tells me. I wouldn't want to be that chamaco.

It's a busy street, I say, and it is. Mornings I find the salt and cut rock that the trucks spill onto the front lawn, little piles of treasure in the snow. Lie down, I tell him, and he comes to me, slipping under the covers. His clothes are rough and I wait until it is warm enough under the sheets before I release the buckle to his pants. We shiver together and he does not touch me until we stop.

Yasmin, he says. His mustache is against my ear, sawing at me. We had a man die today at the bread factory. He doesn't speak for a moment, as if the silence is the elastic that will bring his next words forward. Este tipo fell from the rafters. Héctor found him between the conveyors.

Was he a friend?

This one. I recruited him at a bar. Told him he wouldn't get cheated.

That's too bad, I say. I hope he doesn't have a family.

Probably does.

Did you see him?

What do you mean?

Did you see him dead?

No. I called the manager and he told me not to let anyone near. He crosses his arms. I do that roof work all the time.

You're a lucky man, Ramón.

Yes, but what if it had been me?

That's a stupid question.

What would you have done?

I set my face against him; he has known the wrong women if he expects more. I want to say, Exactly what your wife's doing in Santo Domingo. Ana Iris mutters in the corner loudly, but she's just pretending. Bailing me out of trouble. He goes quiet because he doesn't want to wake her. After a while he gets up and sits by the window. The snow has started falling again. Radio WADO says this winter will be worse than the last four, maybe the worst in ten years. I watch him: he's smoking, his fingers tracing the thin bones around his eyes, the slack of skin around his mouth. I wonder who he's thinking about. His wife, Virta, or maybe his child. He has a house in Villa Juana; I've seen the fotos Virta sent. She looks thin and sad, the dead son at her side. He keeps the pictures in a jar under his bed, very tightly sealed.

We fall asleep without kissing. Later I wake up and so does he. I ask him if he's going back to his place and he says no. The next time I wake up he doesn't. In the cold and darkness of this room he could almost be anybody. I lift his meaty hand. It is heavy and has flour under each nail. Sometimes at night I kiss his knuckles, crinkled as prunes. His hands have tasted of crackers and bread the whole three years we've been together.

He does not talk to me or Ana Iris as he dresses. In his top jacket pocket he carries a blue disposable razor that has begun to show rust on its sharp lip. He soaps his cheeks and chin, the water cold from the pipes, and then scrapes his face clean, trading stubble for scabs. I watch, my naked chest covered with goosebumps. He stomps downstairs and out of the house, a bit of toothpaste on his teeth. As soon as he leaves, I can hear my housemates complaining about him. Doesn't he have his own place to sleep, they'll ask me when I go into the kitchen. And I'll say yes, and smile. From the frosted window I watch him pull up his hood and hitch the triple layer of shirt, sweater, and coat onto his shoulders.

Ana Iris kicks back her covers. What are you doing? she asks me.

Nothing, I say. She watches me dress from under the craziness of her hair.

You have to learn to trust your men, she says.

I trust.

She kisses my nose, heads downstairs. I comb out my hair, sweep the crumbs and pubic hairs from my covers. Ana Iris doesn't think he'll leave me; she thinks he's too settled here, that we've been together too long. He's the sort of man who'll go to the airport but won't be able to get on board, she says. Ana Iris left her own children back on the Island, hasn't seen her three boys in nearly seven years. She understands what has to be sacrificed on a voyage.

In the bathroom I stare into my own eyes. His stubble quivers in beads of water, compass needles.

I work two blocks away, at St. Peter's Hospital. Never late. Never leave the laundry room. Never leave the heat. I load washers, I load dryers, peel the lint skin from the traps, measure out heaping scoops of crystal detergent. I'm in charge of four other workers, I make an American wage, but it's a donkey job. I sort through piles of sheets with gloved hands. The dirties are brought down by orderlies, morenas mostly. I never see the sick; they visit me through the stains and marks they leave on the sheets, the alphabet of the sick and dying. A lot of the time the stains are too deep and I have to throw these linens in the special hamper. One of the girls from Baitoa tells me she's heard that everything in the hamper gets incinerated. Because of the sida, she whispers. Sometimes the stains are rusty and old and sometimes the blood smells sharp as rain. You'd think, given the blood we see, that there's a great war going on out in the world. Just the one inside of bodies, the new girl says.

My girls are not exactly reliable, but I enjoy working with them. They play music, they feud, they tell me funny stories. And because I don't yell or bully them they like me. They're young, sent to the States by their parents. The same age I was when I arrived; they see me now, twenty-eight, five years here, as a veteran, a rock, but back then, in those first days, I was so alone that every day was like eating my own heart.

A few of the girls have boyfriends and they're the ones I'm careful about depending on. They show up late or miss weeks at a time; they move to Nueva York or Union City without warning. When that happens I have to go to the manager's office. He's a little man, a thin man, a bird-looking man; has no hair on his face, but a thatch grows on his chest and up his neck. I tell him what happened and he pulls the girl's application and rips it in half, the cleanest of sounds. In less than an hour one of the other girls has sent a friend to me for an application.

The newest girl's called Samantha and she's a problem. She's dark and heavy browed and has a mouth like unswept glass—when you least expect it she cuts you. Walked onto the job after one of the other girls ran off to Delaware. She's been in the States only six weeks and can't believe the cold. Twice she's tipped over the detergent barrels and she has a bad habit of working without gloves and then rubbing her eyes. She tells me that she's been sick, that she's had to move twice, that her housemates have stolen her money. She has the scared, hunted look of the unlucky. Work is work, I tell her, but I loan her enough for her lunches, let her do personal laundry in our machines. I expect her to thank me, but instead she says that I talk like a man.

Does it get any better? I hear her ask the others. Just worse, they say. Wait for the freezing rain. She looks over at me, half-smiling, uncertain. She's fifteen, maybe, and too thin to have mothered a child, but she's already shown me the pictures of her fat boy, Manolo. She's waiting for me to answer, me in particular because I'm the veterana, but I turn to the next load. I've tried to explain to her the trick of working hard but she doesn't seem to care. She cracks her gum and smiles at me like I'm seventy. I unfold the next sheet and like a flower the bloodstain's there, no bigger than my hand. Hamper, I say, and Samantha throws it open. I ball the sheet up and toss. Slops right in, the loose ends dragged in by the center.

Nine hours of smoothing linen and I am home, eating cold yuca with hot oil, waiting for Ramón to come for me in the car he has borrowed. He is taking me to look at another house. It's been his dream since he first set foot in the States, and now, with all the jobs he's had and the money he's saved, it's possible. How many get to this point? Only the ones who never swerve, who never make mistakes, who are never unlucky. And that more or less is Ramón. He's serious about the house, which means I have to be serious about it, too. Each week we go out into the world and look. He makes an event of it, dressing like he's interviewing for a visa, drives us around the quieter sections of Paterson, where the trees have spread over roofs and garages. It's important, he says, to be careful, and I agree. He takes me with him whenever he can, but even I can tell that I'm not much help. I'm not one for change, I tell him, and I see only what's wrong with the places he wants, and later, in the car, he accuses me of sabotaging his dream, of being dura.

Tonight we're supposed to see another. He walks into the kitchen clapping his chapped hands, but I'm in no mood and he can tell. He sits down next to me. He puts his hand on my knee. You're not going?

I'm sick.

How sick?

Bad enough.

He rubs at his stubble. What if I find the place? You want me to make the decision myself?

I don't think it will happen.

And if it does?

You know you'll never move me there.

He scowls. He checks the clock. He leaves.

Ana Iris is working her second job, so I spend my evening alone, listening to this whole country going cold on the radio. I try to keep still, but by nine I have the things he stores in my closet spread before me, the things he tells me never to touch. His books and some of his clothes, an old pair of glasses in a cardboard case, and two beaten chancletas. Hundreds of dead lottery tickets, crimped together in thick wads that fall apart at the touch. Dozens of baseball cards, Dominican players, Guzmán, Fernández, the Alous, swatting balls, winding up and fielding hard line drives just beyond the baseline. He has left me some of his dirties to wash, but I haven't had the time, and tonight I lay them out, the yeast still strong on the cuffs of his pants and work shirts.

In a box on the top shelf of the closet he has a stack of Virta's letters, cinched in a fat brown rubber band. Nearly eight years' worth. Each envelope is worn and frail and I think he's forgotten they're here. I found them a month after he stored his things, right at the start of our relationship, couldn't resist, and afterward I wished I had.

He claims that he stopped writing to her the year before, but that's not true. Every month I drop by his apartment with his laundry and read the new letters she has sent, the ones he stashes under his bed. I know Virta's name, her address, I know she works at a chocolate factory; I know that he hasn't told her about me.

The letters have grown beautiful over the years and now the handwriting has changed as well—each letter loops down, drooping into the next line like a rudder. *Please, please, mi querido husband, tell me what it is. How long did it take before your wife stopped mattering?*

After reading her letters I always feel better. I don't think this says good things about me.

We are not here for fun, Ana Iris told me the day we met, and I said, Yes, you're right, even though I did not want to admit it.

Today I say these same things to Samantha and she looks at me with hatred. This morning when I arrived at the job I found her in the bathroom crying and I wish I could let her rest for an hour but we don't have those kinds of bosses. I put her on the folding and now her hands are shaking and she looks like she's going to cry again. I watch her for a long time and then I ask her what's wrong and she says, What isn't wrong?

This, Ana Iris said, is not an easy country. A lot of girls don't make it through their first year.

You need to concentrate on work, I tell Samantha. It helps.

She nods, her little girl's face vacant. It is probably her son she misses, or the father. Or our whole country, which you never think of until it's gone, which you never love until you're no longer there. I squeeze her arm and go upstairs to report in and when I come back she's gone. The other girls pretend not to notice. I check the bathroom, find a bunch of crumpled-up paper towels on the floor. I smooth them out and put them on the edge of the sink.

Even after lunch I keep expecting her to walk in and say, Here I am. I just went for a stroll.

The truth is I am lucky to have a friend like Ana Iris. She's like my sister. Most of the people I know in the States have no friends here; they're crowded together in apartments. They're cold, they're lonely, they're worn. I've seen the lines at the phone places, the men who sell stolen card numbers, the cuarto they carry in their pockets.

When I first reached the States I was like that, alone, living over a bar with nine other women. At night no one could go to bed because of the screams and the exploding bottles from downstairs. Most of my housemates were fighting with each other over who owed who what or who had stolen money. When I myself had extra I went to the phones and called my mother, just so I could hear the voices of the people in my barrio as they passed the phone from hand to hand, like I was good luck. I was working for Ramón at that time; we weren't going out yet—that wouldn't happen for another two years. He had a housekeeping guiso then, mostly in Piscataway. The day we met he looked at me critically. Which pueblo are you from?

Moca.

Mata dictador, he said, and then a little while later he asked me which team I supported.

Águilas, I told him, not really caring.

Licey, he boomed. The only real team on the Island.

That was the same voice he used to tell me to swab a toilet or scrub an oven. I didn't like him then; he was too arrogant and too loud and I took to humming when I heard him discussing fees with the owners of the houses. But at least he didn't try to rape you like many of the other bosses. At least there was that. He kept his eyes and his hands mostly to himself. He had other plans, important plans, he told us, and just watching him you could believe it.

My first months were housecleaning and listening to Ramón argue. My first months were taking long walks through the city and waiting for Sunday to call my mother. During the day I stood in front of mirrors in those great houses and told myself that I'd done well and afterward I would come home and fold up in front of the small television we crowded around and I believed this was enough.

I met Ana Iris after Ramón's business failed. Not enough ricos around here, he said without discouragement. Some friends set up the meeting and I met her at the fish market. Ana Iris was cutting and preparing fish as we spoke. I thought she was a boricua, but later she told me she was half boricua and half dominicana. The best of the Caribbean and the worst, she said. She had fast, accurate hands and her fillets were not ragged as were some of the others on the bed of crushed ice. Can you work at a hospital? she wanted to know.

I can do anything, I said.

There'll be blood.

If you can do that, I can work in a hospital.

She was the one who took the first pictures that I mailed home, weak fotos of me grinning, well dressed and uncertain. One in front of the

McDonald's, because I knew my mother would appreciate how American it was. Another one in a bookstore. I'm pretending to read, even though the book is in English. My hair is pinned up and the skin behind my ears looks pale and underused. I'm so skinny I look sick. The best picture is of me in front of a building at the university. There are no students but hundreds of metal folding chairs have been arranged in front of the building for an event and I'm facing those chairs and they're facing me and in the light my hands are startling on the blue fabric of my dress.

Three nights a week we look at houses. The houses are in terrible condition; they are homes for ghosts and for cockroaches and for us, los hispanos. Even so, few people will sell to us. They treat us well enough in person but in the end we never hear from them, and the next time Ramón drives by other people are living there, usually blanquitos, tending the lawn that should have been ours, scaring crows out of our mulberry trees. Today a grandfather, with red tints in his gray hair, tells us he likes us. He served in our country during the Guerra Civil. Nice people, he says. Beautiful people. The house is not entirely a ruin and we're both nervous. Ramón stalks about like a cat searching for a place to whelp. He steps into closets and bangs against walls and spends close to five minutes running his finger around the basement's wet seams. He smells the air for a hint of mold. In the bathroom I flush the toilet while he holds his hand under the full torrent of the shower. We both search the kitchen cabinets for roaches. In the next room the grandfather calls our references and laughs at something somebody has said.

He hangs up and says something to Ramón that I don't understand. With these people I cannot even rely on their voices. The blancos will call your mother a puta in the same voice they greet you with. I wait without hoping until Ramón leans close and tells me it looks good.

That's wonderful, I say, still sure Ramón will change his mind. He trusts very little. Out in the car he starts in, certain the old man is trying to trick him.

Why? Did you see anything wrong?

They make it look good. That's part of the trick. You watch, in two weeks the roof will start falling in.

Won't he fix it?

He says he will, but would you trust an old man like that?

I'm surprised that viejo can still get around.

We say nothing more. He screws his head down into his shoulders and the cords in his neck pop out. I know he will yell if I talk. He stops at the house, the tires sliding on the snow.

Do you work tonight? I ask.

Of course I do.

He settles back into the Buick, tired. The windshield is streaked and sooty and the margins that the wipers cannot reach have a crust of dirt on them. We watch two kids pound a third with snowballs and I feel Ramón sadden and I know he's thinking about his son and right then I want to put my arm around him, tell him it will be fine.

Will you be coming by?

Depends on how the work goes.

OK, I say.

My housemates trade phony smiles over the greasy tablecloth when I tell them about the house. Sounds like you're going to be bien cómoda, Marisol says.

No worries for you.

None at all. You should be proud.

Yes, I say.

Later I lie in bed and listen to the trucks outside, their beds rattling with salt and sand. In the middle of the night I wake up and realize that he has not returned but not until morning am I angry. Ana Iris's bed is made, the netting folded neatly at its foot, a gauze. I hear her gargling in the bathroom. My hands and feet are blue from the cold and I cannot see through the window for the frost and icicles. When Ana Iris starts praying, I say, Please, just not today.

She lowers her hands. I dress.

He's talking again about the man who fell from the rafters. What would you do if that was me? he asks once more.

I would find another man, I tell him.

He smiles. Would you? Where would you find one?

You have friends, don't you?

What man would touch a dead man's novia?

I don't know, I said. I wouldn't have to tell anyone. I could find a man the way I found you.

They would be able to tell. Even the most bruto would see the death in your eyes.

A person doesn't mourn forever.

Some do. He kisses me. I bet you would. I am a hard man to replace. They tell me so at work.

How long did you mourn for your son?

He stops kissing me. Enriquillo. I mourned him a long time. I am still missing him.

I couldn't tell that by looking at you.

You don't look carefully enough.

It doesn't show, I don't think.

He puts his hand down at his side. You are not a clever woman.

I'm just saying it doesn't show.

I can see that now, he says. You are not a clever woman.

While he sits by the window and smokes I pull the last letter his wife wrote him out of my purse and open it in front of him. He doesn't know how brazen I can be. One sheet, smelling of violet water. *Please*, Virta has written neatly in the center of the page. That's all. I smile at Ramón and place the letter back in the envelope.

Ana Iris once asked me if I loved him and I told her about the lights in my old home in the capital, how they flickered and you never knew if they would go out or not. You put down your things and you waited and couldn't do anything really until the lights decided. This, I told her, is how I feel.

Here is what the wife looks like. She is small with enormous hips and has the grave seriousness of a woman who will be called doña before she's forty. I suspect if we were in the same life we would not be friends.

I hold up the blue hospital sheets in front of me and close my eyes, but the bloodstains float in the darkness in front of me. Can we save this one with bleach? Samantha asks. She is back, but I don't know for how much longer. I don't know why I don't fire her. Maybe because I want to give her a chance. Maybe because I want to see if she will stay or if she will go. What will this tell me? Very little, I suspect. In the bag at my feet I have his clothes and I wash them all together with the hospital things. For a day he will smell of my job, but I know that bread is stronger than blood.

I have not stopped watching for signs that he misses her. You must not think on these things, Ana Iris tells me. Keep them out of your mind. You do not want to go crazy from them.

This is how Ana Iris survives here, how she keeps from losing her mind over her children. How in part we all survive here. I've seen a picture of her three sons, three little boys tumbled out in the Jardín Japonés, near a pine tree, smiling, the smallest a saffron blur trying to shy away from the camera. I listen to her advice and on my way to and from work I concentrate on the other sleepwalkers around me, the men who sweep the streets and those who stand around in the backs of restaurants, with uncut hair, smoking cigarettes; the people in suits who stumble from the trains—a good many will stop at a lover's and that is all they will think about while they're eating their cold meals at home, while they're in bed with their spouses. I think of my mother, who kept with a married man when I was seven, a man with a handsome beard and craggy cheeks, who was so black that he was called Noche by everyone who knew him. He worked string-ing wires for Codetel out in the campo but he lived in our barrio and had two children with a woman he had married in Pedernales. His wife was very pretty, and when I think of Ramón's wife I see her, in heels, flashing yards of brown leg, a woman warmer than the air around her. Una jeva buena. I do not imagine Ramón's wife as uneducated. She watches the telenovelas simply to pass the time. In her letters she mentions a child she tends who she loves almost as much as she had loved her own. In the beginning, when Ramón had not been gone long, she believed they could have another son, one like this Victor, her amorcito. *He plays baseball like you*, Virta wrote. She never mentions Enriquillo.

Here there are calamities without end—but sometimes I can clearly see us in the future, and it is good. We will live in his house and I will cook for him and when he leaves food out on the counter I will call him a zángano. I can see myself watching him shave every morning. And at other times I see us in that house and see how one bright day (or a day like this, so cold your mind shifts every time the wind does) he will wake up and decide it's all wrong. He will wash his face and then turn to me. I'm sorry, he'll say. I have to leave now.

Samantha comes in sick with the flu; I feel like I'm dying, she says. She drags herself from task to task, she leans against the wall to rest, she doesn't eat anything, and the day after I have it, too. I pass it to Ramón; he calls me a fool for doing so. You think I can take a day off from work? he demands.

I say nothing; it will only irritate him.

He never stays angry for long. He has too many other things on his mind.

On Friday he comes by to update me on the house. The old man wants to sell to us, he says. He shows me some paperwork that I do not understand. He is excited but he is also scared. This is something I know, a place I've been.

What do you think I should do? His eyes are not watching me, they're looking out the window.

I think you should buy yourself a home. You deserve it.

He nods. I need to break him down on the price though. He takes out his cigarettes. Do you know how long I've waited for this? To own a house in this country is to begin to live.

I try to bring up Virta but he kills it, like always.

I already told you it's over, he snaps. What else do you want? A maldito corpse? You women never know how to leave things alone. You never know how to let go.

That night Ana Iris and I go to a movie. We cannot understand the English but we both like the new theater's clean rugs. Blue and pink neon stripes zag across the walls like lightning. We buy a popcorn to share and smuggle in cans of tamarind juice from the bodega. The people around us talk; we talk as well.

You're lucky to be getting out, she says. Those cueros are going to drive me crazy.

It's a little early for this but I say: I'm going to miss you, and she laughs.

You are on your way to another life. You won't have time to miss me.

Yes, I will. I'll probably be over to visit you every day.

You won't have the time.

I will if I make time. Are you trying to get rid of me?

Of course not, Yasmin. Don't be stupid.

It won't be for a while anyway. I remember what Ramón had said over and over again. Anything can happen.

We sit quietly for the rest of the movie. I have not asked her what she thinks of my move and she has not offered her opinion. We respect each other's silence about certain things, the way I never ask if she intends to send for her children someday. I cannot tell what she will do. She has had men and they, too, have slept in our room, but she never kept any for long.

We walk back from the theater close together, careful of the shiny ice that scars the snow. The neighborhood is not safe. Boys who know only enough Spanish to curse stand together at the street corners and scowl. They cross into traffic without looking and when we pass them a fat one says, I eat pussy better than anybody in the world. Cochino, Ana Iris hisses, putting her hand on me. We pass the old apartment where I used to live, the one over the bar, and I stare up at it, trying to remember which window I used to stare out of. Come on, Ana Iris says. It's freezing.

Ramón must have told Virta something, because the letters stop. I guess it's true what they say: if you wait long enough everything changes.

As for the house, it takes longer than even I could have imagined. He almost walks away a half dozen times, slams phones, throws his drink against a wall and I expect it to fall away, not to happen. But then like a miracle it does.

Look, he says, holding up the paperwork. Look. He is almost pleading.

I'm truly happy for him. You did it, mi amor.

We did it, he says quietly. Now we can begin.

Then he puts his head down on the table and cries.

In December we move into the house. It's a half-ruin and only two rooms are habitable. It resembles the first place I lived when I arrived in this country. We don't have heat for the entire winter, and for a month we have to bathe from a bucket. Casa de Campo, I call the place in jest, but he doesn't take kindly to any criticism of his "niño." Not everyone can own a home, he reminds me. I saved eight years for this. He works on the house ceaselessly, raiding the abandoned properties on the block for materials. Every floorboard he reclaims, he boasts, is money saved. Despite all the trees, the neighborhood is not easy and we have to make sure to keep everything locked all the time.

For a few weeks people knock on the door, asking if the house is still for sale. Some of them are couples as hopeful as we must have looked. Ramón slams the door on them, as if afraid that they might haul him back to where they are. But when it's me I let them down softly. It's not, I say. Good luck with your search.

This is what I know: people's hopes go on forever.

The hospital begins to build another wing; three days after the cranes surround our building as if in prayer, Samantha pulls me aside. Winter has dried her out, left her with reptile hands and lips so chapped they look like they might at any moment split. I need a loan, she whispers. My mother's sick.

It is always the mother. I turn to go.

Please, she begs. We're from the same country.

This is true. We are.

Someone must have helped you sometime.

Also true.

The next day I give her eight hundred. It is half my savings. Remember this.

I will, she says.

She is so happy. Happier than I was when we moved into the house. I wish I could be as free. She sings for the rest of the shift, songs from when I was younger, Adamo and that lot. But she is still Samantha. Before we punch out she tells me, Don't wear so much lipstick. You have big enough lips as it is.

Ana Iris laughs. That girl said that to you?

Yes, she did.

Que desgraciada, she says, not without admiration.

At the end of the week, Samantha doesn't return to work. I ask around but no one knows where she lives. I don't remember her saying anything significant on her last day. She walked out as quietly as ever, drifting down toward the center of town, where she could catch her bus. I pray for her. I remember my own first year, how desperately I wanted to return home, how often I cried. I pray she stays, like I did.

A week. I wait a week and then I let her go. The girl who replaces her is quiet and fat and works without stopping or complaint. Sometimes, when I am in one of my moods, I imagine Samantha back home with her people. Back home where it is warm. Saying, I would never go back. Not for anything. Not for anyone.

Some nights when Ramón is working on the plumbing or sanding the floors I read the old letters and sip the rum we store under the kitchen sink, and think of course of her, the one from the other life.

* * *

I am pregnant when the next letter finally arrives. Sent from Ramón's old place to our new home. I pull it from the stack of mail and stare at it. My heart is beating like it's lonely, like there's nothing else inside of me. I want to open it but I call Ana Iris instead; we haven't spoken in a long time. I stare out at the bird-filled hedges while the phone rings.

I want to go for a walk, I tell her.

The buds are breaking through the tips of the branches. When I step into the old place she kisses me and sits me down at the kitchen table. Only two of the housemates I know; the rest have moved on or gone home. There are new girls from the Island. They shuffle in and out, barely look at me, exhausted by the promises they've made. I want to advise them: no promises can survive that sea. I am showing, and Ana Iris is thin and worn. Her hair has not been cut in months; the split ends rise out of her thick strands like a second head of hair. She can still smile, though, so brightly it is a wonder that she doesn't set something alight. A woman is singing a bachata somewhere upstairs, and her voice in the air reminds me of the size of this house, how high the ceilings are.

Here, Ana Iris says, handing me a scarf. Let's go for a walk.

I hold the letter in my hands. The day is the color of pigeons. Our feet crush the bits of snow that lie scattered here and there, crusted over with gravel and dust. We wait for the mash of cars to slow at the light and then we scuttle into the park. Our first months Ramón and I were in this park daily. Just to wind down after work, he said, but I painted my fingernails red every time. I remember the day before we first made love, how I already knew it would happen. He had only just told me about his wife and about his son. I was mulling over the information, saying nothing, letting my feet guide us. We met a group of boys playing baseball and he bullied the bat from them, cut at the air with it, sent the boys out deep. I thought he would embarrass himself, so I stood back, ready to pat his arm when he fell or when the ball dropped at his feet, but he connected with a sharp crack of the aluminum bat and sent the ball out beyond the children with an easy motion of his upper body. The children threw their hands up and yelled and he smiled at me over their heads.

We walk the length of the park without talking and then we head back across the highway, toward downtown.

She's writing again, I say, but Ana Iris interrupts me.

I've been calling my children, she says. She points out the man across from the courthouse, who sells her stolen calling-card numbers. They've gotten so much older, she tells me, that it's hard for me to recognize their voices.

We have to sit down after a while so that I can hold her hand and she can cry. I should say something but I don't know where a person can start. She will bring them or she will go. That much has changed.

It gets cold. We go home. We embrace at the door for what feels like an hour.

That night I give Ramón the letter and I try to smile while he reads it.

SEFI ATTA

The novelist and playwright Sefi Atta was born in Lagos, Nigeria, in 1964, and immigrated at age fourteen to the United Kingdom, where she later became an accountant. Sixteen years later, she would move once more, this time to the United States, where she received an MFA from Antioch University of Los Angeles.

In 2005 Atta won PEN International's David T. K. Wong Prize, and in 2006, she received the first ever Wole Soyinka Prize for Literature in Africa for her debut novel, *Everything Good Will Come* (2005). Her stories have appeared in the *Los Angeles Review*, *Mississippi Review*, and *World Literature Today*; her radio plays have been broadcast by the BBC. Her most recent novel is *A Bit of Difference* (2012). The short story presented here, "Wal-Mart Has Plantains," was previously published in the *Crab Orchard Review*.

Of the impact different countries have had upon her writing, Atta says, "I suppose I get my need to commemorate from Nigeria, social satire from England, and from America my trust in detail." Sefi Atta currently lives in Mississippi with her husband and daughter.

Wal-Mart Has Plantains

The DPS man asked why I moved to Mississippi. "It's a long way from Africa," he said, as if giving a friendly warning. He was wearing a wig the exact color of my daughter Rolari's stuffed bunny, Poopy. Perhaps this was why she stared at him.

"My husband's work," I said with a smile.

"You military?"

"No."

He scratched the back of his neck. "Where does your husband work?"

"The community clinic," I said.

"He a doctor?"

"Yes."

"What kind of doctor?"

"Children's."

He smoothed the laminate of my driver's license. "Is he from around here?"

"No," I said, already tired of answering him.

"He's from Nigeria too?"

I glanced at Rolari. She shrugged.

"Yes," I said.

The DPS man narrowed his eyes. "Where in Africa is Nigeria?"

"West Coast."

"That near the Nile or something?"

I held out my hand. "River Niger."

"Must be real hot over there."

"As a summer afternoon here," I said.

I took my driver's license from him and checked that my last name, Ogedengbe, was spelled correctly. Rolari stood on her toes and peered at my photograph. "You look pretty," she murmured. The camera lens had caught me wincing. I mimicked my expression in the photograph and she nudged me. Rolari hated for me to disregard her compliments. "Stop," she whispered.

The DPS man lifted his chin in her direction. "Was she born here?" Instinctively, I placed my hand on her shoulder. "She was born in Nigeria."

He noticed the drop in my voice.

"Well, have a good one," he said.

"He has funny hair," Rolari said before we were out the door.

I squeezed her shoulder. "That's okay."

She mistook my indulgence for encouragement. "But it's true, Mama. It had bits like this and stuff sticking up."

She ran her hands over her cornrows and slid them down to her gold hoop earrings. She was almost six and her language was not as specific as her observations.

"People here ask too many personal questions," she said, shaking her head.

I ushered her outside before she could say any more. She'd heard that from me.

We'd been in Mississippi almost three months. I was giving up my New York driver's license; I had no use for one. In New York, I needed a driver's license for out-of-state audit jobs, all within the tri-state area. I told my work friends, Naomi and Sheila, who often traveled farther than me, that I was moving to Mississippi. Sheila covered her mouth with both hands. "Yikes," she said. "They sit on porches and spit tobacco." "Girl," Naomi said. "Mississippi, Louisiana, Alabama, and what's the other one?" "Tennessee," Sheila said, shutting her eyes. "Texas," Naomi said. "Now, you know I'll miss you, but don't be inviting me." Our boss, Jim, thought anywhere outside New York would be an improvement. "You'll have less stress," he said, giving a royal wave. "You'll spend more time with your family. You'll love small-town America. Believe me." My job was always open, he said, in case I changed my mind. Still, within a week, he was ignoring me, and before my notice was up, he'd placed an ad in the Sunday *Times*: Internal Auditor. CPA Required. Limited Travel.

"Watch it," I said, reaching for Rolari's hand. I stepped down a couple of inches from the pavement to the parking lot outside the drivers license office. Her sneakers hit the tarmac and lit up.

"Ow," she yelled.

"Are you okay?" I asked.

She hopped. "I broke my leg."

"You didn't."

"Really, Mama. I'm not faking."

She pointed at her smiley ankle socks. I summoned as much patience as I could; I'd only just picked her up from school.

"Maybe we should take you to Daddy's clinic?"

She spread her fingers. "No! He'll give me a big shot!"

Recently she was complaining about too many ailments, stomachaches especially. Sanwo said he had just the cure.

He came ahead of us, after his residency at New York University Hospital. Rolari and I followed soon after because the school year started early in Mississippi. Sanwo wanted her in the Catholic school across from his clinic: they had a good racial mix. His clinic catered to Medicare and Medicaid patients. He was employed there under a government scheme for foreign-trained doctors. After four years, our family would be eligible for green cards. In another five, we would qualify for U.S. citizenship. Under this scheme, I was not entitled to work for the first four years.

"I'll die of boredom," I said when we found out. I'd assumed I would be able to renew my employment authorization.

The INS telephone assistant I spoke to explained that I was allowed to work as the spouse of an exchange student, but not as the spouse of a Work Permit holder. Sanwo reminded me of the mornings we left Rolari in daycare in New York and I began to cry because she didn't want me to leave; nights she had fevers and vomited on my chest. I moved her to another daycare when she developed a diaper rash that looked like a second degree burn. She once had a cold so bad mucus was seeping out of her eyes. I took a day off to nurse her and cursed Sanwo out when he couldn't do the same. Whenever I got stuck in traffic and I was running late to pick Rolari up from daycare, I called him, on the New Jersey Turnpike, over George Washington Bridge, saying, "I can't, I can't, I can't do this anymore."

"Remember?" he said. "We won't have to go through that *wahala* again."

"But she's older," I insisted. "She doesn't get sick like that. She'll be in school most of the day. You're not on call twenty-four/seven. I have to work. I've always worked. Why can't I work?"

My mother worked. She taught Sanwo when he was in medical school: pediatrics. She had four children. I was her third. Throughout my childhood in Nigeria, I was raised by nannies, drivers shuttled me to and from school, piano, and tennis lessons. My father ran an accounting firm. I worked for him after I graduated from university. Sanwo was a resident when we met and he lived in hospital accommodation. His government salary could barely afford him a suit for our wedding; I was living off my father's generous senior staff allowance and waiting to be promoted to a manager. My father called me his accountant. My sister was a lawyer and my brothers were doctors in private practice. Like my mother, Sanwo was not interested in joining any private practice in Nigeria. He said he'd end up dispensing antimalarials and antibiotics. At his teaching hospital, patients were sent out to buy their own IV drips and wound dressings. The medical association and nurses' union went on strikes because their salaries were delayed. We had to leave Nigeria, Sanwo decided, after Rolari was born. "At least your mother had your old man. Look at me. Who can you say you have? You'll lose respect for me."

"Don't be ridiculous," I immediately said.

"Don't deceive yourself," Sanwo said just as fast.

At the time I was paying our rent, buying Rolari's clothes and diapers.

Sanwo's mother had raised four children on her own. Their father died of cancer when he was eight. Sanwo was the eldest and I thought he behaved more like an uncle than an older brother, though he denied this. Now that he was out of residency, he sent money home through Western Union; I'd never had to.

I strapped Rolari in her car seat and she began to sing the song that never ended.

Fall in Mississippi was not as dull as New York, or as epidemic. I took the bridge over Sowashee Creek to Wal-Mart Supercenter and lowered my window to let in fresh air. A white Ford pickup crawled ahead of us for most of the way. This one had a Proud Mom sticker. In Mississippi, I'd learned not to tailgate proud moms: they accelerated for nobody. I'd also learned that when vehicles pulled over on a street, without a siren to be heard, a funeral procession was approaching. Twice I'd witnessed this, and only once had I seen people sitting on a porch. That was on Old Country Club Road, where the houses were mansions. Not one tobacco chewer had I come across, but I'd seen spitters, especially at traffic lights—they stopped, opened their car doors and leaned over. This was not a small town; it was a small city, with as many trailer parks as secondhand car dealerships; as many instant cash businesses as Dollar Stores. There was a Coca-Cola bottling plant, a cemetery dating back to an 1878 yellow fever epidemic, an old opera house that was being renovated, a new mall that could have been any in the tri-state. Whenever we drove around the city, Rolari looked out for the carousel horses at designated historic buildings. Sanwo was the Hummer spotter in our family; he was vicariously triumphant whenever we passed one: "*Baba ke!* That's my baby!" In his dreams, I said. I was jealous of his attraction to Hummers. I'd stopped being surprised by the number of churches in the city. There was one with every head turn.

I glanced at Rolari in the rearview mirror. "You want jollof rice and chicken tonight?"

She was enjoying singing so much she was rocking.

"How's your stomach?" I asked.

She slapped her knees. "Aw! Now I have to start all over again!"

"Does your belly still hurt?"

She tilted her head. "I already told you, Mama."

I would have to buy plantains, I thought; I couldn't make jollof rice and chicken without fried plantains.

The parking lot at Wal-Mart was packed as usual. Rolari begged to sit in a cart and I refused. "You break your leg walking," I said.

"That's mean," she said, scowling.

I smiled. "Tough."

"Please," she said, placing her palms together. "I won't fall out and break my head."

I carried her into the cart. As I pushed, she started humming the song that never ended with such intensity her nostrils flared.

"Sh," I hissed and headed for the produce department.

When Sanwo got his job at the community clinic, I was relieved to hear there was another Nigerian there, Dr. Makanju. He had a family. I met his wife, Funke, their four-year-old daughter, Bimbo, and son, Dare, who had just had his second birthday. My first thought was that Americans would misconstrue their names. "They do," Funke agreed cheerfully. She rolled up the sleeves of her tie-dye *agbada*. "I keep correcting them. Bim-buh. Bim-buh. Da-reh. Da-reh. They even mess up my own name. They call me Funky. Foon-keh, I tell them. Foon . . . "

I couldn't imagine expending that much energy over names. At work, I'd used my birth name, Coker. My married name, Ogedengbe, would have been a nuisance at clients' meetings. "Dr. Ogy-diggywhat?" Sanwo's patients asked. Some laughed, others crossed their arms in resignation and said, "Uh-oh," as if Sanwo were another Medicare Medicaid conspiracy against them.

I asked Funke if she ever succeeded in correcting people. "You have to be patient with Americans," she said—as though Americans were pets to be trained. Her children were born in America. Why did she choose such Nigerian names? Bimbo especially. These were considerations any immigrant would have, if they wanted their children to go to school in peace. Funke, I discovered, was more concerned about the culinary implications of immigration. "Mississippi is not bad," she said. "Only I can't eat their food. All I can say is thank God they have goat meat."

"Goat meat?" I asked.

"Yes," she said. "They have goat farms here, but they don't kill them like we kill them at home, slitting their throat and all that. You know? You can't find fresh fish in this city either. Fresh from the sea? Only catfish."

"Catfish," I said.

"Yes," she said. "And you know, catfish isn't good for pepper soup. My husband likes his with fresh fish. He won't eat anything else. But they have oxtails here, and okra, and yes, pickled Scotch bonnets. In Wal-Mart. Look for them in the produce section. Habañeros, they call them. They even have plantains."

"Wal-Mart has plantains?" I said.

I was surprised. Hispanics preferred them green, she said, rather than yellow and ripe as Nigerians ate them.

Within a day, Rolari and Bimbo became playmates. By the next, Rolari was teaching Bimbo how to behead Barbies. Sanwo and Dr. Makanju discussed medicine, CMEs, and E-Trade. Funke and I talked about where to find Nigerian food: yams in Birmingham, tripe from a farmers' market in Atlanta, goat meat from a Halal butcher in Jackson. She and Hakeem went to the INS office in New Orleans to get their green cards. I looked after their children for the day. Funke returned with a bag of *garri* for me, a bottle of palm oil to make black-eyed peas, and chin-chin for Rolari.

Now, the Makanjus had moved to North Carolina and Funke had her fresh fish.

In the produce department, I spotted a basket of ripe plantains. I was glad Wal-Mart stocked plantains. I enjoyed Nigerian food; I missed Nigerian food. I would not traverse the South in search of Nigerian food. I wasn't one of those who made regular trips to the Forty-Second Street African food store in New York, either. In Mississippi, my family ate fried chicken, catfish, collard greens, sweet potato, and macaroni and cheese, at Tommy's, for less than five dollars a head, unlike the gourmet prices we paid for soul food in Harlem.

My Wal-Mart assistant was called LaShanda. I placed the plantains on the belt of her counter. She held one up. "These bananas?"

She must have had at least five hundred braid extensions and they were neatly knotted in a bun.

"Plantains," I said.

"Huh?"

"Plantains."

She lifted a corner of her mouth. "These ain't bananas?"

"No."

"Oh. I thought they was bananas."

A woman behind her was holding a loaf of bread and eyeing us. Rolari raised her hands in exasperation.

LaShanda checked her code sheet. "Plan . . . what d'you call them?"

"Tains," I said, leaning over. I could not read the print on the sheet.

She found the correct code. "Oh, here. Tains."

Rolari rolled her eyes.

"How do these um, um, plan . . . taste?" LaShanda asked, tapping the code.

"Like bananas," I said.

She looked up. "Where your accent from?"

"Africa."

"For real? Do you do braids?"

"Nah," I said, Americanizing my voice, as if to confirm my inadequacy.

She smiled. "Who do your baby cornrows?"

"Me," I said, patting my chest.

She smoothed back her extensions. "I'm looking for someone to do my micro braids."

"They're beautiful," I said, sliding a box of Uncle Ben's Rice toward her.

She pursed her lips. "Yeah, but they be costing me too much."

A hundred and fifty dollars. I'd inquired at Y-Not-Turn-Heads salon in my first week of arriving in the city, and the hair stylist there said she could finish them in no less than eight hours. This stylist didn't know how to twist my natural hair. "You mean dreads?" she asked. "Two strand twists," I explained. "Uh-uh, we don't do that here," she said. She couldn't trim natural hair either. I went to JC Penney to get my ends trimmed. "I haven't seen virgin hair in years," the stylist there said. "Y'all don't get hair relaxers in Africa?"

I didn't go natural until I got to New York. Malaika in Brooklyn twisted my hair and it grew long and strong, and she gave me aromatherapy scalp massages, and she burned incense to purify my spirit. I was so frustrated trying to find a replacement for Malaika in Mississippi, I asked Sanwo to take me to his barbers on Fifth Street, where my hair was cropped down to a quarter of an inch. I paid his barber, Mr. Nobles, seven dollars, and so long as I kept my mouth shut, I got to listen to Mr. Nobles's opinions on President Bush's first term, Shaquille O'Neal's game, that Monica Lewinsky woman, West Nile disease, and Genesis, as he maneuvered between his Martin Luther King Jr. poster and pedestal: "Eve was carved from Adam's rib. See? Not the other way round. That's why I believe a woman gotta stay at home and take care of her man and kids. You feeling me, sister?"

Mr. Nobles's stomach was like a pregnant woman's. He shaped my hair with his clippers and put a smile on my face. I looked forward to seeing him every other week. From him, I heard about the tornado season—the city had not been hit in over a hundred years. I heard about the drug dealers around, the school shooting at Pearl, a suicide ruling in a town nearby. "Valedictorian," Mr. Nobles said. "Messing with white girls. They hanged him." "People here love God," he said about the number of churches around. "But they don't love God enough to come together in worship." It was the same everywhere in the world, I said. "I can't speak for anywhere else," Mr. Nobles said. "Except here."

Sometimes I studied his features in the mirror. He had a shiny round nose, on which he perched his bifocals, and wide lips. He could easily be a Yoruba man. Was he? How would he know after so many generations? Did he care about his African ancestry? And here I was with my husband Sanwo, two Yorubas who came to Mississippi voluntarily in the year 2001, and we were grateful for the opportunity to find work.

Rolari wouldn't get out of the cart until I'd finished unloading my bags. I'd promised that we'd stop at Toys "R" Us, but I ended up driving home because I had a couple of Cornish hens in my trunk from Wal-Mart.

Where we lived, a block of apartments next to a radio station, most of our neighbors were families who were on the waiting list for housing at the naval base outside the city. They were called Navy. People sometimes asked if our family were Navy. Rather than explain our circumstance, I was tempted to say yes.

At home, I defrosted the Cornish hens in the microwave and rinsed them; chopped the tomatoes, onions, and habañeros and liquidized them; emptied the liquidizer into a pot and poured in three cups of Uncle Ben's Rice; stuffed the chickens with lemon halves and onion quarters and rubbed them with mustard. Then I dusted them with black pepper and rosemary.

Rolari watched television as the oven preheated.

"Are you playing soccer this Saturday?" I asked.

"Don't know," she mumbled.

"Paige's party, is it morning or afternoon?"

She didn't know either. The party was at a skating rink. I would have to buy Paige a present; a gift bag with a soccer theme and tissues to match. I tapped my forehead. Why didn't I think of this in Wal-Mart?

"I think the party is the same time as your soccer," I said, prodding the Cornish hens. "Will you go to soccer or will you go to Paige's birthday?"

Rolari screwed up her nose. "Paige plays soccer with me."

"What's wrong with me today? I'd better ask her mother what's happening."

The onion fumes stung my eyes. I cleaned my tears with a towel from the kitchen roll and left a black smear of mascara.

Through Rolari I'd met other women. There was Paige's mom, Lynn. She had bangs that flipped up, walked with a boyish bounce, and always had traces of crimson lipstick. She was Rolari and Paige's soccer coach. "Good shot!" she cheered and raised her thumb. "Way to go!" She didn't yell like some coaches and sometimes she even forgot the score. After our games, she hugged the girls and handed them Fruit Roll-Ups. "How do you manage your time, Lynn?" I asked. She was like a CEO without the fraud scandal and million dollar benefits. She carpooled and organized charity walks. She served on the PTA and not even in a nyah-nyah way, that one might despise her. I saw her on local TV serving up at God's Kitchen, another time she was on the news selling tickets for the symphony orchestra. "I don't know," she confessed. "Honestly, my life is like one big circus."

There was Meena. Meena's son, Ali, had a crush on Rolari. "Every time he sees her he pedals so fast," Meena said. "I don't know why, eh, Ali?" Meena was from Pakistan. She was about ten years younger than me and her hair was gray and thinning. In Pakistan, she worked as a psychologist before her family came to the U.S. Now, her husband worked for a state psychiatric hospital and Meena was at home. They lived in our apartment block. True enough, Ali worked his skinny legs on his tricycle, trying to keep up with Rolari, as Rolari urged him, "Come on Ali," knowing full well she was going to win their races. Meena and I came outside to watch them play. Perhaps because we were foreigners, we had the same sense of security about our apartment block. We worried about kidnappers; we talked about going back to school. She wanted to get a PhD. Her mother-in-law was coming from Pakistan to help her with Ali. She thought I should consider an online MBA. "The way I feel?" I said. "Fifteen years out of college. I studied for institute exams at home, state boards here. I can't go back to school, Meena, even if we could afford it. I honestly can't study a paragraph."

At her own school, I'd assumed Rolari would become friends with Kiara. Kiara had her hair pressed and coordinated her barrettes with her clothes. Rolari barely mentioned her name and I kept asking, "Don't you play with Kiara?" "Nope," Rolari said. Occasionally she came home and complained, "Kiara was mean. She went like this: whatever!" or "Kiara was laughing at my name. She said Ogedengbe means Big Booger." Kiara began to bug me. Her mother, Brenda, had introduced herself one morning when I was almost late getting Rolari to school. She was wearing a white linen shirt; I was in gray sweatpants. "Well, hello," she said. "My husband knows your husband. Yes, mine's a doctor too. We should get together sometime. We're not from around here either. We're from Atlanta." Then she whispered before we parted, "I know people say Africans and African Americans don't get along, but we're both doctors' wives."

I wondered—not about Africans and African Americans getting along; that I'd heard before—why she thought we could get along because we were doctors' wives.

At first, I appreciated Brenda because she didn't walk past me as if I were invisible, like most of the other mothers. Then I began to avoid Brenda, because I noticed that if Brenda had a second to spend with me, she would spend that second trashing a kid in the class, his or her mother, the teacher, or teacher's assistant—*Oh, he's bad. Her mother should have taught her better. Is he ADHD or something? I don't know what that woman is teaching them. The Montessori teacher was much better. Much, much better last year. But Kiara says Grandma Pigford never helps her with her reading. It's not just white folk, now. Some of ours can be a little resentful when you're successful. They look at women like us and think, well, she's a doctor's wife. She doesn't have to work.*

"Her?" she said about Chad's mother, Dr. Evans. "She never comes to anything in class. She's from around here. Oh, trust me, she's definitely from around here."

Dr. Yolanda Evans was Chad's mother. Chad was the tallest and coolest boy in class. "He's funny," Rolari said. "He makes me laugh. He says his name is African." Rolari had a crush on him. Chad had freckles on his caramel-colored skin and he had already lost his teeth. Dr. Evans was always in her green scrubs. She dropped Chad off every morning and zoomed off in her convertible. She was responsible for half the smiles in the city, according to Sanwo, and apart from her practice, she ran the dental clinic where Sanwo worked, plus a clinic at the city prison. "What's her name," she said, and snapped her fingers when she referred to Brenda. "The lady from Atlanta? Her husband's a doctor?"

Chad was actually named after Lake Chad, Dr. Evans confirmed on PTA Night. When she was pregnant, she saw the name on a map, on top of Nigeria. She'd never been to Africa. She wanted to, but didn't know where to start. I promised to help. Sanwo and I sat next to her and watched that night as the PTA asked for volunteers for the Fall Fest, Spaghetti Dinner, and requested a show of hands for those in favor of a brown bag lunch on the first Monday of every month.

"Imagine," Dr. Evans said, leaning toward me, "if this is your life."

I laughed, then I waited until she'd left to volunteer for the Fall Fest.

I admired Dr. Evans, I said on our way home from PTA night. I was staring out of the car window at the city lights. I was trying to take stock of my life, assess where I was headed in five years, and all that MBA stuff; I didn't know how. During the day, I was spending three, four hours on the Internet researching schools. I wished I was able to braid hair instead.

Sanwo asked why I admired Dr. Evans.

"The woman has no time."

I had too much time, I thought; too much time for nonsense lately: laundry, picking up toys, cleaning baths, making beds, gossip, and resentment.

"She's divorced," Sanwo said.

"So?" I said.

Rolari tapped my shoulder. "What's divorced?"

The oven preheat light came on. Rolari rolled over on her belly and pressed on the remote control. The television was too loud.

"Turn that TV down," I said.

Rolari didn't move.

"Baby, will you turn that down?"

She jumped up. "Oh, sorry!"

I slid the tray of Cornish hens into the oven and waited to adjust the heat. Sanwo would be back soon.

The PTA night had ended in a showdown between us. We argued even before we reached home. I could not believe he would tell Rolari divorce was "nothing," as if she'd asked the meaning of a filthy word.

"You can't tell me how to parent my own child," he said.

I reminded him that I barely dragged his butt to her PTA meeting. "You're taking advantage of me since I've been at home. Yes, you are. Yes, you . . . "

In no time, we were yelling. At home, he told me he came to Mississippi to give *us* a better life. I circled him as he stood under the ceiling fan. "I did not come to America for a better life," I said. "Hear me? I came to give our marriage a chance. That is why I moved to Mississippi. The only reason. Do you understand? What will I do here for four years?"

"We could have another child," Sanwo said.

"We have a child. I will not have another child for having another child's sake. I will not have another child because I'm bored. I will certainly not have another child to give my child a little brother or sister, as your mother says. I will have a child only because you and I want another child. Hear me? And having another child will not substitute for working."

How much did I like working anyway? he asked.

"That's my business," I said. "My right to hate my work."

Sanwo raised his arms. "What do you want me to do? Tell me what you want me to do."

I glared at him. I wouldn't tell him if I knew. Rolari, who'd been in her bedroom, came out rubbing her chest. "My belly hurts."

"Come here," I said.

I reached for her and patted her stomach. Sanwo slouched off to our bedroom. He'd forgotten about her in his anger. I hadn't, but I couldn't stop myself from losing my temper even though I'd never heard my own parents argue. I was a horrible mother, I thought, as I ran my fingers over Rolari's cornrows that night.

She held on to a button on my shirt. "Just be happy with Mississippi."

I bent to bite her fingers. She made a fist and hid them.

"Are you and Daddy going to get a divorce?"

I faked a laugh. "Why do you say that?"

"Chad's parents got a divorce."

She stood up and began to do her Shake Your Booty dance.

"So?" I said wiggling my hips. "Do I do everything Chad's mom does?"

Rolari turned her backside to me. "You want to work like her."

"So?" I, too, stood up. I was dancing; I wanted to cry. "Are you calling me a copycat?"

We shook and twirled under the ceiling fan and I fell on the carpet. She fell on me and placed her head on my thigh.

"Actually, I have a very good idea," she said.

"What?" I asked.

She was itsy-bitsying her fingers. "Well, if you look after me, at least you won't need a work permit."

My jollof rice was bubbling. I checked that the Cornish hens were roasting.

"Smells good," Rolari said and kicked her legs.

"Will you open the windows?"

Her head popped up. "Are you making plantains?"

"Yep."

She clapped. "Yeah! Hurrah for Mommy! Savior of the Universe!"

I took a low bow. She was loving and beautiful and smart. "When we get our American passports?" she'd asked on PTA night. "Will I be African American or African and American?"

As she opened the window, I said, "Glad your belly is better. We're over that now, aren't we?"

She didn't answer. She was watching the television.

LARA VAPNYAR

At the age of twenty-three, and three months pregnant, Lara Vapnyar (1971–) immigrated to New York from Russia. She says of immigrating, "I didn't expect that much; I didn't plan our life. What I was thinking of was that it's going to be wonderful . . . I will have some kind of amazing job . . . my life will be full of adventure."

While Vapnyar struggled to find a job in the United States she began writing. Her short stories were first published in English in 2002, and her work has appeared in the *New Yorker*, the *New York Times*, and *Open City*. The story presented here, "Fischer vs. Spassky," was first published in the *New Yorker* in October 2012.

Vapnyar's first collection, *There Are Jews in My House* (2003), was nominated for several awards and won the Prize for Jewish Fiction by Emerging Writers from the National Foundation for Jewish Culture. She has since published the novels *Memoirs of a Muse* (2006) and *The Scent of Pine* (2014), and the collection *Broccoli and Other Tales of Food and Love* (2008).

Fischer vs. Spassky

For a long time after her husband died, Marina used to scream. She'd feel the scream rushing up from her stomach, choking her from the inside, and she'd run out of the room, stumbling over her kids' toys, and hide in the hallway, in the narrow space between the coatrack and the mirror stand, biting down on her right forearm to muffle the sound. After the scream had passed, and she unclenched her teeth, there would be little circular marks on her arm that looked like irregular postage stamps. Those scars remained long after Marina had stopped screaming, long after she had ceased grieving for her husband altogether.

Even now, thirty years later, she could feel them tingle at random moments. She felt it when she heard Bobby Fischer's name on the radio. She was driving down a snowbound Brooklyn street on the way to see a client. The radio was on low, but she thought she heard the announcer repeating that name. She turned up the volume and there it was: Bobby Fischer. Bobby Fischer had died. Bobby Fischer had died in Reykjavík, Iceland.

Marina turned onto a side street and started her crawl up the slippery slope that led to Elijah's house. His empty driveway was unshoveled, so she had to park on the street between two caked mounds of brown snow. She knocked on the front door, then opened it without waiting for an answer. Inside, there was the usual picture: Elijah in his chair, tiny, wrinkled, wearing his cancer hat, while his night health aide, a chubby young woman, dozed in front of the blaring TV.

Marina called the night aide's name to rouse her, and she groaned and opened her eyes. Her face was creased. Her mouth had traces of dried saliva. She was embarrassed about being caught sleeping on the job but mostly angry at being woken up. She took her time gathering her things, zipping up her boots, and heading outside, while Elijah sat, staring at the TV.

"Bobby Fischer died today," Elijah said. "Look." And he pointed toward the TV. There was a close-up of Fischer in 1972. An enormous, warty face, twitching with anxiety. "Do you know who he was?"

"Oh yes," Marina said. "I was following that match in Russia."

She went to wash her hands, and when she came back into the room Elijah was slumped in his chair, his face twisted in pain. She gave him his pills, then poured herself a cup of coffee, and sat down on the sofa. On the TV was footage of the 1972 match. Excited crowds in Reykjavík and Moscow. Excited crowds all over the States. Americans cheering for Fischer. Russians cheering for Spassky.

"See how they're cheering?" Elijah asked. "I bet you were rooting for Spassky!" His words were becoming slurred.

"As a matter of fact, we supported Fischer," Marina said, but Elijah was already asleep. His head, too heavy for his withered neck, fell down onto his chest.

In 1972, all Marina's friends had rooted for Fischer.

All the Russian Jews who considered themselves liberal had wanted Fischer to win. For them, the Soviet Union stood for everything that was vile and deceitful, while the United States held the promise of everything that was good. And Fischer was the face of that good. The enormous, warty face of democracy.

Marina's husband, Sergey, was an especially passionate supporter of Fischer. "I can't believe how they're making him look!" he said, slapping a fresh copy of *Pravda* down on the rickety kitchen table, making five-year-old Sasha jump. "Like a fucking idiot! The man is a genius!"

"Sh-h-h!" Marina said, as she always did when Sergey expressed his indignation in front of Sasha, even though she agreed with him a hundred percent.

There were so many things about the Soviet Union that gnawed at them. So many lies, so many humiliations, big and small. The fact that Marina hadn't been accepted into graduate school because another Jew had just been given a spot. The fact that Sergey hadn't been allowed to attend a scientific conference abroad because he wasn't a member of the Party. The fact that they had to stand in line to buy meat or toilet paper or underpants. Plain white cotton underpants—they weren't even pretty! Color was what impressed Marina the most in the glimpses of foreign life that she saw in movies and magazines. Cars painted yellow and blue and green. Pink houses. Azure swimming pools. Red bras. Crimson lipstick. Straightforward envy over everyday objects grew into a kind of existential restlessness. She felt as if she were boxed up in some bleak, inferior world, while other people were outside enjoying bright and wonderful lives. Sergey took it especially hard. Ever since he was a child he'd experienced the lack of freedom as a physical thing. He liked to keep the frames of his glasses a little loose, to avoid even the slightest pressure on his temples. He never wore gloves, not even in the dead of winter, because they stifled his fingers. Sasha grew up to be just like him. Or even worse. He never wore ties or turtlenecks and always bought shoes a half size too big.

In the fall of 1971, Sergey told her that they needed to think seriously about emigrating. Some of their friends were in the process of leaving. Some had already left. They had nothing to lose. Marina's parents were dead. Sergey's parents had two other sons. Sergey was a talented chemist; he was bound to find a good job in the U.S., where the opportunities were unlimited and success required only talent and determination. They could get a visa to Israel, he said, make it to Europe, then try to get into the U.S. from there. It would be difficult, but not impossible. The hardest part was getting the exit visa from the Soviet Union. Many people were denied. Their friends Andrey and Nina Botkin had been denied and now lived in a horrible state of limbo, outlaws in the eyes of the Soviet government, both fired from their jobs, Andrey painting cabins at some remote resort, Nina working as a cleaning lady at a school for the deaf, their son, Kolya, expelled from his kindergarten and left in the care of his psychotic grandmother. Marina was terrified of ending up like that, and she could tell that Sergey was, too.

They spent the entire winter and a good part of the spring discussing whether applying for a visa was worth the risk. In May, when the match between Spassky and Fischer was first touted in the press as a Cold War standoff, Sergey, excited, said that he was willing to let the match decide their fate. If Fischer won, they would apply for exit visas. If he lost, they would stay in the Soviet Union. Marina didn't take this too seriously. She started looking for a dacha for the summer.

She found a tiny house in a village called Oselki, perched on a hill right by the train station. "We'll be able to see you coming home from the porch," she said to Sergey. It was an ugly house. All brown, with chipped pink paint on the shutters. Marina found it touching.

Oselki was thirty-three kilometers from Moscow, thirty-three hundred kilometers from Reykjavík, and four hours ahead. It was Sergey who had calculated the distance and the time difference, so that it would be easier for them to follow the match in real time. "Seven, it's seven here," he mumbled when he woke up. "It's only 3 a.m. in Reykjavík. Fischer and Spassky must be fast asleep."

Marina groaned and got out of bed. She threw a shawl over her night-gown and ran to the outhouse. A warm morning mist rose up off the flowers and the blades of grass, making her feel mildly elated.

They had breakfast on the porch. Sergey was content to eat a little bread and cheese, and then run to the station, but Sasha always asked for farina. Marina cooked it in an old dented pot, then poured it into shallow bowls, and put a lump of yellow butter and some apple jelly at the center of each. They ate their porridge in slow spirals, saving the treat for last.

After breakfast, Marina took Sasha to the woods to pick berries—strawberries in July, blueberries in August. He had a small plastic pail, and Marina carried a large aluminum jug; she loved how the blueberries rapped against the bottom. When they came home, Sasha played with his modeling clay, and Marina tended to the berries. They were small and wet. Some of them were rotten already; others were unripe. It took a long time to clean them, but Marina didn't mind.

After lunch, she undressed Sasha for his nap, removing his clothing in layers: his pants smelled like garden soil, his sweater like modeling clay, and his shirt like apple jelly and Sasha—that distinct Sasha smell that Marina couldn't describe but loved so much.

She used Sasha's nap time to work on her dissertation. The summer of 1972 was exceptionally hot, and his nap fell at the hottest time of the day, but it wasn't too bad in the garden. Marina would spread a blanket under a tree and lie down with a book. She had brought to the dacha a typewriter and five crates of books on behavioral psychology. So far the typewriter had sat unused. Sergey scolded Marina for not working. "I'm doing my research," she'd say. But more often than not she'd drop the book on the blanket, and lie down on her side, staring at the dark, crumbly soil so close to her face. When she was pregnant with Sasha, she'd had a weird craving to eat soil. What she craved now was for Sergey to appear in the garden and fuck her right there, pressing her naked body into the soil. She imagined that it would feel warm at first, but then as she sank deeper it would become colder and colder and smell stronger and stronger until she disappeared into the earth.

Marina never shared these fantasies with Sergey. They never really talked about sex. There was no point in talking.

Every night, Marina would wait for Sergey on the porch. His train arrived at 6:15. It was only 2:15 in Reykjavík, not that she really cared what time it was in Reykjavík. Sergey carried bags (bread and butter, chicken and fruit—the country store had little to offer), but he always kept his back very straight, as if he wanted to pretend that the bags weighed nothing at all. He wore a long bushy beard that summer, which looked ridiculous on his young face. His white shirt was soaked with sweat, stains spreading under his arms and over his back, making him appear even thinner than he was. Marina always marveled at how brittle he seemed, when she slid into his arms and clasped her hands around his back. She could have counted his vertebrae.

Sasha would jump out from behind a bush and shoot at Sergey with his toy gun, or wave a caterpillar under his nose, or just clutch onto his leg, screaming, "Papa! Papa! Papa!" Then he'd run off to play again, while Marina stayed, as if frozen, in her husband's arms.

"Masha. Mashen'ka," he'd say and bend to kiss her neck, while she pressed herself to him tighter and tighter.

Sometimes he called her "my buttermilk cow." She didn't know why.

"Mom, that's horrible," Marina's daughter said, when Marina told her this years later. "He meant you were fat!"

No, he meant that he loved her. But Marina didn't know how to explain that to her daughter. He called Sasha a "maestro of farts" and a "hidalgo of snot," and loved him more than anything.

For dinner, they had foods appropriate for the heat: green *schi*, cold potatoes, compote, and berries with sour cream. Sergey ate so fast that bits of food got stuck in his beard, and soup often dribbled down his shirt.

After the soup, it was time for *Pravda*. Every day brought fresh news from Reykjavík, so every dinner conversation was dominated by the subject of chess.

"Look, look at that!" Sergey said, pointing at the page with his fork. "'It is still unclear whether the match will take place. Today R. Fischer presented the organizers with new outrageous demands.' They're trying to paint him as a money-greedy bastard!"

Back in May, when Sergey had said that he would let the outcome of the match decide their fate, Marina had assumed that he was joking. Now, seeing his growing anxiety, she understood that he hadn't been.

"We lost! Fischer lost. I'm sure they were putting too much pressure on him."

"We lost again! Fischer refused to play, and Spassky won by default. That is so unfair!"

"I think the Soviets must have done something to him in Reykjavík."

"They say that Fischer is threatening to cancel the match, because he suspects that his room in Reykjavík is bugged. I'm sure his room is bugged!"

Soon, Sasha had learned to say Reykjavík. He pronounced it as if it were the name of some fairy-tale beast: "Rrryk Yavík."

Their dinners usually ended with Sergey picking up the scissors, cutting *Pravda* into squares, and taking them to the outhouse. He marched there with Sasha, singing a military song, making this look like a courageous anti-Soviet act, not simply a necessity caused by the scarcity of real toilet paper.

Marina's secret pleasure was to read these pieces of *Pravda* the next day. Their outhouse was exceptionally roomy and clean, with the bare minimum of stench. In the daytime, light came in through a tiny overhead window, just enough to read by. Marina had always read newspapers for entertainment, rather than for information. She hated the urgency with which some people (Sergey included) read newspapers, their belief that the mere knowledge of certain events—belated, incomplete, and often false knowledge—made them active participants in society. She was fine with the outhouse version of the news, soggy with the humidity, sliced into uneven pieces, perfectly random. "A tenth grader, Galya Kolbasina, won the competition for young tractor operators. Her skill and knowledge of the tractor's technical characteristics impressed the judges." "Slobodans will celebrate the 450th anniversary of their glorious city, Sloboda." "The Bolshoi Theatre will show 'Madama Butterfly' in the morning, 'Swan Lake' at night." "Proletarians of all countries, unite!"

Reading these scraps of *Pravda* filled Marina with a strange sense of comfort. Here she was, alone in a cozy little place, calm and untroubled, while other people went about their lives. Children competed in tractor competitions, ballerinas danced, Slobodans celebrated Sloboda, and proletarians united. It was there that Marina realized that she didn't really mind the Soviet Union so much. She decided that she wouldn't be too upset if Fischer lost the match.

One night in mid-July, Sergey came home, tapping a folded *Pravda* against his thigh.

"We won!" he yelled, as soon as he saw Marina. He picked Sasha up and spun him in the air.

She took the copy of *Pravda* and flipped through it, until she finally found a tiny notice about the match at the bottom of page 6. "It doesn't say that Fischer won," she said.

"Of course it doesn't!" Sergey said, laughing. "I heard it on Radio Liberty."

"But why are you so sure that Liberty has the right information?" she asked.

"Don't tell me that you trust *Pravda* more than Liberty!" Sergey said, mocking.

"You know I don't. It's just that Fischer's first win is a big thing. I think they would've mentioned it in *Pravda*. They couldn't just ignore it."

"Oh, really?" Sergey asked. He stared at her face as if he were seeing it for the first time, studying her features with cold precision. Marina had a glimpse of what it would be like if Sergey stopped loving her. Despite the heat, her skin broke out in goose bumps.

She took *Pravda* and ran out of the house, ran to the place that never failed to provide peace.

She sat in the outhouse leafing aimlessly through the newspaper, until Sasha knocked on the door with a stick. "Mama, are you coming out soon?" When she didn't answer, he knocked again. Then he pressed his face to a crack between the boards and said, "I can see you! You're not doing anything. You're reading."

Marina had to come out.

The fight with Sergey progressed well into the night, until they lay in angry silence on their warm bed. Sergey complained about Marina's tossing and turning. She kicked him. He rolled over and asked what it was that she wanted. Some brief sex followed. It wasn't good. Afterward, Sergey fell asleep, but Marina got up and went outside.

She stood on the porch, looking into the dark garden and listening to the cicadas. She didn't want to emigrate. That was perfectly clear to her now. Another thing that was perfectly clear was that she'd lose Sergey if she didn't.

The heat wave reached its peak. The peat bogs near Moscow were on fire, and smoke was creeping closer to the dacha. At the village store, the fires were all that people talked about. There were reports of houses burned to the ground, of hospitals crowded with burn victims. Marina asked Sergey if it wouldn't be smarter for them to return to Moscow. Sergey said no. The entire city was now shrouded in a yellowish smog, and it was so hot that he saw people faint on the subway. "Here we have some fresh air, at least," he said.

Pravda didn't say much about the fires. Marina kept looking for coverage of the disaster, but all she found was a piece about ice cream: "A new production line was recently installed at Ice Cream Factory No. 3. This will allow more people to enjoy sweet, cool refreshments."

Marina studied the photograph of a smiling ice-cream engineer holding a tray filled with ice-cream cones. She imagined Sergey reading the paper over her shoulder and gloating: "Sweet and cool, huh?"

On July 24th, Sasha got sick from the heat. He was crying, complaining that the neighbors were "roasting chickens." Then he vomited. It was so hot in the house that the walls were warm to the touch. Marina carried Sasha into the garden and gave him some cold tea. Toward the end of the day, he felt better and asked Marina to help him make some clay animals, but by then she was too tired and irritable. She could barely make herself prepare dinner.

Sergey came home from work shaking with happiness. The day before, it turned out, Fischer had won Game 6, taking the lead in the match. "See, see? Even *Pravda* acknowledges Fischer's victory," Sergey told her. There was a large headline on page 6: "SPASSKY'S MISTAKES LEAD TO DEFEAT."

At dinner that night, Sergey praised Marina's *schi*, then raised the bowl to his mouth to drink the last dregs of the soup. He kept talking about the Queen's Gambit and the Tartakower Defense, and kingside pawn structure, attacks and counterplays, and other chess nonsense—and how gutsy and brilliant Fischer had been to do what he did. They didn't have a chess set, so he took out the box with Sasha's clay animals and arranged them on the table to explain what the Queen's Gambit was; Marina got the feeling that he had only a vague idea himself. The blue catlike monstrosities became knights, a misshapen red dog was the queen, and the green pig (which had actually come out quite well) was the bishop. The animals were clammy in the heat. The cats stained Sergey's fingers. The pig stained the table. The more Sergey talked about chess and the more he praised Fischer, the angrier Marina became. She didn't want Fischer to win. She really, really didn't. She hated Fischer with all her heart. She had an urge to scoop the animals up and knead them together into an ugly mass.

After she had put Sasha to bed, she went and stood on the porch. It had cooled down a little. The smoke was less pungent than it had been, more like the smell of a campfire or of potatoes baking in coals.

Sergey came out to find her. He hugged her and whispered, "Mashen'ka, aren't you happy?"

She hugged him back and said that she was.

Elijah opened his eyes. "Something to drink?" Marina asked. "Tea?"

He declined the tea, but asked Marina to turn up the volume on the TV. The program was now dealing with Fischer's later years. There were close-ups of him from the nineteen-nineties, bearded and insane. What he liked to talk about was the Jews: Jews were parasites. Jews were evil. Jews needed to be exterminated. All of them.

Elijah chuckled and said, "Yep, that's Bobby Fischer for you."

Marina wondered if Sergey would have been disappointed.

He had died of a heart attack a year after they got to the U.S., when Marina was three months pregnant with their daughter. It would still have been possible for her to have an abortion, but she had decided to keep the baby.

She felt a draft on her feet, probably coming from the front door.

"Do you want a blanket, Elijah?"

He shook his head and pointed at the TV. "I was there, you know."

"Where?"

"In Reykjavík, in 1972."

"You saw Fischer?"

"Yes, and Spassky. I was working for the *New York Times*. Iceland is a beautiful country. I didn't care for Fischer, though."

"No?"

"He was a crazy fuck, even then. All the reporters hated him. All the chess people hated him. I rooted for Spassky. He was a decent guy. Do you know what he did when he conceded Game 6?"

"What?"

"He stood up and applauded Fischer. Now that's sportsmanship for you. Not like that crazy bastard."

Marina was suddenly overcome by an urge to protect Fischer. In those last interviews, he looked like a lost old man, scared and sick. She felt pity and something like perverse affection for him.

"I think you're too hard on Fischer," she told Elijah. "I used to hate him, too," she wanted to add, but Elijah had closed his eyes again.

REESE OKYONG KWON

Reese Okyong Kwon was born in Seoul, South Korea, but raised in the United States. She earned a BA from Yale and an MFA from Brooklyn College.

Narrative magazine featured Kwon on its list of "30 Below 30" writers, and published her story "Superhero" in 2008. Her stories have since been published in *Ploughshares*, the *Southern Review*, and the *Kenyon Review*, while her nonfiction has appeared in the *Believer*, the *Rumpus*, and other publications. "The Stations of the Sun" originally appeared in the *Kenyon Review* in 2011.

When asked about being identified as an Asian American writer in a recent interview with *Ploughshares*, Kwon responded, "[Saul Bellow says] his instinct is to say that he's a writer first and Jewish second. I like that, and I agree with him, while also recognizing that this could sound like too facile of an answer in a world in which, when people look at me or my name, the inclination could be to see an Asian woman first, and a writer second. On the other hand, there still haven't been that many Asian American writers—though there are more published every year, thank goodness—and maybe this relative scarcity is freeing."

The Stations of the Sun

1. Another god, another artist

According to Chinese mythology, the goddess Nugua formed the first mortals from yellow mud. An artist, she sculpted each limb, pressed closed each fingertip, contoured each nose, creating individuals. But at some point she became impatient with the demands of craftsmanship and dipped a vine in darker soil, flung it every which way. Lumps of mud fell from the skies, and became human.

And so the land was divided into two races: the hand-formed pale-skinned nobles, and the darker commoners who had never known the goddess's touch.

Chinese people, Annabel's mother said, shaking her head. Such snobs. But in the lamplight, her mother's face shone paler than the moon.

2. Heliophobia

Annabel Lin was born Korean, not Chinese, but Nugua was a powerful goddess and had spread her mud far beyond the borders of present-day China. As she grew up, Annabel was forbidden from playing in the sun. Since fate and the vagaries of her father's medical career had placed her and her family in a sunlit town in California, its every street flashing the spokes of children's bicycles, this was no small feat of parenting on her mother's part.

But everyone agreed that her mother, Haemi Lin née Haemi Sung, was a remarkable woman. In Seoul, her family had flourished for centuries, its men governors and ferocious generals, its women famous for their high-nosed aristocratic beauty. Now her mother stayed at home and directed all

143

her energy at Annabel's upbringing. She sang to her, she told her stories of shape-changers and heroes, centaurs and gods, she schooled her in musical instruments and other necessary disciplines, she taught her everything. Against the enchantments of her mother, the sun stood no chance.

As a matter of course, her mother also shunned the sun. Every morning, she applied sunscreen. If it rained, she put on more. To retrieve letters from the mailbox, ten steps from the house, she wore a vast white hat. Though her husband purchased only convertible sports cars, she never once put down the top. She drove with gloves on. Even when she filled her car with gas, gloves whitened her hands. In the house, she kept the shades down. The other Korean women of the town marveled at her mother's consistency, envied the even white of her complexion.

3. Of shibboleths and thieves

When Annabel's father ran off one day with a Chinese nurse, the fact that most tormented her mother was the shade of the other woman's skin. Her mother had met the nurse once, years ago. There had been a barbecue at the house of the chief surgeon and when Annabel's father introduced the young nurse to his wife, Haemi had felt, as if with a sixth sense passed down by generations of wronged Sung women, a shiver of anger.

From behind her sunglasses, Haemi looked closely at the nurse, who gazed at the ground. With a loose braid that snaked down her back and a broad, dark face, her nose slick with oil, the nurse looked like a farmer. Her analphabetic ancestors would have worked the ground; this would be an unwanted daughter shipped to America who still sent money back to her peasant parents. She was no competitor to a Sung woman. Almost imperceptibly, Haemi shrugged her thin, elegant shoulders. Then she smiled and said in her perfectly enunciated college English that it was a pleasure.

But she looked like a peasant, Annabel's mother said, afterward, her hands over her face. Tears splashed through the cracks between her long, white fingers.

4. Milk for gall

Had they still been in Seoul, had the times been different, the governors and generals of the fierce Sung family would have hired a gangster to shoot Annabel's father like the animal he had proven himself to be. Not because of the infidelity, of course, but because of the desertion. Korean men of honor did not abandon their wives. And for such a woman. A Chi*nese* woman, not even a Korean. A presumably low-*class* Chinese woman.

But moving to America, crossing the wide sea, had turned the six Sung brothers' blood to water. They knew no gangsters here. They knew no judges, either, and no governors to issue pardons if they were found guilty of bloodshed. Unprotected themselves, they could not protect their Haemi. Besides, Annabel's father promised to pay a sizable alimony. And she had her daughter, already almost a young woman, for companionship.

They knew, though. If they weren't acting dishonorably, they weren't acting honorably, either. So during their meeting they avoided looking at the eyes of their sister, and they drove away fast in their expensive cars, painted red as if to flash their altered rage.

5. Our Lady of America

Both of the dominant mythologies of the Western world, the Greco-Roman and the Judeo-Christian, warn of the perils of looking.

In the Bible, no one can see the face of God and live. When Moses asked as an especial favor to be allowed to see the Lord, He only showed him His holy backside. The prophets of Apollo, less mollycoddled, might look at their Lord as they liked, but as a consequence their eyeballs would be burned away. Semele, another of the women chased by amorous Zeus, insisted on seeing him in his true and glorious form and was incinerated by the sight.

Nevertheless, thousands of people gather every year in Rome City, Indiana, expecting to see the face of the Madonna. The sun burns their eyes so that, each year, people damage their vision, but still they turn their faces up to the sun, hoping for her.

6. What the Lord giveth, the Lord taketh away

A week after her husband left, Annabel's mother shut herself in her car and drove. She left the house as the sun was rising and returned hours after the sun had fallen. She opened the door and found Annabel sitting panic-stricken on the kitchen floor, the phone cradled in her lap. Her mother looked back at her. Her hair was windblown and the parts of her body exposed by her nightgown—her face, her throat, her hands—shone so brightly red that, at first, Annabel thought her mother had daubed herself with paint.

But then she understood. Did you drive without . . . did you drive with the top of your car down? Annabel asked.

Annabel's mother nodded. I wanted to see, she said. She drifted out to their garden. Annabel followed her out. Silently, her mother broke off aloe vera stalks and smeared the gel over her sunburns.

7. Colonized

A stripe of dark skin: that was how her mother discovered the sickness. She had been applying her usual libations to her body, the creams with which she softened her white skin. And maybe because she was alone without her husband in the large and empty bedroom, that morning she looked more closely at herself than she had done in years, and in the course of her looking she found, hiding near her hairline at the base of her neck, a blackish mark she had never known was there. Its borders were irregular, an enemy growing in the night.

A week later, she went to a doctor, a new one, as for years she had gone to her husband with her medical concerns. She asked the new doctor to take a look.

8. Monday, Tuesday, Wednesday, Thursday, Friday, Saturday

She died in six days.

From the diagnosis of melanoma to brain death, the decline was swift.

As she sat by her mother's body, Annabel could not stop thinking that if her mother had been properly loved, if her father had been the kind of husband who occasionally lifted his wife's hair and kissed her neck, then surely the sickness would have been discovered in time.

9. What the children thought

At the funeral, nobody said what everyone but Annabel was thinking: that her mother, pale with death, was still more beautiful than she had ever been. Her beauty had always seemed misfit, otherworldly; now that she was no longer of this world, it was as if she had found her rightful place.

Annabel sat stiff-backed in the front row, staring ahead. Her father sat next to her, though out of deference to community opinion he left his Chinese girlfriend home. The Sung men were there, their broad shoulders squared, their black heads bowed. Their wives sat next to them and cried silently, decorously. All the Koreans of the town attended, as did her father's doctor colleagues. Some of the wives wore black veils to hide the pleasure in their eyes. That pure face, that haunting skin would soon be cast into the ground. The death of Annabel's mother had left each wife safer.

As they watched the white figure in the coffin, some of the children permanently lost their ability to believe in God. What sort of a fiend would create something so beautiful, only to destroy it? Even they, the children, knew better.

10. The girl who became a tree

Though in almost all known stories of Attic mythos it was perilous for a human to be loved by a god, such love tending to end in death or persecution, it's possible that of all the amorous Greek deities, Apollo in his lust was the most dangerous. Daphne, Acantha, Castalia, Coronis, Leucothea, Hyacinth, Cassandra: transformed into a tree, a shrub, a fountain, shot dead, buried alive, killed by a discus, made to tell prophecies whose catastrophic truth no one ever believed. It should have been the kind of curse to spit at a mortal enemy: may you be loved by the sun god.

In the Villa Borghese of Rome, there stands a life-sized marble statue of Apollo and Daphne. According to the Ovidian myth, Daphne was a nymph determined to run free in the forest all her life, recognizing allegiance to no one but herself. Men begged for her hand and she said, Absolutely not. Peneus, her river-god father, asked for children and she said, Forgive me, but no. Then one afternoon Apollo looked upon her and, desiring her, ran after her. Daphne fled but she was only a nymph and he was the god of the sun. Soon, he was gaining on her. She felt his breath on her hair and she prayed to her father. Open the earth to enclose me, she cried. Or, father, change my form!

Bernini captures her at her moment of transformation. As Apollo tries to drag her to him, her feet become roots. Her arms, branches. Her skin, rough bark. Loose hair splits and flattens into laurel leaves. Her mouth opens in anguish and she twists away from him. Even the tree bark shrinks from his touch, but it's no use, he presses her close. Annabel's mother had seen tourists put aside their cameras and start to bawl. They turned their heads from shape-changing Daphne, frozen in her fear. Couples groped for each other's hands, but gently, wishing to force nothing. One day, you'll see this, her mother had said. One day, I'll take you there.

11. The necessity of following the proprieties

Annabel set her lips once more on her mother's forehead and it was as cold as stone. She saw how large the coffin was for the body and understood that her mother needed company. She could climb in with her. She could hide herself until the end of the world from the killing glare of the sun.

But as soon as the thought came to mind, she was swept into the arms of the Sung men and their gently weeping wives. Immediately afterward, her father pulled her to his side so that she could thank people for having come to say goodbye.

Thank you for coming, she said, obediently. Thank you for coming, she said. Thank you for coming, she said. Thank you for coming, she said. Thank you for coming, she said. Thank you for coming, she said.

12. Like mother, like daughter

After the reception at her father's house, as soon as the last guest had left, Annabel went out the door and got into one of her father's convertible cars. The Sung impulses ran hot in her blood. And so, like her mother, like her uncles, she drove.

She steered blindly, not caring where she went. It seemed that if she could drive fast and far enough then she could outrun herself. But it was too quiet, she could still hear her thoughts, so she opened the roof to the sky. For the first time in her life she raised her face to the sun, the wind screamed in her ears. She was fifteen years old and had never before driven alone. The sun wheeled to the edge of the world and she drove through the night.

In the morning, a white-lettered sign told her she had come to Death Valley. She lurched left onto a side road, parked, stripped, laid her body on the open desert floor, and spread her arms and legs.

13. The revelations of the sun

She lay in the stillness a day and a night. She watched the sun she had been taught all her life to fear. She held her hand in front of her to see the steady movement of her blood, the skin shot through with light. The sun rolled from east to west. Her body brightened, turned red. Blisters rose like revelations. Constellations shivered and spun to the rhythm of her blood. She expected at any time to burst into flames.

But in the end, it was not the blaze of the sun but the burning inside her that urged Annabel up and into the car. At the first gas station she poured water down her throat until she spat up, laughed, then fell unconscious to the ground.

14. The art of storytelling

Because Koreans have an old proverb that says it is better to leave your child a book than a fortune, and because Korea, like other frequently invaded small countries, invests its proverbs with an almost oracular significance, each visitor who came to see Annabel during her extended convalescence brought her yet another book. The selections varied by the visitor. A Sung uncle brought her a volume on the breeding of the Jindo dog and the importance of the purity of the bloodline. A second uncle, whose father had been a governor, brought her books on Korean folklore. A third uncle, a Protestant, brought the King James Bible. A fourth uncle, a Catholic, brought Butler's *Lives of the Saints*. A fifth uncle, who read Latin, brought Ovid and Virgil. Her sixth uncle and the youngest, the one who had loved her mother most, never came to visit.

She was badly and dangerously burned. Her uncles jollied her, asking if this was what white people called a suntan, but her father sat in silence and stared at her as if he was trying to read her bandages. But Annabel, how on earth did you end up in the desert? her father said. I got lost, she repeated, and turned away, back to her book.

As she read, she recognized some of the stories as tales her scheherazadian mother had told her. Tales of the founding of the universe. Tales of people who tried to save the world. She read and she looked for her mother.

15. The disadvantages of being underage

When the doctors told her that thick scars would mark her skin, Annabel was glad. Now her outside would match her inside. But her father went red and huffed out of the room, holding his small phone up, and within hours one of his doctor colleagues had come to see her.

Can you give my daughter a new skin? her father asked his colleague.

I can, the colleague said, and both men disregarded Annabel's screams about wanting to keep her scars. The sun, they thought, must have gotten to her head.

16. For Daphne, in memoriam

But her father's colleague turned out to be wrong. His new skin covered much of her face, her arms, and her legs, but the rest of her body was more difficult to repair. Some parts looked like standard fifteen-year-old

THE STATIONS OF THE SUN

skin, smooth and undemanding, but there were as many parts of her that declared themselves as scar tissue, stripes shining in recognition of her past injury.

As Annabel grew older, she gave herself to men who held the sun in their hair. In bed, they told her she was beautiful, then fingered the damaged skin on the cradle of her hip, in the crook of her neck. They always asked the same, shocked question. What happened?

Then she could tell some piece of the story. To a few of the men, she said her mother had carried her out of a burning house and had died while saving her. To others, she explained that a careless hired nurse had splashed her with boiling water. To the one or two men who most gently asked the question, she leaned in and whispered that she once had been loved by the sun god and had lived to tell the tale.

17. The stations of the sun

At the height of the summer equinox, Annabel became pregnant. When she was close to giving birth she went home to visit her father, who still lived with the Chinese nurse. They were married now, with three braided children who shouted in the sun.

In the afternoons Annabel went out to her father's garden, sometimes wearing a hat, sometimes not. She was so heavy with her child that she had trouble walking, so she sat under a laurel tree and sang, and told her baby elaborate stories she made up as she went along. Her father's wife, a woman so kind she could not be hated—Annabel knew, she'd tried—often joined her and asked if she could offer a glass of iced ginseng tea.

Out in the garden on a hot day, Annabel gasped. What is it? asked her father's wife. Nothing, Annabel said, the baby kicked. You know what they say about a baby moving, said her father's wife. No, what? Annabel said. Well, said her father's wife, her broad, appealing face opening into a smile, they say that some infants in the womb turn their faces away from sunlight, and you can tell how dark or pale the baby will be based on just how quickly he turns. Annabel's expression must have changed, because her father's wife looked alarmed. It's only a story, she said. Again Annabel gasped, and put her hand against her stomach. See? her father's wife said. Maybe the baby is turning again, this time toward the sun.

LAILA LALAMI

Laila Lalami was born in Rabat, Morocco, in 1968. She attended Université Mohammed-V in Rabat and University College in London. She came to the United States in 1992 to attend the University of Southern California, where she earned a PhD in linguistics.

Lalami is the author of the short story collection *Hope and Other Dangerous Pursuits* (2005), which was a finalist for the Oregon Book Award, and the novel *Secret Son* (2009), which was on the Orange Prize longlist. Her essays and opinion pieces have appeared in *Newsweek*, the *Los Angeles Times*, the *Washington Post*, the *Nation*, the *Guardian*, the *New York Times*, and in numerous anthologies. She is currently an associate professor of creative writing at the University of California at Riverside.

Her short story "Echo" was first published in the *Guardian* in September 2011. Lalami says of immigration, "Many of us face the pain of being in one place, but not of it. Those we have left behind have to contend with another pain: the absence of a loved one. Deciding to leave one's homeland affects all of us."

Echo

The deliveryman came at lunchtime, when Mona, still in her bathrobe, was rummaging through the pantry, looking for something to eat. Three packets of pasta, all of them half-empty and sealed with blue plastic clips, sat on the top shelf. On the bottom one were two bags of lentils and a jar of preserved lemons from the specialty store down the street. Then, behind a bottle of balsamic vinegar, she found a packet of instant oatmeal, which she held up as if she'd won a prize. There was no need to go out. "Be right there," Mona called when she heard the doorbell. She tightened the belt of her robe, ran her hands over her mass of tangled hair, and shuffled to the front door of her house. She looked, she knew, exactly like the kind of woman she had once promised herself she would never become.

A tall, well-built man in a brown uniform was waiting at her door. He seemed surprised when he saw her—she was usually at work at this time of day.

"Afternoon," he said cheerfully. "I have a package for you." His nametag, unstitched on one side, read "Perry." He had a wide forehead and his face was dotted with freckles. Long, carefully trimmed sideburns emerged from his cap, ending at the jawline. Just two days earlier, he had dropped off a box of books on Mona's doorstep and was already on the other side of the white picket fence when she opened her door. But today he had waited for her to answer the bell. "You need to sign for it," he said.

Mona saw that the package was from her sister Amal, in San Francisco. Amal was always sending things: birthday cards, photographs of her family, announcements that her oldest had finished grade school or that her youngest had earned a Girl Scout badge, even colorful boxes of homemade petits fours. Where Amal found the time for these things, Mona didn't know. Amal was a scientist for a company that manufactured medical devices—heart valves, stent grafts, and pacemakers—a job that involved long hours in the lab. And yet she still ran three miles every morning, attended PTA meetings, wrote thank-you notes, and sorted paper and plastic in the appropriate bins.

"It's gonna be a hot one," Perry said, handing Mona a pen. A red, woven bracelet was strapped to his wrist. Along the back of his arm was a long scar, reaching all the way to his elbow.

"Isn't it always?" she replied. She signed her name on the electronic clipboard.

"That's why we live here, right?" He regarded her with gentle eyes, eyes that said he wanted to continue the conversation.

But Mona reached for the doorknob. "Well, thank you," she said, closing the door.

She shuffled back to the kitchen to start the coffeemaker. The package contained a photo album, one of those keepsakes you could design and order from an online photo-printing service. Amal had sent albums before—pictures of her and her family on holiday in Hawaii, on Crater Lake, or at Yellowstone—but this one was different. On the cover was a portrait of Mona and Amal's parents, taken when they were still a young, childless couple. Everything about this photograph struck Mona as exotic. Her father, Taher, had a thick beard and wore oversized plastic-rimmed eyeglasses; her mother, Zahra, was in a dress with a psychedelic pattern, her hair gathered in a low ponytail on one side. They were seated on a damask-covered sofa, Taher's right arm slung over Zahra's shoulders, a lit cigarette dangling from the fingers of his left hand. Mona had never known her father smoked.

Still, it wasn't the 1970s fashions or the period's vices that accounted for Mona's surprise—it was the expression on her father's face. All her life, he had been a shy, quiet man, but here he stared straight at the camera. He seemed full of passion, animated by a fire that could overcome any obstacle or setback. And Mona's mother, too, looked different. She had always been the outspoken one, the family member delegated to sort out any disputes over insurance claims or unusual bank charges, though in this portrait she looked timidly away from the lens. Mona took a sip of her coffee and sat down in the dining room to leaf through the album. Inside it were photographs from that mysterious era in her parents' lives: on a long wharf by a lake, at dinner with a group of friends, at a rally against the regime, on a beach in Agadir, in a horse-drawn carriage in Marrakech. Mona and her sister were nowhere in these pictures, their existence not yet planned, or perhaps not even imagined.

She called Amal on the phone. "Where did you find these?" she asked, leafing through the album again, this time from end to beginning. In the yellow ceramic bowl, her instant oatmeal was getting cold, its surface hardening steadily even in the warm air.

"I was cleaning out the attic last week, when I found them," Amal replied, her voice ringing with enthusiasm. "They were in the pocket of an old suitcase I had when we moved into this house. The pocket is the same color as the lining, which was why I hadn't noticed it before."

"You haven't used that suitcase in all this time?"

"No. I mean, yes. Once or twice. But it's too big to take on plane trips, especially now that everyone has carry-ons. Dad had packed some things in it for me when I got married; it's been sitting in the attic for thirteen years." She paused. Mona could hear her typing on her keyboard, could imagine her sending a memo or wrestling with FDA paperwork while also carrying on a phone conversation. "Anyway, I'm glad I found them. A few of them were scratched or torn, but I managed to scan them and put together the album. Do you like it?"

"Of course, I like it. I love it." Mona took another sip of coffee; she craved a cigarette, but she had run out two days ago and hadn't yet gone out to replace them. "Mom and Dad look so young here."

"Don't you think Zach is starting to look like Dad?" Zach was Amal's oldest child, a boy of eleven whose given name was Zakaria, after his paternal grandfather, but whom his classmates—and now his mother, too, apparently—called Zach.

Mona couldn't quite see the resemblance, but she forced herself to say something. "I suppose he has Dad's eyes."

"Wait," Amal said suddenly. "What are you doing at home anyway?"

Mona held her breath, looking up from the album to the turquoise sky outside, nearly violent in its perfection. Beneath it, the jacarandas that lined the back of the yard were blooming. The neighbor's cat ran along the side fence, stopping suddenly when he spotted a hummingbird fluttering over a tree branch. A blue jay landed on the white chaise lounge and surveyed it for crumbs. Mona was never around during the daytime, to witness all of this. I should spend more time outdoors, she thought, like my sister. Go out for a run every day, or at least a walk.

"I mean," Amal continued, "I see you're calling from your home number. Don't you have class at this time?"

"Actually," Mona said, but even before the last syllable of that word left her lips she knew she would conceal the truth from her sister. "It's the last week of the spring semester. My students are working on their final projects. So, no class."

It had been nine days since Mona had been told she would not be offered the tenure-track job she had hoped to get at Columbus College, where she had been a visiting assistant professor of history for the last three years. The word "visiting" suggested that the three years on her contract were a trial period. Now, it seemed, the trial was over and she had been found unsuitable. The department chair had said that the college's endowment—considerably reduced after the stock market crashed—made long-term hires difficult, but Mona suspected that his decision had more to do with her searing criticism of the War on Terror in a popular newspaper. "Mona has an agenda," one of her colleagues sniffed at a faculty party. There had also been an angry phone call to the dean from a prominent donor, asking him about the "indoctrination" of students in her classes. Columbus was a private college on the California coast, a place that prided itself on decorum and propriety. So there had been no official complaint or rebuke. But now she would need to find another job.

"You're not teaching all this week?" her sister said. "It must be nice to have a vacation."

This vacation Mona had spent in bed with her laptop, looking for jobs, sending resumes, and canceling subscriptions to journals and magazines. The day before, she had counted all the places in which she had lived since she'd left home, at the age of eighteen. There had been the two dorm rooms and the noisy apartment she had rented when she was studying English and history at Barnard; the pest-infested condominium she shared with another master's student at Georgetown; three small cottages at Berkeley, where she completed her PhD; the university-subsidized townhouse when she was an adjunct professor in Ann Arbor, Michigan; and now, this house in Bay City. The thought of another job, and another move, made her nauseous. So it was difficult to announce the news to Amal, who had spent her entire college years in one apartment near

Stanford, had lived in the same suburban home for thirteen years, and had held the same job for ten.

"I captioned all the photographs," Amal said, "but there is one that I can't quite seem to place. Maybe you would know. It's on the next to last page. Do you see it?"

Mona turned to the appropriate page. The black-and-white photograph showed her parents at what seemed to be a dinner party. They were seated together at a large table, but they each had their faces turned to the people next to them. Her father was smiling at another guest, perhaps listening to a joke or a funny story; her mother was speaking to a handsome man in dark eyeglasses, her hands raised before her as if she were emphasizing a point.

"What year do you think this was?" Amal asked.

Mona looked again at her mother, admiring the sleek, long hair and wishing she had inherited it. "Mom's wearing her pearl necklace," Mona said. "Dad bought it for her when he went to Switzerland for treatment after his second arrest. So this is at least 1974, maybe a year or two later."

"Great eye," Amal said, approvingly.

Mona smiled to herself, sitting back in her chair and putting her feet up on the chair next to her.

"I'll add a caption before I print another one," Amal said. "I want to send it to Dad for his birthday."

Taher's sixty-sixth birthday was in two weeks. Mona was planning on giving him a book about modern architecture, a subject he had mentioned a few times when she had visited him in Los Angeles. Though he had cut back on his hours, he refused to retire from his position as accountant for the school district; instead, he had taken on a string of new hobbies. But her gift, she now feared, would pale in comparison to her sister's. "That's a great idea," Mona said. "Dad will love it."

"Do you know who the man is that Mom is talking to?"

Mona turned the picture toward the sunlight and looked more closely at the guest seated next to her mother—he was a handsome man with sharp eyes, high cheekbones, and a thin nose.

"No," Mona said. "He looks familiar, though."

Growing up, Mona had only heard vague echoes of her parents' youth, of their work for dissident organizations, or even of their incarcerations in Morocco. Those were things that had happened in the old country, her father said, before they had moved to the United States, in 1981. While their fellow exiles had settled in France, Taher and Zahra had landed at JFK with two little girls and ten suitcases, rented a car, and driven it westward for weeks, exploring the country and trying to decide on a place to live. They had stopped only when they had reached the Pacific Ocean, the furthest any of them had been from their home. One of Mona's earliest memories was being carried in Zahra's arms to the beach and the feeling of ice-cold water touching her toes. But aside from that, Mona had scant memories of the cross-country trip, and none of Casablanca, the city in which she had been born, something for which she had always envied her sister. With the industry and optimism of immigrants everywhere, Taher had found a job in Los Angeles, and gone about fashioning new lives for his family. But Zahra, the keeper and teller of all the family stories, had died of complications from hernia surgery when Mona was thirteen. Perhaps it was that feeling of loss, and her father's resolute silence about the past, that had driven Mona to study history and, later, to teach it.

"Anyway," Amal said. "It doesn't matter who he is. I only wanted the year for the caption."

Mona stood up from the table. "Well, if I can remember where I've seen him, I'll call you. Thanks again for sending me the photos. I'll let you get back to work."

"You're still driving up here next month, for Zach's birthday?"

"Yes, that's the plan. Give the kids a kiss for me."

She took her bowl to the sink, where she placed it on top of the other dirty dishes, wondering why she had lied to her sister about her job. She wanted to believe it was to spare Amal any further worry about her younger sister and her precarious university career. Often, Amal asked Mona if she was seeing someone, and she always sounded disappointed when the answer was no. Mona, who had impulsively married a fellow student at Berkeley and was divorced by the time she defended her thesis, dreaded these questions. She didn't want to hear her sister's advice, which was so much like their father's, about planning for the future.

It was nearly six o'clock when Mona decided to take an evening walk. She had stopped going to the coffee shop in the morning, when it was filled with students and professors; she avoided the campus gym; she no longer picked up the college newspaper, the *Sandpiper*. Now, she walked out, exploring the streets that she ordinarily saw only from her car. She waved at Mr. McKenzie, her white-haired neighbor, as he pulled into his driveway with his windows rolled down and his radio set to the local classic-rock station; she noticed two new "For Sale" signs peeking out above the trash cans on the sidewalk; further ahead, she smiled at another walker, an old man whose yellow Labrador came to smell her shoes. Eventually, she looped back and found herself in front of her darkened house.

It was a California bungalow, which she had bought three years earlier, after her department chair, a man who dressed in checkered shirts and often made humorless jokes, had said that a tenure-track job was "a near certainty." The house was painted a soft white, with green trim, and had a heavy wooden door—a 1941 original—that had immediately caught Mona's eye. She liked to think about the people who had built this house, liked to imagine the rattle of their milk bottles in metal crates on the porch, liked to wonder what could have caused the scar on the tree in the front yard. Her homes for the last fifteen years had been so transitory that, sometimes, she had trouble reconciling certain events in her adult life with the apartments in which they had taken place. Now this house she had grown to love would have to be sold and she would have to prepare herself for the pain of parting.

Walking through the hallway, Mona noticed that the photo album was still on the dining room table, where she had left it. She looked again at the picture of her parents, ran her index finger along the outline of her mother's face. She turned the overhead light on and sat down again to leaf through the album, stopping once more on the photo of the mystery man. She was sure she had seen him somewhere, but every time she felt close to placing him, the memory faded away like a wisp of smoke. After a few minutes of this, she turned off the light and went to bed.

The next day Mona woke earlier than usual. She had slept poorly and no amount of coffee seemed to cure the throbbing pain she could feel on her temples. She was sweeping the porch when the deliveryman came. At least this time, she thought, I'm fully dressed, even if it's only in white Bermuda shorts and an embroidered Mexican shirt. She leaned the broom against the nearest beam and received the box. The label indicated that it was shipped from a small bookstore, from which Mona had ordered an expensive out-of-print book a few weeks earlier. It was an expense she could not afford now.

"So," Perry said, his hands resting on his hips, "Mona—is that an Arabic name?"

She looked up from the box. She had that peculiar feeling she sometimes did, of looking at herself through the eyes of others—taking note of the black hair, the olive skin tone, the khamsa charm that dangled from her silver necklace—and of the ambiguity of their interest. Their gaze could mean hate or contempt or disgust; it could mean pity; it could even, sometimes, mean desire. But it was never neutral or dispassionate. "Yes," she said. "Why do you ask?"

"It sounded like it was," he said. "I was in Iraq"—he pronounced it Ai-raq—"for three years."

"Ah," she replied. "But now you work for UPS."

"I drove a hummer in Baghdad; now I drive a truck in Bay City." It seemed to be a line he had used more than once, and it was said with a tone whose intention she could not interpret with certainty. Was he being wistful or ironic? She couldn't tell.

"Well," she said after a moment. "Thanks again."

She watched him leave, closing the picket-fence door behind him. When she went back inside she was momentarily blinded by the darkness in the hallway; she stopped and waited for her eyes to adjust. She thought about Baghdad. The city on the Tigris; the metropolis the Persians called God's gift; the setting of so many stories from the illustrated *One Thousand and One Nights* her mother had given her when she was nine; the city now buried in rubble. Her father had gone there once, hadn't he, in the early 1970s. She went to her study, scanning the shelves for a volume whose title she couldn't remember, but which she was sure had a chapter on prominent Egyptian dissidents. Her own scholarly research was on sixteenth-century American history, so her library didn't have many books on the Middle East. But eventually, she found the book, recognizing it by its red spine and pulling it out from the dusty shelf. Flipping through the pages, she finally found the photograph she had in mind.

She called her sister. "Remember the guy in the photo with Mom?" Her voice, she knew, betrayed her excitement. "I think I've found him." She cradled the phone against her neck and smoothed the page, which showed a photograph of the mystery man giving a speech, his forefinger raised in the air, his expression full of raw passion. "His name was Mahmoud Abdallah. He was a Marxist—a doctor by training, I think—who was fiercely critical of Anwar Sadat. He was a charismatic speaker, quite popular among students, which was why he often traveled abroad, gathering support for the opposition. Then Sadat emptied his prisons of Islamists and started arming them—covertly, of course. Abdallah was disappeared in 1975, kidnapped in broad daylight in Cairo and never seen again."

"Huh," Amal said. Mona could hear the metronomic sound of a machine somewhere in the background, perhaps a heavy-duty stapler or a copy machine. She felt as though she were competing with it for her sister's attention. "That's interesting."

Mona continued, "Dad must have met Abdallah at a conference in Baghdad back in 1971; I didn't know Abdallah had visited our parents later in Morocco."

"Are you still driving up next month for Zach's birthday?"

"Did you hear what I said about the man in the photo?"

"Yes, I heard," Amal said. "I heard. And I said it was interesting. It's just . . . " There was a series of abrupt sounds and then the machine in the background finally stopped. In the silence that followed, her sister's voice came through more clearly. "I already have the date for the caption, that's all."

"So you already sent Dad the album?"

"Yes, it went out last night."

"It'll be a blast from the past. That's the sort of thing he"—she drew out the next word—"loooooves."

"What's that supposed to mean?"

"Nothing."

"You sounded, I don't know . . . sarcastic or something."

"Did I?" Mona said. She closed the book with a snap and slid it back on the shelf. "I just meant he doesn't like to talk about the past, that's all. And apparently neither do you."

"Hmm," Amal said. "Well."

"I'll let you get back to your lab, then."

"Your students are still working on their projects?"

Mona felt her heart skip a beat. "Yes," she said, releasing a breath.

With nothing edible anywhere in the house, Mona had to go to the grocery store three days later. She went at eight in the morning, just when the store opened, to lessen the chance of running into colleagues—or, rather, former colleagues—who might ask about her plans. The chair's decision not to hire her had come extraordinarily late in the academic year; that was why he had taken over her classes for the last week, to give her more time to look for a job. But the best she could hope for now was an adjunct position. The hours she had spent sending out letters and resumes had yielded only one phone interview, for a position in a small college in rural Montana.

When Mona pulled into the parking lot, she saw that the store had been vandalized—students had sprayed shaving cream on its windows, spelling out the name of the college football team—another one of the juvenile acts that their $40,000-per-year tuition entitled them to perform, with disturbing regularity and with little consequence. The campus police rarely apprehended anyone and the town itself was too dependent on the business brought in by the college to demand much accountability. An employee was already cleaning one of the windows with a rubber blade, his movements smooth and repetitive. A woman stood by the entrance, holding an iron pot and ringing a bell. "Help the needy," she called. "Help the needy!" As Mona pushed her cart down the aisles, filling it with groceries, she continued to hear the ringing of the bell. Its echo faintly followed her all the way to the refrigerated-foods section, in the back of the store. Even after she got back in her car and drove away, it seemed to her she could still hear it in her ears, ever so faintly.

She was carrying the groceries into the house when the deliveryman came again. "Morning," he said, in the cheerful tone she had already learned to expect from him. He handed her a long box. It was from her sister. "Again?" she said.

"You need to sign for this one." He handed her his clipboard.

She signed distractedly, wondering what it was her sister had sent this time.

"Need help with those?" he asked, pointing to the bags of groceries on the porch.

"I should be fine."

"Are you sure?" he asked, his blonde eyebrows raised. "I don't mind at all."

"All right, then."

He carried four bags, two in each arm, and followed her inside, through the dark hallway, to the lemon-colored kitchen she had painted with such hope when she had moved in. One wall was lined end-to-end with a high shelf, which she had filled with books and mementos from her travels. Beneath the shelf was a wide mirror, an antique Mona had bought at a garage sale. The glass door leading to the yard was locked, and the blinds drawn.

"You can just set the bags anywhere," she said. The brown box was still in her hands. She pulled out a paring knife from the wooden block on the counter and opened it. Inside, wrapped in silk tissue paper, was a desk sign spelling out, in graceful letters, the words, "Professor Mona Benyahya." On one side of the sign was the logo of Columbus College and on the other was its motto: *historia vitae magistra est*. It was made of brushed nickel and felt heavy in her hands. What was she to do with this? What was she to do with it now?

"That's nice," Perry said.

Mona looked up from her present; she had forgotten that the delivery-man was there. With the grocery bags everywhere on the tiled floor, with the glass door closed, and with him standing so near, the kitchen was cramped. Only the mirror gave the room any depth. "I don't need this," she said, holding the sign up. "I don't need it anymore." She felt suddenly aware that he was witnessing an intimate quarrel with her sister. Then, thinking that she sounded ungrateful, she added, "My sister is always sending me things."

"You teach at Columbus," he said, as if he were answering a question he had asked himself before. "That's where I went to school."

Mona blinked. She put the tissue paper back inside the box and set it down next to the garbage bin. She felt her face get warm and gathered her hair into a loose knot on one side.

"You seem surprised," Perry said.

"No," she said, a bit too quickly. "Of course not."

"But that was years ago. Before I was shipped out."

"Oh." Mona wiped the dust off the counter with her hand. The delivery-man appeared to interpret this gesture as a request to move the grocery bags to the counter. He reached for one, but its handles broke. "Oh," she said again. "There's no need," she said. "Thanks for bringing them in."

"No problem."

She walked him to the door and sat down for a long while before she gathered the courage to pick up the phone. "Thanks for sending me the desk sign," she began.

"Do you like it?" Amal replied. And then, without waiting for an answer from Mona, she continued, "You sounded a bit strange on the phone last week, so I thought it might cheer you up."

"Listen," Mona said softly. She looked out of the dining room window. The day was grimly lit and the colors in the backyard were duller than usual. Even the jacarandas had begun to shed their blossoms. She could see her reflection framed in one of the windowpanes. With her hair pulled to one side and her color washed out by the bleak light, it seemed as if her likeness were coming to her from another era. "There's something you need to know."

She told her sister that she had lost her job. She would have to sell the house; she wouldn't be able to see her nephews as often; she might have to miss their birthdays next year. Once more, she was adrift. This long confession, she knew, was the last thing Amal wanted to hear. But the truth, when it came out, was a relief, for it reminded Mona that every life, including her own, was tethered to that of others, to all the living and all the dead.

CAROLINA DE ROBERTIS

The author and translator Carolina De Robertis grew up in England, Switzerland, and California, the daughter of Uruguayan and Argentinean parents. De Robertis worked for ten years in women's rights organizations before publishing her first book. Based in Oakland, California, she teaches creative writing in the Latin America MFA program at Queens University in North Carolina, and is currently coproducing a documentary about people of African descent in Uruguay.

De Robertis is the recipient of a 2012 National Endowment for the Arts fellowship, and her books have been translated into sixteen languages. Her novel *The Invisible Mountain* (2009) was an international bestseller and won Italy's Rhegium Julii Debut Prize; her stories and translations have been featured in *Granta*, the *Virginia Quarterly Review*, and *Zoetrope: Allstory*. Her second novel is *Perla* (2012).

On her roots in Argentina and Uruguay, and her literary fascination with both countries, De Robertis says, "I've written one book about each country, [and] I feel like I've only begun to explore the richness of their cultures and narratives. Maybe one day I'll write a novel that has nothing to do with Uruguay or Argentina, but right now, I find this difficult to imagine. There is too much still pulling me there."

No Subject

The e-mail from my daughter arrives in a crush of messages, so I almost delete it without realizing it's there. I'm moving quickly, the lights are off, and the lab is quiet; it's the end of a long day and the postdocs have all gone home. It's her name that stops me. It glows in the "From" column, and once I see it, I sit and stare at the screen for a long time. Thinking. Not thinking. Trying not to think. Totaling the years in which I haven't seen my daughter: fourteen.

The subject line reads <no subject>. There is an attachment: a little paper clip hovers beside her name.

I gave her that name. Angela. Angelita. I will myself not to open that e-mail. Don't you dare. But still it taints the room around me, leaking out rage, accusations, or else untenable questions. Or something else, I don't know what, I don't want to know.

My hand reaches for the mouse, moves the cursor over her name, still bold and unread. I don't click. I watch the cursor move away from her, then back again. Away. Back. Hovering. I don't want to open that e-mail, but I'm not sure I can be trusted to sit at this computer much longer without doing so. I have to get away from it, as far away as possible. Fuck her for invading my lab, my refuge. Fuck her for all of it. Time to get out of here. I spring up from my desk, find my keys, and close down the lab. I walk quickly across campus to the parking lot and make my escape, forgetting for a moment that in these days of ubiquitous Internet access, e-mails, like pain itself, will follow you home.

On the way, I stop at a grocery store off Sunset for two bottles of good whiskey. The checker looks bored. He's balding and paunchy and doesn't know or care that I've been dry for eight days, that I promised Marta before she left for Uruguay that I wouldn't drink while she was gone. The whiskey catches the light. Gold. Liquid gold. The sight of it unties something in me and the swigs I take before resuming my drive untie me more, and next thing I know I'm gliding smooth and fast along the curves of Sunset Boulevard, humming some old tango from my childhood, a tune with no purpose and no end.

Do you know what it's like, to be gone from your country for so many decades that you start to think you dreamed the whole place up?

Or maybe this is the dream-place. This Los Angeles. With a house minutes away from movie stars. You don't have to see them every day to know they're there, to feel their power—or, at least, their power over the relatives back home.

When I first got here I secretly thought they might find me. The movie people. See me walking down the street and beg me to come act for them, to grace the cameras, and I'd be forced to sacrifice science on the altar of the silver screen. And why not? You hear all sorts of things about Hollywood, stars rising up out of nothing and all that. But it didn't happen. I'm still a chemist. We rarely even see celebrities, though you'd never know it from the way Marta talks to her family on the phone. To her sister, brother, mother, cousins, she's the star of a glamorous California life, the one who soared, the one who got out.

Which may be why she refuses to retire in Uruguay. I try to entice her with promises, vacations in Punta del Este, the swankiest house to make her relatives green with envy, even though the thing I most want to do is walk the Rambla like all the poor old fools who stayed. Walk and sit on a ledge or bench to stare at the river without talking to anyone, just be alone with the sight of the water and the humid Montevideo air and the cream and maroon promenade that snakes along the whole edge of the shore, listening to waves and traffic and the steps of people around me, blending in with those people as if the whole place belonged to each of us, as if the past forty years hadn't changed a thing. Not even the dictatorship years. Marta says what I want is to go back to 1960s Uruguay, and maybe she's right. She tells me I'm crazy for wanting to retire there.

"The country's changed. There's nothing there for us."

"Your mother," I say.

"She can move here."

"She'll never leave Uruguay."

"I'll talk to her, when I visit. Try to change her mind."

"And the rest of your family?"

"Hmmpf. We have our own family here, our sons."

She has learned to say the words our sons with a steady tone that cuts out our third child, our youngest, Angela. Speaking as if we'd never had a girl. I admire Marta's ability to do this, but it still stabs me every time, and then I'm angry it stabbed me and curse Angela for it in my mind.

"And one day," she goes on, "we'll have grandchildren."

This also stabs and impresses me. The resoluteness of her one day. I pretend that I feel nothing, follow her script. "Don't hold your breath for that. Last time I talked to Álvaro, he said—"

"—Forget what they say. They're going to have children and we should be here for it."

Marta and I have been married for forty-two years. She's the closest thing I have to a friend. I know she's more ruthless than I am, and I know not to argue with her when she takes that tone. So I change the subject. "I dreamed about Montevideo again."

She says nothing, listens.

"That we went back and found a house there. It was right on the river, something like a houseboat, only enormous. All the rooms were white and had high ceilings that opened to the sky."

"Some house. No roof?"

I try to explain it to her, the way I'd seen it in the dream. "The ceiling slanted upward like the inside of a pyramid but it was open at the top, it let in starlight."

"I bet it let the rain in too."

"It wasn't raining in the dream."

"It always rains in Montevideo. Every winter. That's the shittiest house I've ever heard of."

I give up on trying to describe the house's beauty. Its opalescence. The heft of the river beneath the floor, pushing calmly forward. Glowing white walls. Endless corridors that led to room after room after room. And much less do I tell her what I found in those rooms: stairs that led to convoluted basements and corridors, then more rooms containing snakes, trinkets, broken fishing rods, a gutted wolf, Angela. Over and over, Angela. She was a little girl or a grown woman, crying or smiling or raking her fingernails violently along the walls, but no matter what she was doing, in every room she turned to me and held my gaze until I looked away.

I arrive home to an empty house and an empty glass that I fill with the good whiskey. I go outside to listen to the night. From our balcony, you can glimpse a sliver of the Pacific Coast Highway and, beyond it, the ocean. At this hour, though, the water is black and bleeds right into the sky. The wind rustles in the eucalyptus trees and traffic moans on the highway, drowning out the waves. Some days, you can hear chants from a place down the hill called the Self-Realization Fellowship, a bunch of crazy people, as American as it's possible to be, who sit cross-legged and Om and I don't know what else. When Angela was in high school, she snuck out to go there once. I raised a big stink about it at the time, but if I'd known then what I know now I might have counted my blessings and kept my mouth shut.

We could never have seen any of it coming. She was a good little girl. She looked just like the pictures of my mother when she was small. Big eyes, thick dark hair you could get lost in. The boys became tough early on as they had to, but Angela loved me with a sweetness I hadn't known existed in the world.

The thoughts crowd in and I need to fill my glass again, so I go inside and turn on the television. On Fox News, the pundits are still bewildered by the election, enraged that Republicans lost. I'm enraged too, and the rage is a source of comfort and distraction for a good while until they turn to the subject of gay marriage, the states where it won, more bewilderment. Where is this country going when two men or two women can call what they do a marriage, when traditional families are not respected?

Where, indeed?

Angela's wedding, if you can call it that, took place in 2002. It was before gay marriage was happening all over the place, infesting state after state, the way it is now. It was one more crazy idea from our crazy daughter, just like when she took up the sitar or read all those books about the goddess crap or volunteered to walk women into abortion clinics. The fights between us took over family dinners, days, nights, everything, and when she went away to college it only got worse. By the time she told us she was with a woman—and a black woman no less—we couldn't stay on the phone for five minutes without yelling to break the heavens. So when the wedding invitation arrived in the mail, all cursive writing and two women's names, Marta and I were united in our outrage. We won't answer. We'll stop taking her calls. We'll tell her she's excommunicated until she comes around. It can't last, a stupid thing like this. Of course she'll come around. She'll come back.

But she never did.

After the first year, Marta took out all the family photo albums and cut Angela out of the pictures. Every one.

For a long time I couldn't stop thinking about them together. There's nothing worse than picturing your own daughter doing perverse things. Believe me, it will keep you up at night.

What could she have written in that e-mail? Perhaps a long blaming letter. Perhaps a begging for forgiveness, at long last, I'm so sorry, you were right, I'm not a lesbian anymore, I've found a husband, please Daddy let me back in.

I reach for the whiskey bottle to pour myself another one, but it's empty. How did that happen? The pundits have given way to commercials, and the room feels crushed somehow, pressing in from all sides. Nothing is solid. Everything can die. I'm sixty-four, not dead yet, not even retired, but I can feel death encroaching slowly from the inside (and that's what they never tell you about aging, that your bones start to whisper their own death) and I may never see her again. Once, I was a young man, slender and strong, Uruguay still fresh inside of me, bright as the future, bright as the baby girl who looked so much like my mother and loved for me to tuck her into bed at night, stroke her hair, and tell her stories, long convoluted epics with her as the heroine. Her face lit up with delight as if I were offering her, not just words, but a map of reality. As if I were the center of her world. Or more than that: its source.

I turn the television off. The darkness envelops me so fast I have no time for terror. Its plush shape is a comfort. The message. She's written me a message. It could contain terrible things, but suddenly, for a moment, it seems even worse not to look.

I go to the den, turn on my computer, and log into my e-mail. Find her name. Click. Inside is only one line, no greeting and no goodbye:

Here are the kids. I thought you might like to see.

The attachment is a photograph. And there they are: the ones Marta and I never talk about. I've never seen them before. The girl is five now, the boy is two. They smile brightly for the camera. They are darker-skinned than Angela, but those are her eyes on that five-year-old girl.

Do you have grandchildren? An innocuous question, or so people think. Even strangers at the supermarket feel entitled to ask.

No, I say. No and no, every time.

But I know they exist. That they live in Brooklyn. That the family in Uruguay accepts our version and either doesn't know about the children or pretends not to know. That my sons call themselves their uncles and visit them and love them and refuse to listen to me when I try to have them do otherwise. And now, I also know that they are almost beautiful enough to cut you up inside.

I scroll back up to Angela's words and study them closely, try to crack their code. Is there hope in them? An invitation? Or a kind of reproach, a slap? For a second I think of answering her. I could tell her to leave that woman, start a new life, raise the kids in a decent home and then maybe I could see them. But Angela has not offered to redeem her life. She has only shown me a picture. Nothing more.

I sit in front of the computer for hours, looking back and forth between the photo and the line of words above it. Finally dawn light creeps in and pulls me to the balcony. The eucalyptus trees are stark and still. There are no Oms rising up through the valley. The Pacific Coast Highway hums with cars, and beyond it the ocean is gaining back its color, as is the sky; the line between them seems almost impossibly sharp, a thin blade guarding the far edge of the earth.

YIYUN LI

Yiyun Li was born in Beijing in 1972 and studied mathematics and physics. Before coming to the United States to study immunology at the University of Iowa, she served in the Chinese army. Li received an MFA from the Iowa Writer's Workshop and has now been published in the *New Yorker, Best American Short Stories*, and *O Henry Prize Stories*. She has released several books, including the novels *The Vagrants* (2010) and *Kinder Than Solitude* (2014). "The Science of Flight" was published in the *New Yorker* in 2010.

Li has won many awards, including the Frank O'Connor International Short Story Award, the PEN/Hemingway Award, and a MacArthur Foundation Fellowship. Li currently lives in California and teaches at the University of California, Davis.

On writing about China from overseas, Li says, "When I write about China from a distance, I need to research for information on the surface but when you know the people, when you understand human nature, it is possible to enter their world from any place."

The Science of Flight

At lunch, Zichen told her two coworkers that she was considering going to a new place for her vacation. Feeling more adventurous this year? Ted said. Since Zichen had begun to work with Henry and Ted, thirteen years earlier, she had taken two weeks off every November to visit China—her hibernation retreat, as Ted called it. England, she said now when he asked, and she wondered which would be more adventurous in her colleagues' opinion, England or China.

Henry had been sent to Vietnam at eighteen, and had returned to Iowa six months later with ruptured intestines; at nineteen, barely recovered, he had married his high school sweetheart. Every summer he and Caroline spent three weeks in a lakeside cabin in Wisconsin with their children and grandchildren. The farthest place Ted had traveled to was Chicago. A few years earlier, he had accompanied his daughter there for a high school volleyball tournament; her team had lost in the final match, and with his daughter now a senior at the state university Ted still held Chicago responsible for the disappointment.

What's there to see in England in November? Ted asked. Zichen did not answer, because anything she said would fall short of his expectations. In previous years, he had wondered belligerently what there was to see in China, and Henry had been the one to shush Ted. Like Zichen's other acquaintances in America, they had been led to believe that in China she had a pair of parents, and that, like many, she had wedged some distance between herself and her parents, reducing her filial duty to an annual two-week visit.

What about China? Henry asked, laying out his lunch—a sandwich, a thermos of soup, and a banana—on a paper napkin. His time in the army must have taught him to keep the contents of his life in good order. Henry was a neat man, his lab coat clean, what remained of his hair combed and parted precisely; he was quiet, but said enough not to seem sullen.

Her parents were taking a tour to Thailand with a group of retired people, Zichen said. Why couldn't she meet them in Thailand? Ted demanded, and predicted that she would see nothing in England but rain and coldness and people who were too polite to ask her to repeat her name.

There was a reason to visit a place where one's name was unpronounceable, Zichen thought, just as there was a reason that her parents continued to share a life in their daughter's mind. A month from now, rather than telling Henry and Ted about England, Zichen knew she would be relating tales of her parents' trip to Thailand: the crowded marketplace after nightfall, the cabaret show that they disliked but felt obliged to enjoy because it was said to be the highlight of their tour, the hotel bed that was too hard, or perhaps too soft. There were other moments, also imagined, though these she would keep to herself: her father's insistence on splitting a dish in a restaurant because he was unwilling to pay for two, her mother eying a grain of rice on her father's sleeve without pointing it out. They would've been one of those couples who had married young, and had, over the years, developed their separate ways to live with the mistake, he with his tyranny, she with her wordless contempt.

Henry, Ted, and Zichen worked in an animal-care center, in a two-story brick building next to a research facility that a hundred years ago had been an infirmary for tuberculosis patients. Because they were on the edge of a university town—the facility, a satellite site that housed some projects from the medical school, was in the middle of cornfields—the three of them had over the years become a more or less autonomous unit. Janice, their supervisor, a tall and angular woman who took pride in her extreme fairness and efficiency, came for a routine inspection once a week; Dr. Wilson, the attending veterinarian, a genial and absent-minded man, was about to retire any day now. The only crisis since Zichen had begun to work there—if one did not count the time the water was contaminated and fifty cages of mice contracted hepatitis, or the occasions when breeding went wrong, and the due date passed without a litter, or worse, with a disturbed mother mouse feeding on her own babies—was when a group of animal-rights activists had tried to break into the building on the eve of the new millennium. They had given up when the alarm went off, and instead liberated cages of minks from a farm thirty miles west on the country road. The farmer and his family had recovered less than a third of their loss, the local paper had reported. The rest of the minks, the farmer had told the *Gazette*, would not survive the Midwest winter and their many predators.

Zichen had been reading the newspaper in the office, pondering the fate of the homeless minks, when Henry, looking over her shoulder, said that he and the farmer had gone to the same high school. She was about to express her sympathy for his old classmate when Henry mentioned that the guy had once pursued Caroline when he was in Vietnam. She was glad that Caroline had not married the mink farmer, Zichen said, and Henry said he was, too, though come to think about it, perhaps Caroline wouldn't have minded a mink coat. Ted, entering the office with a stack of yellow death slips to file and overhearing the conversation, reminded Henry that a mink farmer's wife does not wear mink, just as cobblers' children have no shoes. What does that mean? Zichen asked. When the expression was explained to her, she thought of the way her grandmother used to clip her hair shorter than a boy's in summer or winter, but this would not make a good office tale.

Zichen had grown up in her grandmother's hair salon—a small shack really, at the entrance of an apartment complex, with a wooden plank propped up by two stacks of bricks that served as a bench for the waiting customers, a folding chair in front of a mirror that hung from a low beam, and a makeshift washstand, next to which a kettle of water was kept warm on a coal stove. On the curtain that separated the salon from the bed shared by Zichen and her grandmother, there were prints of bunnies, white on a green-and-yellow background. There was no window in the shack, and a fluorescent light was turned on the moment her grandmother opened up the shop and continued buzzing until the end of the day, giving everything a perpetual bluish-white hue.

That her grandmother could have had an easier life in her old age was made clear to Zichen from her first years: Zichen's two uncles—her mother's elder brothers—would have dutifully taken in their mother, and between the two families they would have seen to it that she had a decent retirement. But how could you burden your own sons with a child like that? her grandmother used to ask her customers, as though the time

Zichen had spent in the shop learning to sit up and then to walk, and later to assist her grandmother, handing her warm towels or cleaning the ashtrays—two blue-and-white china bowls placed at either end of the bench, the rims chipped, filled with smoldering cigarette ends and streaks of ash—had never softened the shock of a child's existence. It would have been a different story had she been an orphan, her grandmother would say; it would have been sensible for any uncle to take in an orphan, a statement her audience readily agreed with. Indeed, a woman who had run away with a man against her family's wish, who had given birth to a baby out of wedlock, and had then been abandoned by the man—that mother would have done her baby more of a favor had she died during childbirth.

It hadn't taken Zichen long to piece together her own story from the parts alluded to by her grandmother and uncles and customers and neighbors: that her grandmother had agreed to raise her on the condition that her mother sever all connections with the family; that a couple had once come to the shop to look her over, but then decided not to adopt her; that she owed her life not only to her grandmother, who had to toil at an age when other women could rest, but also to the patrons of the shop, who remained loyal to her grandmother because of the responsibility they felt toward her.

Sitting on a bamboo stool in a corner and listening to her own luck, both good and bad, discussed, Zichen would clandestinely move her feet and make piles of hair according to a system known only to her. Inevitably the game would be interrupted by the strokes of her grandmother's broom, but even that did not disturb Zichen, as the disassembling of the small hills of hair could also be part of her scheme. Quit grinning like an idiot, her grandmother would sometimes tell Zichen, turning from her clipping, and Zichen would straighten her face, but when her grandmother turned back to her customer she smiled again at the back of a man's half-shaved head, or at the shoelaces of someone waiting on the bench. Where on earth did the girl get that smile? her grandmother complained to the customers. One would think a child like that should know how to make people forget her for a moment.

Hydrangea House, a sixteenth-century timber-framed house, had served as a family home for generations before it was turned into a B & B; Zichen wondered, reading the information provided on its website, how such a change had come about. Perhaps the owners would tell her when she asked—if not the whole story, then bits and pieces would nevertheless delight her.

On the website, there were no photographs of the kind that other places, with more business-minded management, displayed: blooming flowers in a garden or soft-colored curtains lifted by unseen wind. Instead, a small sketch of the house, made in ink or perhaps pencil, showed little except a whitewashed front wall and four rectangular windows. It was said to be "never a grand house"; two rooms, the Rose Room and the Lilac Room, were available upstairs.

The modest, almost apologetic way that Hydrangea House advertised itself made it easy for Zichen to choose it. The trip to England, despite Henry's bafflement and Ted's disapproval, was becoming a certainty in her mind. Tomorrow she would buy the plane ticket; next week she would call and reserve a room.

Contrary to Henry and Ted's beliefs, Zichen was neither an experienced nor willing traveler. The summer she had begun to work at the animal-care center, Ted had invited her, along with Caroline and Henry, to a picnic on the Fourth of July. She had apologized and said that she needed to go to the East Coast to visit her husband, who had finished graduate school earlier that year and moved away for a job.

Before the holiday weekend, she had purchased more food than she could consume, and for four days she had hidden herself in her apartment and worked slowly through a Latin reader of Cicero's speeches. She had picked up the book from the library not for any grand ideas she might glean from the text; sometimes she forgot a sentence the moment she figured out its meaning. But the effort of making sense out of something that was at first glance indecipherable satisfied her, as did the slowness of the activity; an hour or two would pass as she made her way through one passage on a war; a day that would have otherwise been long was shortened.

Her interest in the dead language had been one of the things her husband had held against her when he asked for the divorce, which to Zichen had come neither as a surprise nor as a disappointment. There was a practical order of things for an immigrant couple like them, he had once explained to her. They would start a family when they had finally made it, he'd said comfortingly when the baby that Zichen so desired, who must have sensed itself unwanted by its father, miscarried. He'd had plans for her to go to graduate school to become a statistician, or an accountant, or a nurse, part of that order of things that would help them make it in the new country; he was finishing a PhD in mathematics, and had a goal of working on Wall Street. Zichen, never arguing, for arguing was not in her nature, nevertheless dismissed his blueprint for her career with unconcealed resistance. There was no use in her copying Latin vocabulary onto flashcards, he had yelled at her—only once, as yelling was not in his nature, either—when she had outraged him by missing the GRE test he had registered her to take, wasting more than a hundred dollars, half a month's rent.

The marriage had ended shortly before he moved away, but Zichen had used him to excuse herself from two years of social life. The cheek of it. When she lied to Henry and Ted, she could hear her grandmother's words, those she would say after Zichen had read her report card aloud in the shop. Unable to concentrate, the teachers commented every year; a lack of interest in both studying and participating in school activities. Her grades were meager, barely good enough for her to proceed to the next level. What will you do with your life if you don't catch up with your schoolwork? her grandmother's customers ceaselessly asked her; not knowing the answer, she would smile as though she did not understand the question, and it was her smile more than her grades that had marked her as beyond teachable.

Zichen had given Henry and Ted a skeletal account of her divorce the third year into her work, as it had not felt right to continue to lie about a marriage that no longer existed. But an ex-husband was easy to be done with and never mentioned again, while a pair of parents, even if they lived on another continent, needed careful maintenance: an annual trip; phone calls that brought news from China; presents to take home—Wisconsin ginseng for her father, anti-aging cream for her mother.

She could easily take the usual trip back to China this year, a routine unbroken, thus causing little concern or suspense, but the truth was the shack that had housed her grandmother's shop had been demolished, her grandmother reduced to an urn of ashes. Her grandmother had lived in the shop until a month before her death, at ninety-three, and Zichen knew that for as long as her grandmother had lived there the shop door was opened every morning, the fluorescent light kept on till closing time, as it was during her annual visits. The news of the death had reached Zichen after the funeral; she had not been invited to it, as she knew her mother had not been. Together they, rather than an early widowhood, were blamed for her grandmother's harsh life; together they had been the old woman's disappointments, a daughter who had brought humiliation to the family, a granddaughter who had rashly married a man she had met twice and then been unable to stay married for longer than three years.

The B & B was in a village called Neville Hill, some distance from Brighton, but to simplify the matter Zichen told Ted and Henry that Brighton was her final destination. They were eating lunch together, savoring one of the last warm autumn days before a cold front set in. She described the places she wanted to see: the promenade, the beach, the English Channel.

"Now, explain two things to me," Ted said, and for a moment Zichen thought Henry looked relieved that someone was going to confront her as he would never do. "First, why do you want to go to the beach in the winter?"

November was not winter yet, Zichen argued, and Ted merely nodded at her with a triumphant smile as though he had cornered a runaway rat that Zichen wasn't able to catch. It was rare that a mouse or a rat slipped through her grip, and when it did happen—a few times over the years—Ted would talk about it for days afterward with a childlike glee. When you touch an animal, it can tell right away if you are nervous or if you are the master, Henry had explained to Zichen when he trained her. Ted, during the first weeks, had liked to seek her out and tell her gruesome tales; his favorite one concerned a homemade rat guillotine that he and Henry had once built for a neurologist's study. But to her coworkers' surprise Zichen had never been jittery. She had applied for the opening because she had no other profitable skills, but in retrospect she wondered if she had found the right job out of blind luck. From the beginning, she had clipped a mouse's ear or prepped a rat for a skin graft as deftly as if she had always worked with animals. Even the bigger mammals had not distressed her: the monkeys that clamored in the cages and made faces at her when she came in with feed or a hose, the forlorn-looking dogs that rarely barked. After her training, Henry had told her that he and Ted would split the care of bigger mammals because they thought her too small, for instance, to dispose of a thirty-pound carcass by herself. The Rodent Queen—on her thirtieth birthday they had left a toy crown on her desk, the words scrawled on with permanent marker.

"Now, winter or not winter," Ted said. "Why do you want to go to England all by yourself?"

People traveled alone all the time, Zichen said, and there was nothing wrong with that.

"But what are you going to do in a place where you don't know anyone?"

"How do you know I don't know anyone there?" Zichen said, but the moment the words came out she regretted them. Over the years she had become accustomed to who she was in other people's eyes: she knew she would be considered a loser by her Chinese acquaintances in America, a divorced woman toiling her life away in an animal-care facility, someone who had failed to make it; in her landlord's and neighbors' eyes she was the quiet, good-mannered foreigner who paid her rent on time, who every Halloween put out a couple of pumpkins, uncarved but with drawn-on eyes and mouths, and who had no visitors on weekends or holidays, so there was no conflict regarding the guest parking; for her grandmother and her aging customers, who spent their days in the shack for conversation and companionship more than for the care of their thinning hair or balding heads, she was—despite being a baby who should have remained unborn, a child with little merit and an unnerving manner, and a young woman who had no respect for marriage or her own future—a proof, in the end, of the ultimate mercy of life. She had been able to build a life out of her failures, to wire dollars to her grandmother, to return every year like a loyal homing pigeon and sit with the old customers, still with that unnerving smile on her face although they no longer cared; simply sitting and listening to them had absolved Zichen of all possible sins.

But it was who she was in the eyes of Henry and Ted that she cherished the most: sure-handed and efficient at her job, quiet yet at times chatty, uncomplicated. That she had memorized passages from *Winnie-the-Pooh*, that she had read its Latin translation before reading the English text, she did not share with them, because that would make her an eccentric in their eyes. The things that gave her pleasure—the pile of wood shavings meant for the animals' bedding, which she assembled into small hills; the time she spent imagining her ex-husband in a pale-blue suburban house in New Jersey, his two sons growing up and looking more like him each year, his new wife unaging; the marriage she had given her father, whom she had never known, and her mother, whom she had only met once, in a small one-bedroom apartment in an older neighborhood in Beijing—these she did not share with Henry and Ted, because they would have made her a person with a history, in this or that time, this or that place.

"So, you are meeting someone in England?" Ted said.

"No," Zichen said. "Why should I?"

The unusual confrontational tone in her reply made Ted flinch, as though he had trespassed. He shrugged and, with a theatrical gesture, threw a half-eaten sandwich to a squirrel. Years earlier, Molly, Ted's wife, had asked Zichen if she wanted to meet someone she knew who was available; Henry's wife, Caroline, had mentioned once or twice her Chinese dentist, divorced, according to his office manager. When Zichen had not followed up on either lead, the women had not pressed her. Henry and Ted had never asked about her personal life. The ease into which the three of them had settled left her life outside work irrelevant, and she liked to imagine that for them it was as natural for her to cease to exist the moment she left work as it was natural that she could handle the animals with confidence and calm. The only time they had experienced discomfort was when Henry first trained her to breed the mice—he had asked Ted to be present when he showed her how to detect vaginal plugs, the evidence of successful copulation. Beet red, Henry had grabbed a few females to display their private parts to Zichen, then explained that sometimes the plugs did not guarantee pregnancy. Ted, rearranging the charts on the cages with a look of concentration, had remained uncharacteristically quiet on a subject that he might otherwise have joked about with Henry.

Had Ted been offended by her abruptness, Zichen wondered, but she could not find the words to soften the tension as he continued to whistle to the squirrel, which was ignoring his generosity. She had unwisely opened a door and then clumsily slammed it shut, but perhaps some harm had already been done.

"You'll do just fine," Henry said when it was apparent that Ted would not fill the rest of the lunch break with one of his favorite topics, the upcoming basketball game or a wrestling match. "When you think about it, I've seen my share of pictures of China but never any of England."

Zichen took pictures when she traveled to China, of things she imagined Henry might like to see, or of strange sights that would offer Ted an opportunity to criticize. Yes, she agreed. England would be a good change.

She then dusted off the crumbs from the picnic table so that they would not find ants crawling over their space the next day. Before she had joined them, Henry and Ted used to eat in the office, the door open to the hallway with its constant odor of bleach and rodent pellets and damp bedding and dead animals; they did not seem to be bothered by this, but when Henry noticed that Zichen often sat on the steps in front of the building to eat her lunch, he had requested a picnic table as an improvement for their work environment.

Josephina, the proprietress of Hydrangea House, had been easy to talk with on the phone. If she had felt curious as to why a woman from America with an unpronounceable Chinese name would want to spend two weeks in Neville Hill she had not shown it. Zichen wondered, after the phone call, whether the thought would be shared with Josephina's husband; she wondered if they would decide that such a question did not matter in a bed-and-breakfast.

When she got to Neville Hill, Zichen would explain to the owners that she had come in memory of an elderly woman who had befriended her when she first moved to America. Margaret was the woman's name. She had spent her childhood in Neville Hill before marrying an American pastor, John Hubor, and had lived in the States for fifty-three years. Would the couple at Hydrangea House try to locate a girl in the village's past, one who had left, taken away by a marriage after the war? Perhaps they had heard of a girl named Margaret, or perhaps they would apologize for having no such recollection. The truth was, the name Neville Hill had never been mentioned in Zichen's conversations with Margaret, yet it was Neville Hill that Zichen had decided to go to, her research fitting the village to an old woman's descriptions: the school trips to Seaford taken on foot; the car rides to Brighton for special family occasions.

It was in the spring of 1994 when Zichen had met Margaret and John, in a supermarket; the autumn of 1995 when Margaret had been buried in a hillside cemetery. In the aisle between shelves of sugar, flour, and cooking utensils, Margaret had mistaken Zichen for a Chinese student she knew, who had recently graduated and moved to California; John had invited Zichen to become their friend, as the woman before her must have been invited, whose name Margaret had used for Zichen for as long as she had visited the house.

She would describe Margaret to the couple at Hydrangea House, and tell them how Margaret had tutored her in English when she first arrived in America because she had wanted Zichen, a young woman who had left her country for marriage, to have a friendship.

Growing up, Zichen had never had a close friend. A bastard was what some of the children at school had called her, the word learned from older siblings. Once, when Zichen was ten, and tired of being teased by her classmates, she had pointed to a neighbor who was passing by on the street and said that he was her real father. The man, overhearing Zichen's claim, had paled but said nothing—he had recently divorced, and his twin daughters had moved away with their mother.

The cheek of it; her grandmother would have been shocked by her shamelessness. The man Zichen had appointed as her father, a week later, asked her if she would like to see a butterfly exhibit that he perhaps imagined his own daughters would enjoy. Across the street from the park was the Friendship Hotel, and after the exhibit the man took her to the hotel entrance. It was one of only two hotels where foreigners were allowed to stay in Beijing, he explained; once, when he and his daughters were there, an American had given each of the girls a chocolate. It was ridiculous to stand in front of a hotel for the prospect of chocolate; still, Zichen smiled at the two armed guards, and, later, at a pair of foreigners walking out of the hotel. The couple, both with pale skin and straw-colored hair, must have assumed that the man and Zichen were father and daughter, for they signaled and made it understood that they would take a picture of them. It was the first Polaroid Zichen had seen. The man had offered it to her, but she had refused to take it, the unspoken agreement being that their lives would go on as though the outing had never happened.

As a teenager she was one of the girls no one wanted to be close to; she was too strange and unpredictable to be a confidante, too inconspicuous to be a subject of any confidences. At that age, friendship had to offer drama or ease; she had been unable to provide either, and later, as a young woman, had been unable to provide either to attract a boy.

Yet it was ease she had offered in Margaret's brightly lit sunroom, giving the old woman the impression that she was tutoring Zichen, although the language they were studying was not English but Latin. Margaret's mind by then had been tangled, and Zichen, working by herself through *Wheelock's Latin*, nonetheless allowed the old woman the luxury of

185

repetitions: farmer, farmer, of the farmer, to the farmer, by the farmer, O farmer. Repeated, too, were the memories of Margaret's childhood village, which she must have known by then she would not be able to visit again: the trail that led to a secret pond, the couple in the red-roofed farmhouse giving birth to a baby who had six fingers on one hand. Every spring saw a batch of new chicks in the yard; in the summer the fluffy clouds sometimes stayed motionless for hours; any month could be called a rainy season, and the rain seemed to keep their house perpetually damp and chilly.

It was kind of Zichen to come and sit with Margaret, John had said the first time he drove her home at the end of the afternoon, apologizing for Margaret's confusions. She had come from a seaman's family, he had told Zichen on another ride home, as if that explained the fact that Margaret had picked up fourteen languages, when all of them, other than Latin and French and English, had been learned during her decades of marriage in America. Toward the summer of her last year, Margaret had shown signs of the approaching end, her words sometimes ungraspable even for John. Out of the blue one day she had produced a copy of *Winnie Ille Pu*, the first edition of the Latin translation, for Zichen as a present; the translator, like Margaret and Zichen, was a man who had left home and settled in a foreign land, but that fact Zichen discovered only later.

No, she had not heard of *Winnie-the-Pooh*, she had told John in the car that day. She had not had any children's books when she was growing up. It must have been the gentle sadness in John's eyes that had made her tell him other things, of being called a bastard when young, of having miscarried a baby, of not loving her husband. John, a careful driver, had removed a hand from the steering wheel and held hers for the rest of the drive. Had that been a moment of deception? Zichen wondered sometimes; had she betrayed Margaret's friendship?—not because Margaret had ever learned of the moment from Zichen or from John but because Zichen had relived it now and again, long after Margaret had been buried and John had moved away to Sioux City, to be close to his children and eventually, as he had explained to Zichen after Margaret's funeral, to be placed in a nursing home.

Once a year in December, Henry took Ted and Zichen out for a drink in a nearby village called Tiffin, since none of them liked the places in the university town, where the music was too loud, and the college students made heartless noises. The bar was on a country road and was never full. The men there were older; some of them, the more talkative ones, had once played in a paintball league with Henry; others remained reticent. The bartender, a former wrestler who had been a state champion in high school, liked to tease Ted; every year, he asked him what color underwear he had on that day, for Ted, being Ted, had once bragged that he bought only two kinds: black and gold for the university's colors, and red and white for his high school, which was also his wife's and his daughter's alma mater. The men at the bar had always been courteous toward Zichen, but as the years went by they had grown more relaxed, raising their glasses to her when she arrived, calling her the Rodent Queen.

A mail-order bride she was, she had told the bartender one year, when she had drunk more than she should have. It was not true, for there had not been any business transaction in her marriage: she and her ex-husband had agreed to marry after meeting twice in a teahouse near her grandmother's shop, he choosing her because she had grown up in a harsh environment, which would make her a good companion in America, she choosing him because of America.

It had made her feel happy for a moment, voicing the words "mail-order bride" and watching the bartender take in the information with an acknowledgment that felt neither aloof nor unnecessarily concerned. It would make her happy, too, she knew, when she told the story in Hydrangea House about Margaret and reading *Winnie-the-Pooh* in Latin, about how she herself, inexperienced with the language, had let the pooh bear's head thump and thump again on the stairs.

"Your father and I did what we could for you," Zichen's mother had said, the only time they had met, perhaps the only time, too, since giving birth to Zichen that she had put herself and Zichen's father in the same sentence. Zichen did not know why her mother had agreed to see her before her departure for America, but she had recognized, at the first sight of her mother, the sternness and stubbornness she had grown used to in her grandmother's face. One's parents could only do so much, her mother had explained, and a child was responsible for her own life. Her mother had not told her anything about her father, saying only that they had long since lost contact; she had not said anything about her new family, either, even though Zichen had known there was one, with a husband and two children. That Zichen's grandmother had kept her in order to spite her rebellious and humiliated daughter Zichen had always known; that her mother had given birth to her in order to spite her father had become evident when they met.

Every year, on the drive back from the out-of-town bar, Zichen sat in the back of the car and quietly wept. Henry drove cautiously, both hands gripping the steering wheel, as he always did after a drink, while Ted, in the passenger seat, talked with expert knowledge about a coming basketball game. She blamed the alcohol for her tears—that, and the cold moon in the winter sky.

One year when Ted had asked to be dropped off first, to attend a wrestling match, she had told Henry that she had grown up without knowing her parents' love for each other. Through the windshield she watched the frozen rain rushing toward them, and when the sound of the windshield wipers seemed too loud she said that her parents had stayed in the marriage because of her; and they had learned to tolerate each other for her sake. It was as close to the truth as she could get—she wished she could tell Henry about the man in front of the Friendship Hotel, or John's hand holding hers, but those stories would make her a different person in Henry's eyes—and afterward he patted her on the back as he walked her to her door, saying it was all right, because that was all he could say.

In Hydrangea House, perhaps she would tell the owners about her grandmother and her mother, the two women in her life whose blind passions had sustained them through the blows of fate, but even as she imagined that she knew she wouldn't. There was no way to leave herself out of their battle stories, and she knew that in all stories she must be left out—the life she had made for herself was a life of flight, of discarding the inessential and the essential alike, making use of the stolen pieces and memories, retreating to the lost moments of other people's lives.

EDWIDGE DANTICAT

Edwidge Danticat was born in Port-au-Prince, Haiti, in 1969. Her parents immigrated to New York and Danticat was raised by an aunt until she joined her parents at the age of twelve. After receiving a BA from Barnard College and an MFA from Brown University, she published her acclaimed first novel *Breath, Eyes, Memory* (1994).

In 2007 Danticat received the National Book Critics Circle Award for her memoir *Brother, I'm Dying* (2007) and in 2009 was awarded a prestigious MacArthur Foundation Fellowship. Among her many works is her essay collection *Create Dangerously: The Immigrant Artist at Work* (2010), exploring art, exile, and the role of the author. Her latest novel is *Claire of the Sea Light* (2013).

"In Haiti, they call people like me part of a black diaspora," Danticat said in an interview with *LA Weekly*. "They say, 'Look at her, she's diaspora.' But when I go back, I don't feel so much like an outsider as I do like someone who's been away for a while. Time passes, and I say to myself, 'Okay, I'm in. I'm back.' If we are honest with ourselves, we must say, 'I am different. I have a different relationship to this place than people who still live here.'"

Hot-Air Balloons

Sherlon, my former philosophy professor, calls and says, "Clio, my dear, I need a big favor from you."

I can tell by the way he drags out my name and slurs on the word "dear," that his nostalgia for our long nights on the bright red velvet couch in his faculty apartment has been inflamed by a great deal of alcohol. What I can't tell is whether he's just missing me, drunk-dialing to flirt, or has gotten himself into serious trouble. Maybe he's taken too many sleeping pills while polishing off a bottle of Chardonnay, thinking that this will bring either me or his estranged daughter back.

"What do you need?" I ask, sounding off-putting on purpose, even while calculating how long it would take me to get out of bed, slip out of my pajamas into real clothes, and drive the fifteen minutes to his place.

"It's Polly," he says.

He had foolishly convinced his daughter to leave her mother and her life in New York to attend the small private college in West Palm Beach where he was the philosophy chair. He had done it, in part, to have his daughter close to him, but she'd interpreted it as a desire to save money and she had dropped out in the middle of the second semester of her second year to join a small women's organization called Kenbe, Hang On, which ran a rape crisis clinic in Port-au-Prince, Haiti. He had not heard from Polly for weeks and neither had I, even though we'd been good friends before she discovered, from a casual remark he made while cooking a dinner for the three of us, that he and I were sleeping together. Her disappearance had given me an excuse to stop seeing him, something which I could never quite find the courage to do, even after a year of saying to myself that what we were doing was wrong, because he was my professor, because he was twenty years older than I was, and because his daughter was my roommate. Polly's absence made us both feel dirty and any conversation about her took away our desire to touch one another. Still, every now and then he would call me in a drunken stupor, in the middle of the night, to complain about some unrelated problem, mostly his students and classes, and I would listen to him while talking myself out of going over to his place and just holding him and apologizing for pushing his daughter out of both our lives.

"What's going on with Polly?" I ask. The fact that he was saying her name at all meant that something had changed either in her status, or ours.

"Her mother's not heard from her," he says. "She's not been calling me, but at least she had been calling her mother."

The mother had long changed status, where he was concerned, from being his ex-wife to simply "Polly's mother." The way he said the word "mother," especially when he was sloppy drunk, made me feel that Polly's mother had reached the lowest point of gradual erasure. It was dangerous to fall from his good graces. He could easily eradicate you with words; wipe you out of his life by merely shifting a pronoun or placing emphasis on a verb.

"What do you need me to do?" I ask.

Part of me is hoping to hear him say, "Get in the car and come to me. Don't bother changing out of your nightgown. I need you now and only you can save me."

Except that he would never put it that way. If it came to that, he might say more professorially, "For everyone's highest good, please come over." This would give him a chance to tap into the past lessons he'd tried to teach me both in and out of the classroom: to entertain thoughts that I didn't completely accept, to find truth not in certainty but in ambiguity.

"You know Polly's mother's heart is not very good," he says. Unlike most people who liked to trash their exes, he preferred to point out her myriad health problems as though they were weaknesses in her character.

"You know she has that strange condition where her gall bladder shoots small stones into the rest of her body," he used to tell me. "You know one of those stones nearly shut down her kidneys." "You know she nearly inhaled one of those pebbles into her lungs." "You know one of them attacked her heart." He said this as though she had left herself wide open to all of that, as though she'd simply decided to commit gradual suicide by initially neglecting all the stomach- and backaches that signaled the beginning of her decline.

"You know Polly's mother can barely walk now," he says. "She's being looked after by a nurse, and insurance being the crap it is in this country, she's paying out of her own university pension for the care. She's sick and nearly destitute and supremely depressed already, the last thing she needs is more complications in what's left of her life."

He had married Polly's mother when they were both graduate students at the City University of New York. Her specialty was Caribbean history, which, according to him, she'd decided to study as a way of better understanding their Trinidadian background. They married in their early twenties, he told me, reasoning that it would be easier to live on very little if they merged into one household. Polly came early in the marriage, a surprise that would cause research papers to be late and classes to be missed and dissertations to be delayed by several years. He and his wife didn't agree on many things. Unfortunately, he realized this after the marriage, and even more so after Polly was born. The only thing they could agree on was their approach to parenting, which was loose and relaxed and resulted mostly from their being too busy with their academic work. Polly became as uninterested in them as they had appeared to be in her, throwing herself into her schoolwork with a zeal that they, scholars both, should have admired. Instead, as she had herself told me, they kept encouraging her to explore what they vaguely termed her "artistic side," offering no guidance or direction, or even a suggestion.

Ambivalent parenting, she had called it, in her merely above a whisper of a voice. "Should I have just woken up one morning and written a novel? I was never sure what they wanted from me. I had a feeling that if I stayed out of their way, they'd consider me a good daughter." Still, when her father suggested after the divorce that she attend the small liberal arts school where he was teaching, she had been eager to give it a try.

"At last, he told me what to do," Polly had said.

"There are plenty of children who come out fine *because* their parents didn't bully them," he said. "This is just who she is."

His judgment was particularly cloudy for someone who considered himself a philosopher, but ask anyone about the tip of their noses—if they try too hard to study that island of skin, the rest of the world becomes blurry.

"Don't you think Polly is now complicating her mother's life?" he asked me.

"Do you really want me to answer that?" I said. He relished in the rhetorical even when it didn't make sense. I felt like diving into an argument about it just to annoy him. Of course I didn't think Polly was complicating her mother's life. She was complicating her own life more than anyone else's. But he knew both Polly and her mother better than I did and maybe he was right about all of this in a way that I would never understand.

"What do you want me to do?" I settled deeper into my bed, while searching in the dark for the outline of the identical oak bed that had been his daughter's. It was still as well made, with hospital corners and fluffed pillows, as she had left it the night she'd walked away. Her books were still neatly lined up on the small bookshelf on top of her ink-stained desk. Crowding her bookshelves were novels for her Latin American literature class. She had bought an entire semester's worth of books using one of her father's credit cards. He had only come to our room to pick up her laptop, which was open to a half-written page on what she was calling the Death of Magic Realism. Could magic ever be real? she had noted, or reality ever be magical? She seemed to have been brainstorming and had gotten stuck. Maybe it was the magic realism paper that had driven her out of our lives. Maybe her father and I had nothing to do with it. That thought was only comforting for a moment. The rest of the time I would imagine her locked up in a room somewhere, hostage to some evil do-gooder who'd lured her with promises of saving poor Haitian women, only to keep her handcuffed to a bed. During more lucid moments, I'd imagine her leaning over a pew in a stone-walled open-air cathedral, wearing a nun's habit. I still couldn't understand though, what he wanted me to do. The long silences between sentences were not helpful either. Was I supposed to guess what was in his heart? What was in hers?

"Clio, I lied to Polly's mother and I told her that Polly had called me," he said in his most professorial voice. He had that rare gift of sobering up quickly, or seeming to, like someone who had emptied a cup only so he could fill it up again.

"Should you have done that?" I asked rhetorically.

"Are you asking me something?" he said.

This was the way we always spoke. He could have the most violent reaction, slamming the phone down on me, if I told him straight out what he should or should not do. Now that we were broken up, I could say whatever I wanted. His punitive silences were not supposed to affect me.

"I don't think you should have lied to your ex-wife," I said.

"There's a grave real possibility that something terrible might have happened to my daughter," he said. His voice cracked and for a second it sounded as though he was crying. Then he broke into a loud laugh and I realized that he was doing both, laughing and crying at the same time.

I have replayed over and over in my mind the night Polly left his apartment. He was nearly done with the salad and pholourie balls that would accompany his stewed chicken and rice, when she asked in the type of timid voice that one might use to address a stranger, whether he was going to be leaving town during his sabbatical the following year or whether he would be one of those professors who stick around and come to the department a few times a week and end up working anyway.

"Maybe I'll do something wild," he replied. "Join an ashram or get a butterfly tattoo on my ass cheek like Clio here."

I could tell that he wished the words hadn't come out of his mouth as soon as he said them. Her face softened, as if to relax her eyes for tears; her pointed cheekbones seemed to melt. She got up, picked up her fading camouflage backpack from under the coat rack, opened the door and walked out. She was so skinny that her clothes never quite fit her and that night they seemed even looser as she slipped through the door.

"Should I go after her?" I said, turning to face him. The fact that I was even asking meant that I didn't want to go. And I could tell from the way he placed the wooden salad bowl on the table that he didn't want to go after her either. It occurs to me now that I was stepping into her mother's inactive role, practicing ambivalent parenting.

I had been parented much differently. My anxious migrant-worker parents took an interest in everything I did. They had only allowed me to hang out with the children of their ambulant colleagues, fellow captives, with whom I'd never really forged a bond. I suppose I could have tried to be a brilliant student and, like many of those kids, plotted my escape via an Ivy League education. But my unstable adolescent life had left me longing for so much that, had I not been accepted to the one college that had taken me, I would have joined the army.

Even now, I try not to make a big deal about it, but Polly's father—in my own version of partial erasure, no longer my college professor but

Polly's father—was the first man I ever had sex with. This was something he seemed so proud of that I was afraid he would blurt it out in the two back-to-back classes I took with him my first year of college.

"One of the last virgins in the world," he would occasionally whisper in my ear, "and I had her."

One of the millions of asses in the world, I would think, and I love him.

After an evening at his apartment, I would feel guilty when I returned to the room I shared with Polly. Each moment with him felt like something I had stolen from her. I would be dying to tell her what we had just done, substituting another name for his, but in the end I decided to lie, telling her I'd been at the library, studying for exams I was failing because of my borderline obsession with my own body and these new sensations I was feeling.

"Do you have a phone number for Polly?" I asked, after he had been silent for a while. So silent that I feared he had fallen asleep.

"Her phone is now disconnected," he said.

He didn't know this, but Polly had learned about Kenbe, the Haitian women's group, from me. I had gone to the Global Experience office and had picked up a small, matte fold-out brochure and had brought it back to the room with me. She had taken it from my desk and had slept with it on her chest that night and many nights after that. How ironic it would have been for me, I thought, to have tried everything possible to escape my parents in rural Georgia only to end up farther from them physically but even closer to their past in Haiti. But their country, the one they had lived in and had left with me as a baby, cradled in their arms, and the country I would now see, the one in the brochure, would not be the same. That country would have long days of consoling wounded women and rocking the enormous heads of their hydrocephalus-stricken offspring and preemies that would barely fit in the palms of my hands. My parents' country would still be green and beautiful, just as they'd vaguely described it to me now and then. Their country would have no need for people like Polly and me to interrupt our lives to go and help.

In the end I didn't volunteer. Instead I spent my spring break working extra hours at the cash register at Whole Foods. I had relieved myself of any guilt by clinging to the possibility of the last line in the brochure, that one did not need to volunteer during spring break, but could do it at any time.

Sherlon had fallen asleep. I could hear him snoring loudly on the other end of the line.

"Sherlon," I shouted his name several times, but he did not answer. Is this what it was like, I wondered, to be his daughter?

I was about to hang up the phone when I heard him mumble my name.

"Clio," he said, "do you know where my daughter is?"

I did, but I wasn't sure I was ready to tell him.

The walls of the Kenbe office in Miami's Little Haiti neighborhood were covered in photographs of sad but hopeful-looking women, their eyes aimed like laser beams at the camera which had hoped to capture their image, to elicit pity and sympathy. Unlike the Haitian restaurant and barbershop next door, which blasted lively music from giant speakers into the street and had people walking in and out, the two-room Kenbe office, though it was completely visible from the street, was quiet, and you could see Polly and another woman in profile as they worked at their desks. Even in the eighty-degree-plus heat, Polly was wearing a thick brown velvet jacket that looked at least thirty years old. She had probably picked it up from one of the many Salvation Army and Goodwill thrift stores that provided most of her wardrobe. Her face was even more gaunt now than when I had last seen her and she was stooped over, reading files through a fragile-looking wiry pair of glasses.

I watched her for a long time from a wobbly table outside the coffee shop across the street. She spent hours staring at her computer screen and only occasionally stopped to file a few pieces of paper in what seemed like small filing cabinets beneath the desk. A while ago, I had suspected that she might be here, based on the way she had carried the Kenbe brochure around for days. She wasn't there that day, but the woman at the other desk, her boss, had told me that she would be back in a couple of hours. I had left and never returned.

Finally, Polly got up, strolled over to the other woman's corner desk, exchanged a few words, then walked to the front door and out onto the street. She walked down the short block, keeping her eyes on the sidewalk as if searching for something. Moving closer to the curb, in between some parked cars, she picked up some cigarette butts and, after sorting them, packed the rest into her pocket, cupped her hands around her mouth and lit one. She had not been a smoker when we were roommates, but then again she might have been without my knowing it. Maybe she was one of those smokers who only smoked the remainders of other people's cigarettes. I finished my coffee and crossed the busy street, still hoping somehow that I could make our meeting seem accidental.

"Hey, Pol," I said, when she looked up and saw me.

"Hey." She opened one of her palms, spat in it and put out the stub with her spit and then put it back in her pocket.

"What are you doing here?" she asked. She didn't sound angry, just surprised.

"So you went on the spring-break trip?" I asked.

She turned toward the window, the office, and her desk and nodded. She had left one of the drawers on her small cabinet open and she suddenly seemed torn between going back in to close it and standing there to talk to me.

"How are you?" I asked.

Pointing to her flat chest, she said, "Me?"

Accustomed to her delay tactics—avoiding eye contact and repeating questions—I repeated the question.

"I am fine," she answered then.

I followed her gaze. She was watching a fox terrier, which was tied to a parking meter in front of the coffee shop across the street. The fox terrier was mostly white, with black patches, and it looked old. Or at least I thought she was watching the terrier. I remembered telling her how, soon after I had turned fifteen, I had convinced my parents to let me get a learner's permit. One day I was driving with my mother on a dirt road when a stray dog came out of nowhere. The window was down in the car because my mother was teaching me to drive the way she claimed people learned in Haiti, including how to signal with my hands. When the car hit the dog, I heard the crash then the long whimper. It was not exactly what I had expected a wounded dog to sound like. Maybe an eternal bark—the equivalent of a scream—even a barking at the sky, but not a pleading moan like the one my mother and I were both hearing coming out of the dog as the car was passing over it. I had pleaded with my mother to stop, but she'd refused, even as we looked back and saw the dog vainly try to stand on one hind leg as the other three crumbled underneath it. There was no blood, which I found strange, but I wondered how long it would take that dog to die. And I wondered how long that image of the dying dog would remain a secret between my mother and me.

"I'm sorry," I told Polly.

"Why?" she asked, still watching the dog.

"Because of your father," I said.

"Come and have a coffee with me," she said. She turned back to look at the open drawer and at the other woman in the office who was also watching us. The woman was a few decades older, maybe our mothers' age, but she was beautiful, eggplant-colored with bright red fingernail polish, which neither of our mothers would wear. She waved at us and, jealously, I didn't wave back. Holding up one index finger, Polly pointed at me then at the coffee shop. The woman nodded her approval.

I felt like holding Polly's hand as we crossed the street and I would have, I think, if she weren't walking a whole lot faster than me. Neither one of us stopped when we passed the old terrier, which appeared listless on the hot sidewalk concrete. I followed Polly to a table in the back of the coffee shop, near the bathrooms. The air was cooler in that spot, but it was also dark and the aroma of cocoa and coffee was strongest there. A man came over and seemed both annoyed and disappointed when we only ordered two hot chocolates and none of the paninis and sandwiches and desserts he kept recommending.

Sitting there, it suddenly felt as though our time together had no limit, as if we might be silently sipping our hot chocolates forever.

"I'm not seeing your father anymore," I told her.

"Why not?" she asked, matter-of-fact, as though we were talking about someone who had been living in the dorm room across from ours.

"Because of you," I wanted to say, but perhaps that was only a part of it. "Because," I said, "it was wrong."

"Didn't my father teach you about moral relativism?" she said. "Or did you ever even talk to each other?"

I thought she was going to throw the rest of her drink in my face and storm out, but we both sat there saying nothing as we calmly emptied our cups.

"Touché," I said, "and well deserved," all the while marveling at our relative calm and reserve. We were close to being adults now, both of us, no longer young women, almost real women.

"Have you been in touch with your parents?" I asked.

"No," she said.

"Shouldn't you be?"

"Shouldn't you be?" She was mocking me.

She covered her face with her hands and rubbed so hard it seemed as though both her palms and her cheeks might be burning when she stopped.

"The spring-break trip was awful," she said.

"So you went," I said.

"It wasn't the trip itself that was awful," she said. "It was the circumstances."

"How so?" I asked.

"I went to work at a rape crisis clinic, in a slum between a sewer ditch and a landfill, in one of the saddest places in the world," she said. "I saw women there who'd had their tongues bitten off by the men who had raped them."

She saw girls, she said, eight, nine, who had vaginas as large as the top of the cup she was drinking from, girls with syphilis scars running down their legs. She saw five-year-olds who had been raped by six or seven men, and saw mothers who took their thirteen-year-old daughters to tents where they sold them by the hour for sex while waiting to take them back home to give them a bath and comfort them and feed them the food that the survival sex money had just bought. These mothers would have offered themselves for the survival sex, except the men did not want them anymore.

"People there," she said, "live so much of their lives on the edge. You walk into a cracked concrete building and you say to yourself, am I going to die? Then you see people sit on top of overloaded trucks going seventy, eighty miles an hour, accepting what we should all know, that life and death are beyond our control."

I was the one who was now avoiding her eyes. I couldn't even look at the cups from which we had been drinking.

"Why didn't you go?" she asked.

Because I was afraid of exactly what she was talking about. I was afraid to see it. I was afraid to know it.

"But you are privileged now," she said. "You can give something."

My parents had never talked about it, but my sense was that they had given everything. They gave everything so that I would never have to see this place Polly was talking about, experience it the way she had.

She had seen a few hopeful things though, she said, and when she came back, she had one of them tattooed on her chest, close to her heart so she wouldn't forget. Knowing her, I was afraid to ask what it was. I knew it would not be a tree, a beach, a hill, or mountain, a flower, or a butterfly.

One morning, she said, she woke up in the rape crisis clinic, where she was also living, and in the open window frame she saw clear plastic bags filled with water. The patients had strung them to the windows to keep out the flies. The flies and their many eyes, saw—it was believed—distorted, magnified reflections of themselves in the water and fled.

"How do you tattoo that on your chest?" I asked.

"The same way you tattoo a butterfly on your ass," she said, raising her eyebrows to make sure that her point had hit home. "But I had someone incompetent do it after I got back," she added, "and my tattoos look more like hot-air balloons than water bags."

It was the first time I had seen her smile that afternoon. I reached for her hand as she started for the door, but she felt my fingers brush against hers and moved ahead. As she walked out, her back seemed a bit straighter than when she had walked in.

Outside, the old terrier at the parking meter was gone.

Standing where it had been, she said, "My father would call my saying this redundant, but there is so much suffering in the world."

"What do you do there?" I asked, pointing at her desk across the street.

"I recruit more volunteers," she said.

"One day I'll have to go with you," I said.

"If you can handle it," she said.

"Can I come and see you again?" I asked.

"Sure," she said.

Then she raised both her arms as if reaching for something above me. Her fingers landed on the back of my neck, clammy and shaking, nervous. They traveled up my neck toward my ears then over to my cheeks, even as her face was moving closer to mine. She smelled like chocolates and cigarettes and I didn't think I would, but I parted my lips when hers landed on top of mine and right there in the middle of the street, with puzzled people walking around us and staring, we kissed.

I was shaking and my head felt like it was on fire and for a moment it seemed as though she was trying to pour into my body, through her mouth, everything that she was feeling, everything she had ever felt, things that she had said and things that she could not say, things that she had done and could not do. I tried to keep us linked that way for as long as I could, clutching her back and inhaling her tongue, but then, pounding both her palms against my chest, she pushed me away.

The rest of the world was there again. I still felt feverish and naked, as she turned around and calmly walked across the street. I watched her go through the office door, sit down at her desk, and turn on her computer. She turned her chair away from the street and said something to the other woman in the office and they laughed, a necks-pulled-back, mouths-open-to-the-sky type of laughter. I waited for her to look back and wave goodbye to me. She never did.

GOING BACK

EMMA RUBY-SACHS

Lawyer and writer Emma Ruby-Sachs (1982–) immigrated to the United States from Canada and currently lives in Chicago. Born in Toronto, she graduated from the University of Toronto law school as well as Wesleyan University in Connecticut.

Ruby-Sachs's writing has appeared in the *Huffington Post*, the *Guardian*, and the *Nation*, among other publications. Her first novel, *The Water Man's Daughter* (2011), explores issues of water access in South Africa, where she worked in 2003.

"I always felt like an outsider," says Ruby-Sachs. "But writing made me realize that being an outsider can be a force for creativity. It's something to be cherished, to be sought after."

Home Safe

He has cancer growing in his stomach, Ahmed tells me, laughing, through drags of the American cigarette he says tastes too light.

"They got Gauloises?" he asks.

"No, sorry."

"Well, what can you do." He takes another drag. Exhales slowly, staring at the sky as it darkens behind the thicket of maple trees.

"You going to Turkey after this?" I ask.

"Nah, going home first. I have some things to take care of."

"Family?"

"Yes, Dad's birthday, then a few meetings. Then Turkey if I can swing it for the National Council meetings."

"You don't want to just hang out here for a bit?"

He chuckles at that, but I'm not joking. I have the urge to wrestle his huge body to the ground and hold him here in the backwoods of Vermont, tie him to a country where I feel safe and he can too.

"How serious is it?" I wish I could take the question back the minute I ask it.

"Surgery. Then we'll see. I'll call when I know more."

I reach up and tear the cigarette from his mouth just as he is taking a drag. I feel my nails scratch his face and am immediately embarrassed.

"What the hell?" He looks annoyed for a moment and then softens, "It's stomach cancer, not lung cancer." He pulls out another slim smoke and lights it, breathes in, puts one rough hand smelling of ash on the back of my neck and exhales. "Nothing tastes good here. Everything is bland."

"You jerk. I just cooked you dinner."

"Yeah." He smiles. I take a step closer to him. The smoke swirls around us both and rises up into the clear night sky.

* * *

This conversation is what I think of when I hear the gruff voice on the phone line in the middle of the night. Our fixer from Turkey wakes me up from a dead sleep. He has Ahmed on the other line.

"They've locked his bank accounts, the city is under siege, they're kidnapping Syrians, Hezbollah might take Beirut tonight."

"Where is he?"

"At his apartment. They turned him back at the bank when he tried to cash a check and handed him a personal summons to the Minister's office."

"Was he followed home?"

"Yes. There's a car still outside. He said it was an obvious tail, no intent to hide themselves, probably just supposed to scare him."

"Okay. Call the U.S. embassy, call the Turks," I tell the fixer. "Let's get him out by boat tonight if we can. And get him to call me."

Later, when I talk to Ahmed on the phone, he sounds tired. He's not interested in talking through the next steps.

"I'm going to my parents' house in the mountains as soon as it's light. I've moved the rest of the team to the Christian neighborhood just outside of the city."

"We're organizing for a boat to take you out before then. Just sit tight and wait for word to move."

"I'm not going on any boat." He's amused. "I'm going to see my family."

"You have to get out. They'll arrest you if you hang around."

"They'll arrest my family if I leave."

"Then we'll move them too."

"You can't just move them; they live here."

He doesn't offer any further explanation. The quick back and forth is the same as always between us. My urgency does nothing to change his demeanor. I can picture him looking out over Beirut from his apartment window. I've stood there next to him and seen how the city moves in waves, spills onto the sidewalk at all hours, bleeding light from street to candle to shop window. All silent and black now. Hushed and blotted out by roving bands of men hell-bent on terrorizing a city for a conflict miles away.

The black car outside on the street has its motor running, just in case he makes a run for it. Just to let him know how ready they are. I hear a rustle, imagine him rubbing his forehead.

"Staying is not an option. You are tired, you've been traveling for too long, you're not thinking straight. Let's get you out until this dies down. Then you can go back."

"That will be months."

Years, I think.

"I can't do that. My work is here."

"You can work from Turkey."

Ahmed doesn't answer immediately, and in the silence I hear him thinking, hear the things he means to say:

> *You don't understand. You don't know what it is like to board a plane in an airport hot and full of men with guns and worry that you'll never see the tiled floor under a flag of home, never smell the smell of disinfectant and mixed spices. You don't know what it's like to run away from a movement of people who have so much less than you, and nowhere to run. Leave my family, leave the house where my father first taught me how to ride a horse and how to cook za'atar and how to play dominos. Leave the winding dark roads that take me in and out of Beirut, that weave so far into the sand that they end up on the border with Syria and I can spit on the land my family came from. I can smell home in the air here. I can taste it in the sand and the warm wind and in the sweat smell that seeps from the armpits of men at the bus stop. I can taste it in my food, in the water that never gets cold, in the coffee that is thick, black, and sweet. You can't ask me to steal away on a boat in the middle of the night. My feet wouldn't take me, my eyes would refuse to see the path, my heart would stop before leaving without knowing I could return.*

But instead, all he says is this: "If I leave, it will be seen as running away. People will talk."

"Ahmed, you don't have a choice here. You have to leave. I'm not letting you make this decision based on the opinion of a bunch of idiots who might use this to attack you behind your back." I take a deep breath. "Look, I know what this means. I know how it feels to run away. But it's the right move. Despite all the loss. You are lucky, we can get you out. You'd be crazy not to go, we've all made this hard choice, but it was the right one."

"I don't want your life!" His voice gets high pitched, like a teenager; the phone crackles. "You are literally disappeared, erased, nothing is left.

You have no music, no smells, no home, no family. You have nothing but this phone line to the rest of us who are still alive. You are dead and you are trying to kill me too."

At another time, this would have enraged me. I would have responded with an impassioned defense of all we do organizing human rights efforts worldwide, of all I do, living with the voices of people on the front lines who call for food and equipment and cars and doctors and money. But I'm too tired now. Maybe I have been for years. Maybe the memory of home is too far away to inspire anything but bare reason.

"If they capture you, they *will* kill you."

"I'm dying already."

True, I think, and my voice catches in my throat.

"This place is cold as shit." Ahmed doesn't move to go back inside out of the Vermont air, preferring to complain. He's leaving tomorrow. My lobbying has failed miserably; he says I should have known. I keep thinking one right word will convince him to change his flight, have the surgery here, let America swallow him up in all its safe, clean whiteness.

"It's chilly tonight," I respond.

"I bet it's always cold here. I know you chose to live here, but I don't get it. Everything is so spaced out, you are all whirling in these wide open spaces without talking or touching. Like you have to use it up without thinking about what it's costing you."

"You don't get it."

"Help me understand."

"I sleep here. The trees eat the noise, the grass soaks up the work day and erases it. This place erases everything. It's clean. It's safe. The phone works. Always. The phone literally never does not work. You couldn't imagine that if you tried."

"You ever miss home?"

"You're looking at it."

"I mean *home*. Don't be cranky with me."

"Yes. I miss my mother's cabbage rolls. I miss the way winter makes everything stark gray. I miss the church bells in Kiev. But there's lots I don't miss, too."

We fall silent. Vermont twinkles, mostly dark so that Ahmed's cigarette seems electric bright. I'm thinking about what blood looks like on snow.

The contrast of a red so light against the dirty speckled gray and white. I breathe in so the cold hurts my chest. It eats everything else away. I breathe out.

"I'm ready to get back," he says with a sigh, taking a last drag before stamping out the smoke.

I try once more: "I'd rather you stayed for a while. You could use a rest. You need to take care of yourself now, especially with this." I wave at his bulging stomach. He responds by shaking his belly up and down like a jolly old man. "I'm serious. I can give you a few months off and a chance to recover. I'll feed you. I promise."

"I can cook better than you."

"Probably, but the offer still stands."

"I love you, you know."

"I love you too."

"I'll be back soon for a longer visit. As soon as all this dies down. It will be soon."

"I'll be waiting for you."

He holds my hand and we walk back inside the wood-framed lodge. The fire is dying under the broad stone of the chimney's base. Here, they even give the fire too much room, I think. And then I am filled with the urge to pull it all in close, the fire, the great big room with stone walls, the windows fogging where the heat meets the cold.

A siren sounds softly, the only sound out of what must be a terrifyingly silent Beirut night.

"I'll leave by morning, before sunrise. I'll call when I get somewhere safe." My silence has ended his anger. His voice is familiar again.

"Bring a friend, rent a car. Don't just get in your damn Honda and drive into the open road where anyone can stop you and disappear you to god knows where."

"I'll be fine."

He sounds resolute, stolid like the mountains he is running to. Too big to wrestle to the ground.

"I love you."

"I love you, too."

He hangs up. I pull the blankets around my shoulder. It's so damn cold. Only September and it's already so cold.

LAWRENCE LA FOUNTAIN-STOKES

The author, scholar, and performer Lawrence La Fountain-Stokes was born in 1968 in San Juan, Puerto Rico. He moved to the United States to study at Harvard University. He received a PhD in Spanish from Columbia University in New York City and is currently an associate professor of American culture, Romance languages and literatures, and women's studies at the University of Michigan, Ann Arbor.

La Fountain-Stokes specializes in LGBT, Latina/o, Puerto Rican, and Hispanic-Caribbean studies and has published several books, including *Queer Ricans: Cultures and Sexualities in the Diaspora* (2009), about LGBT Puerto Rican migration and culture. His first book of fiction, *Blue Fingernails* (2009), was published in both English and Spanish. *Abolición del pato* appeared in 2013.

La Fountain-Stokes has written about "the incommensurability of language and experience for individuals who live between languages and cultures . . . and who have self-chosen or been molded by the dominant hegemonic language, English." His solo and ensemble performances for stage and video have been featured at venues in both Puerto Rico and the United States.

SJU–ATL–DTW
(San Juan–Atlanta–Detroit)

Mickey is a man, one might say, lost in a sea of contradictions. But are they really contradictions, or just a lack of sensibility? What exactly is Mickey's problem?

"Mickey: that's not a very Hispanic name," says Charles, a new friend he's just met at this party.

"You can call me Miguel."

"Very well, Miguel, how long have you been in Detroit?"

"Nine years now, going on ten. But I didn't know how to drive the first two. This is my first time in Indian Village."

"Is that so?"

"This is a spectacularly beautiful neighborhood."

"It's all right."

How long should you be in Detroit? Should you spend more time back home in Puerto Rico, or in other nearby cities like Chicago and Toronto? What ever happened to New York, where Mickey spent most of his twenties and a good chunk of his thirties? What would it mean for him to call Detroit home?

"How do you feel about Puerto Rico becoming a state?" Charles inquires.

"It's not going to happen," Mickey responds curtly.

"But the recent plebiscite . . ."

"About a quarter of the electorate left the ballot blank. And the pro-statehood party just lost the elections."

Charles is a handsome, middle-aged, white Detroit lawyer and self-declared political junkie who is fascinated by the possibility of seven more Democrats in Congress. Perhaps he imagines plucking one or two more from the island. Just then, our host, Robert, interrupts. "Miss Cindy Elmwood will be delighting us in the living room with some carols," he announces.

Miss Cindy Elmwood, with her black bouffant hairstyle and matching bow barrette, gorgeous black crushed velvet dress with a slit up her leg from here to infinity and a huge ruffle at the shoulder revealing a bit of creamy skin, eyes made out with green and white and yellow shadow, and a multistrand diamond choker holding it all together. She's accompanied by the incomparable Robert M. Nelson, self-styled comedian and entertainment impresario, the white queer mayor of Detroit—the very same one who stole the prize at Motor City Pride with his "Robert M. Nelson Presents a Salute to Robert M. Nelson, with Robert M. Nelson and the Detroit Friends of Robert M. Nelson" blue buttons and open-top blue-and-white convertible float featuring none other than Robert M. Nelson and the very incredible Miss Cindy Elmwood in a skintight maple leaf outfit that even made it onto the *Detroit News* website.

Now it's Christmastime and this lovely home in Indian Village is the setting for a sophisticated tree-trimming party, where Charles and Mickey and numerous handsome gay men in black tie and elegant ladies in evening gowns have gathered to listen to ravishing drag queens perform at the upright piano—that is to say, to behave like a charming audience until they lose interest and start chitchatting among themselves or just wander off. The handsome, alternative, multiracial gay men of Detroit—some of whom Mickey encountered just recently at a rather sordid bar, the infamous R&R Saloon, where they had gathered to dance to the beat at Mike Trombley's and Scott Zacharias's Macho City, with special guest DJ Gay Marvine, but instead ended up rushing to move cars parked in the wrong lots across the street before the rival bar called the tow truck.

"I just drove here straight from the airport," Mickey tells Charles.

"Really? Where are you coming from?"

"San Juan. I was there for Thanksgiving."

This is the story of Mickey's life, the back and forth between here and there, at a loss about where he is, or rather, unable to keep up with the demands of being here and there at the same time, not really knowing how long he wants to be in Detroit, but then again not really going anywhere else except for a week or two at a time, or perhaps just a few days, flying down to San Juan on Delta, stopping in Atlanta to change planes and eat some soul food at Paschal's in Concourse A before they closed that location and left him stranded. Where is he supposed to have his biscuits with gravy in the morning, or fried chicken with collard greens and black-eyed peas and corn bread and sweet tea in the afternoon? Fortunately, there's a new place in Concourse E in Atlanta—it might not be that new, but it's new to Mickey—Nature's Table Bistro, which miraculously serves cheesy grits and scrambled eggs for passengers who leave their homes at 4:30 a.m. in order to get to the Detroit airport by 5 a.m., hopefully without a traffic ticket from the disreputable police on the prowl for speeding motorists. Mickey now parks in the eight-dollars-a-day Green Lot, which is way on the other side of the airport, conveniently located close to the North Terminal—but that is not where Delta flies from so you have to add another fifteen minutes just to get to the right gate. But who cares? Who cares about Mickey's travails to avoid the twenty-dollars-a-day parking lot right next to his terminal, or about his thousands of dollars in credit card debt, a good chunk of which came precisely from constantly flying back and forth?

Ah, the lonely life of the gay Puerto Rican man in Detroit, who doesn't actually live in Detroit but rather in Ann Arbor, forty-five minutes away, a charming college town with a growing number of Mexicans and Salvadorans but so few Puerto Ricans, where his Dominican friends sometimes get stopped by the cops. That lovely city of trees, sitting calmly on the banks of the winding Huron River, cold and distant from tropical longings and swaying palm tree breezes.

"I love Thanksgiving! Did you see your family?" Charles asks.

"Yes. I went down for a literary conference and decided to stay an extra six days. Didn't make sense to come back just for a couple of days of work. How was your holiday dinner?"

"Fine. I've had two so far, and will be having the third tomorrow," Charles says.

"Have you cooked for all of them?"

"No, just for tomorrow."

"I haven't had a single piece of pie this whole Thanksgiving, just tons of flan: pumpkin flan, pistachio flan, cheese flan, coconut flan. Don't get me wrong, I love flan. But I would like to have some pie," Mickey admits.

"Puerto Ricans don't eat pie?"

"I think we do, just for some reason, no one was serving any."

While he was in San Juan for the literary conference, Mickey went to a reading featuring Giannina Braschi and her partner, Tess O'Dwyer, taking turns reading Giannina's work and Tess's translations and some of the crazy discussions in *Yo-Yo Boing!* where partners scream about looking at each other and not saying anything, and Tess and Giannina looked just like a bickering couple except it was all fiction read off the page. Giannina's new book *United States of Banana* has a section about the three political status options in Puerto Rico: wishy (independence), washy (statehood), and wishy-washy (commonwealth). Just like that, she has a character called Giannina who speaks with Hamlet and Zarathustra and Segismundo from Calderón de la Barca's *Life Is a Dream* and they battle it out between wishy and washy and wishy-washy and Giannina pleads for resolution and decolonization and clarity and an end to madness but you know it's not going to change.

When it was all over Mickey said hi to Giannina and she asked about their mutual friend Clara's mom, Doña Alfonsina, who had come back from the comatose Alzheimer's cloud they had her in. They all thought she had lost her mind but it turned out it was just the medicines they were giving her; three years in a complete daze. And when Mickey told his own mom, she smelled foul play and suspected it was all about getting Doña Alfonsina's inheritance money now that her daughter Clara is dead and there is no one to help poor Doña Alfonsina with her affairs.

It's just like the status of Puerto Rico, but in this case the haze was provoked by prescription drugs.

Giannina's reading was at the brand-new convention center in Miramar, which is not that new anymore—it must be a couple of years old—named after a rather corrupt former governor of the island, but that didn't matter to the overjoyed literary-convention attendees who competed with the National Dog Show and a local rum and beer expo to get to their sessions.

"This museum is fantastic," Mickey kept saying the first day, confused because of all of the great contemporary artwork on the convention center walls. "That's an Arnaldo Roche Rabell. And those there are by Carlos Cancio. I've been to his studio in Ocean Park."

He couldn't stop gushing about the quesitos they were selling at the concession stand, how you just can't leave Puerto Rico without eating one, whether there or at Kasalta.

"How can you possibly not live here?" a renowned Native American scholar asked Mickey later in the day at a Chicana lesbian book party in a Condado penthouse in a building off Baldorioty de Castro that was actually just outside of Condado (across the street, so to speak), smack in the middle of transvestite-hooker Santurce. "This place is just gorgeous."

"And a mess. I got mugged walking to the convention center last year on my way to see a French electronic band ironically called Justice. The mugger had a gun. And he was pretty handsome. But I hope you have a very nice time here."

"Oh, stop," the Native American scholar pleaded.

Mickey got caught up in the contradiction of agreeing with her about the wonders but not having any real job prospects on the island, not to mention the awkwardness of living near his family.

Several days later, he rolled his Rollaboard suitcases across the San Juan Luis Muñoz Marín International Airport on the way to security but not before stopping at El Mesón Sandwiches to have yet another quesito and a strong cup of espresso with hot milk for half of what it would cost closer to the gate. The restaurant was decorated with murals depicting the airport as it looked in the early 1960s, as it appears in that classic of Puerto Rican and Mexican cinematography, *Puerto Rico en Carnaval*, with the Mexican comedy superstar Tin Tan, the very extraordinary Johnny Rodríguez dressed as Doña Fela, the mayoress of San Juan, and Velda González in her signature role as La Criada Malcriada, driving everyone crazy at the airport with her lumpenproletariat ways. But there were no television or movie stars at the airport, none whom Mickey recognized anyway, even if the country's heart was heavy with the death of Héctor Macho Camacho then and about to be caught up with the drama of his wake in Santurce and funeral in New York.

My life resembles that of a boxer, Mickey thought to himself, although he hasn't been shot to death yet (Mickey, that is), and he's just struggling with his doctor's diagnosis of high blood pressure and high triglycerides, coping with a new regime of medications that have unpredictable side effects such as the painful leg cramps that snuck up on him while he was having sex with a guy he met at Aut Bar in Ann Arbor a couple of weeks ago, a jittery guy with a woman's name who seemed slightly out of it and kept asking for poppers.

My life is like that of a boxer, he thought, constantly dodging these punches, getting on and off that plane, walking down these airport corridors, losing my patience with the poor Delta employees who are just trying to do their jobs, finding comfort in my favorite restaurants as if they were my own personal hangouts. Hanging out in airport terminals the way some people hang out at the mall. Getting to know them like the palm of my hand, riding their automated people movers to get from one gate to another in yet another mad dash to not miss that tight connection, trying to squeeze in a meal when there is more time. But boxers probably get to fly first class, don't have to worry so much about getting a hot meal before a flight to and from this island that is and is not part of the United States—a country not foreign enough to warrant an international flight that would serve food.

"I don't understand why Puerto Rico doesn't want to be a state," Charles says at the party in Indian Village shortly after Miss Cindy finishes with her caroling and Robert M. Nelson brings the house down with a rousing rendition of "You're a Mean One, Mr. Grinch."

"Aren't Puerto Ricans tired of living in a colony?"

"It's complicated," Mickey responds, feeling like he's had this conversation too many times but willing to go at it once again. "It's a question of cultural autonomy. Look at what happened in Hawaii after annexation, and in the entire Southwest. Puerto Rico is a Spanish-speaking country with an Afro-diasporic population. Most people have serious concerns about what would happen if we became a state. And the historically pro-statehood party is currently linked to the Republican Party. There's also a progressive pro-statehood movement that talks about radical statehood, but they are not currently affiliated with a party. We have six political parties in Puerto Rico right now, and they don't line up with U.S. parties."

"You're afraid a bunch of white people are going to move there and take over?"

"It wouldn't be the first time, now would it?"

"So what do you really want? You, personally?"

"Well, for starters, I would do away with capitalism."

"That's not going to happen."

"Well, in my ideal world, Puerto Rico would be an independent country that is not subjected to the same poverty and abuses of power we have witnessed in neighboring Caribbean islands. It would be a place where people have the right to work and receive a living wage and live a decent life. And where drug trafficking to the U.S. does not dominate the national underground economy, and where people don't live in fear for their lives. And where LGBT rights are respected. That's what I want. And I will also let you know I voted for the Green Party in last November's elections."

"You threw away your vote."

"Thank you very much. I feel happy I voted my conscience. I live in a heavily Democratic district, where I knew Obama would readily win. I've been voting Green for quite a while now, except in the 90s when I voted for Joan Jett Blakk of the Let's Party Party. She's a black drag queen, you know."

"You don't say."

"Her name was not on the ballot, she was a write-in candidate. After Jesse Jackson's time but before Barack's."

"Miguel, let me give you my card. Look me up on Facebook. I'm going to get another drink and then I think I'm heading home."

So much for chatting with Charles, Mickey thinks. But there's still some hope; maybe an invitation to look him up on Facebook is more than a polite way to say goodbye. Mickey watches Charles fill a plate with meatballs at the buffet table where Mickey had previously had a coconut macaroon or two and dipped some marshmallows into the chocolate fountain to messily eat with graham crackers while he chatted with Robert's charming sister-in-law and Robert's brother and their friends.

Then there's that brief, awkward moment of not really knowing what to do, and restarting the mute CD player in the living room seems like a really good idea, as well as trimming the very prickly, cactus-like Christmas tree with antique glass ornaments.

"Are you having a good time?" Robert asks Mickey.

"The best, Robert. Thanks so much for inviting me."

"Of course! So absolutely delighted you could come."

Then it's time for Mickey to drive back to Ann Arbor, and Robert feeds him a baby carrot for the road.

PABLO HELGUERA

Born in Mexico City in 1971, Pablo Helguera is an artist and educator living in New York City. From 1998 to 2005, he served as the head of public programs at the education department of the Guggenheim Museum in New York, and in 2007 he was appointed the director of adult and academic programs at the Museum of Modern Art, New York. He is a former resident of Location One in New York.

Helguera works with installation, sculpture, photography, drawing, and performance. His art has taken many forms, including musical composition, performance text, fiction, and socially engaged art project.

Helguera's works include *Endingness* (2005), an essay and installation about the art of memory, *The Pablo Helguera Manual of Contemporary Art Style* (2007), a tongue-in-cheek manual of social etiquette within the art world, and *The School of Panamerican Unrest* (2006), a traveling schoolhouse that made stops along a route from Alaska to the tip of Chile.

Diógenes

Every man is born as many men and dies as a single one.
MARTIN HEIDEGGER

"Oh no!" little Diógenes screamed as he lost his grip on the blue string. Dancing like an angry serpent in the air, it quickly flew away, receding into the horizon line on the highway.

Many years later, Diógenes would ask himself many questions. What did it mean, exactly, to be constantly on the move and to live far away while knowing that another person, who he was convinced was none other than himself, would be sitting always in the same age-old diner, doing absolutely nothing? Was he waiting for himself to come back? The thought worried him. If there was something he feared, it was the idea that something would make him go back and embrace anonymity, immobility. He knew that, deep down in his heart, he was profoundly lazy and reactionary, and it wouldn't take much for him to assume that role.

That seemingly meaningless but actually life-defining incident with the string, and that peculiar case of waiting for himself back in some office-worker's diner in his old hometown were, without a doubt, directly connected to the lessons that Diógenes received from his much older brother. When Diógenes had not yet completed the first decade of his life, his brother was already a dedicated philosophy student at the university, philosophy being his lifelong fascination. (Not coincidentally— indeed, Diógenes's name was given by his parents because of the stubborn insistence of his then-teenage brother, who already loved philosophy and wanted a brother named after Diogenes of Sinope, the cynical philosopher who lived inside a jar. Nobody gave much thought to the symbolism of the name; the matter was settled because it had a nice ring to it.)

Diógenes's brother—who at the time was writing his thesis about phenomenology and Heidegger's concept of *dasein*—would overwhelm the poor kid with explanations about the German philosopher, as well as Sartre, Husserl, Wittgenstein, Bergson, and many others, with a sprinkling of modernist poetry à la T. S. Eliot. They shared a bedroom, where the older brother would study and type his papers on their dad's rickety Remington while the younger one would play with action figures. Diógenes barely understood all the complex philosophical concepts his brother would talk to him about (mainly a way for him to review for exams). In Diógenes's mind they took the form of epic narratives where the characters became some kind of superheroes. Diógenes particularly remembered the period when his brother was studying Kant and subjected him to never-ending explanations of the *Critique of Pure Reason*, the *Prolegomena*, and his transcendental aesthetics and metaphysics, most of which became a blur to Diógenes. The only two things he always distinctly remembered from all those lectures were, first, the simple fact that Herr Kant, who was a feeble man, would wear an elaborate contraption of blue straps to hold his stockings to his waist so that they would not cut off the circulation in his ankles, and, second, that Kant never left his little town of Königsberg during his lifetime, and yet still managed to change the world of ideas. That biographical fate was not too different from that of his namesake, Diogenes of Sinope, at least in the sense that both philosophers stayed put in the same spot throughout their lives.

Now, you might imagine that Diógenes would be inspired by such role models to be more homebound than not. In all fairness, Diógenes did have a particular affection for stability: he always loved the idea of going to sleep knowing that others were awake for him, as if they were guarding his sleep. Which is why he liked twenty-four-hour restaurants.

But as often happens with kids, when he became a teenager he rebelled precisely against the thing he was given as the lead to follow. And in Diógenes's case, it was that a priori sense of staying put that his own name seemed to suggest that he needed to do everything in his power to defeat. Furthermore, for all the things he wasn't sure about, he was certain he did not have the intelligence, talent, or eccentricity of any of those philosophers to pursue such a sedentary path.

So when the time came for Diógenes, the adolescent, to decide whether to stay or go, he decided that life could not be merely the acceptance of appearances and second-hand truths, but instead was a quest for what he considered "an authenticity that can only come from a yet unknown, lived experience" (this last phrase he thought he had borrowed from some philosopher, like Dewey, but it really was his own concoction). He needed to get away and feel a kind of triumph, a prodigal son type of achievement. It was thus paramount for him to leave his country.

But before we go back to the blue string incident, and Diógenes's fateful departure and subsequent odyssey, we should now perhaps talk about Diógenes's father for a minute. Diógenes's father was extremely generous and caring, bordering on overprotective. He was a businessman with a public persona that even during the greatest of intimacies felt businesslike. In truth, he was deeply introspective, with the extreme impenetrability of a fortress. He had no qualms about being emotional when he experienced art—he would weep, for instance, when listening to a Brahms intermezzo that Diógenes's grandmother used to play. But when it came to traumatic experiences, when he faced the death of his close ones, even his own death, his father's response was the opposite, becoming instead completely emotionless, numb. This attribute, which at times felt incomprehensible and even offensive to most people, Diógenes always understood perfectly. Diógenes agreed with Wittgenstein that what we cannot speak about should remain in silence.

Now, to the string: it is a universal fact that when you are a kid riding in the back of the car and playing with a string and you stick your arm with it out the window to see how it flaps with the force of the wind, it may so happen that you will accidentally let go of it, and it will be gone forever. That lost string incident becomes one of the first and most crucial lessons of childhood: the realization that when you drop something it may never come back. It is our preparation for understanding the concept of definitiveness. And what is also interesting is that, if you don't learn the lesson when you are supposed to learn it, then it may be too late when you finally get around to grasping its meaning. Which leads to a paradox, one that Diógenes was unfortunate to experience firsthand.

It's not as if Diógenes had not heard his brother talk about permanence and change. They'd had plenty of those bedroom sessions where his brother talked about pre-Socratic philosophers like Heraclitus, the philosopher of mutability, and his counterpart, Zeno. When his brother talked about Heraclitus, who argued that we are different people in each moment, Diógenes didn't quite understand. To explain, his brother read him a baroque sonnet by Quevedo that included the line "presentes sucesiones de difunto." This, he explained to Diógenes, meant that we are the current successions of the dead, that in a way we all die and are reborn every second.

But his brother preferred Zeno's philosophy. Zeno favored staticism, as exemplified by the famous paradox of Achilles and the tortoise, which went something like this: The philosopher asks us to imagine that Achilles and a tortoise are in a race, and that the tortoise is given a slight advantage at the start. In this scenario, Zeno argued, the speedier Achilles would never be able to pass the tortoise, as he would need to first cover half the distance the tortoise has already reached, and before that he would need to run half that half distance, and before half that, ad infinitum, thus preventing Achilles from advancing, and proving, in Zeno's view, that movement is nothing but an illusion.

You can imagine that when Diógenes would go to school the next day and explain these kinds of things to his classmates, who at the time were more interested in the Smurfs and Soda Stereo, they considered him, at best, a nerd, if not crazy or intolerably pedantic. Which is why he started to shut up in school, becoming isolated. He was convinced that he was smarter than them, but that was no comfort because he also knew he was vastly stupider than Kant and Heidegger and all the other superheroes.

Going back to that paradox: The fact is that Diógenes did not lose the string that time. He was holding it out the window to see it shudder in the wind while his father drove and his mom sat in the front passenger seat. They were crossing an overpass, part of the familiar route from their house to his grandparents' or school, or any of several other destinations. And then, at that very moment, the course of Diógenes's life was forever altered when the string flew out the window.

His father, always patient and benevolent to a fault, hit the brakes in the middle of the busy highway, amidst the protestations of his mother. He stepped out of the car and walked back a hundred feet. Diógenes saw his father in the rearview mirror, with his bright white shirt and tie, picking up the string in the middle of the furiously busy highway and walking back, holding it with both hands, smiling.

That was the beginning of a slight curse: from that moment on, nothing he would ever intentionally leave behind would accept its own abandonment and, instead, would come back to find him in some magnetic fashion wherever he was; these entities became, in a way, extensions of himself, starting precisely with that very string: it became his security blanket, kept discreetly hidden so that no one would ever make fun of him. A philosopher would have called it the string paradox.

A decade or so later, the day when he was on the way to the airport, moving to study abroad, he had spent the day packing, somewhat melancholically. The sun was setting and the sky was orange brown. In typically adolescent and melodramatic fashion, he thought this might be the last sunset of his native life. And then it actually ended up being true. (Sometimes when we are young we happen to be wiser than when we get old.) What would be strange, though, is the peculiar form that the splitting of his previous and future life would take.

Diógenes's brother, who was much more sedentary, never left their country. As a writer, he didn't want to live in a place where a different language was spoken, not even slightly different dialects. He was the true Greek Diogenes, the Emily Dickinson who almost never left her bedroom, the Kant of the two of them. As for Diógenes himself, he still didn't know who he was.

Diógenes sat in the left back seat of the car as they made their way to the airport. Night was already falling. He looked out the window at the last images of his country. Forced exile is definitive, and it likely carries more pain, but self-imposed exile is misleadingly gentle at first and perhaps more cruel in the end: by thinking that we can always come back, we lose sight of the likelihood that we may never actually return and that if we do, we will be someone else by then. Or that we may finally be the person we were meant to be all along, but it won't make much difference, as we will still be different from the person who left.

The streetlights became time-delay mirrors that seemingly absorbed the sky's orange-brown color of a few minutes before. They hit slow traffic as they started to cross that same overpass that they had crossed a million times. Under this overpass, there was a very familiar, if not particularly interesting, view: a large parking lot with a supermarket on one side and a twenty-four-hour diner for office workers on the other that Diógenes and his brother used to love, where they always had watery coffee and pressed ham and cheese sandwiches (they had very pedestrian tastes in food), and where, it being the only twenty-four-hour restaurant in town at the time, they could go at two in the morning when nothing else was open (although Diógenes never went there at two, he always found it comforting to know there was a place in the city that was open all night).

Diógenes looked at two office workers sitting at a table, having dinner, and at someone else out in the parking lot, stuffing plastic grocery bags in their car, happy family faces printed on them. He found himself envying these people profoundly; they were people who in some way were unaware of themselves, happy to be unquestioning victims of the circumstances of their uncomplicated lives. Who would have said that he would one day want to be under the lights of that supermarket parking lot, among those undistinguished and forgettable office workers who drink black coffee and chain smoke through the workweek? But he really did want to be them, to exist in that permanent parenthesis of life that was, in the end, life.

He profoundly hated the idea of leaving his friends, his family. He was afraid, nostalgic, on the edge, perhaps, of freaking out. And yet, he felt he would perish intellectually if he stayed. He couldn't live with himself. He wanted to leave but he also wanted to stay.

He had packed the blue string in the outside pocket of his bag—he had never separated from it since childhood. But that moment crossing the overpass felt very auspicious for enacting a departure ritual. He had the impulse to pull the blue string he had kept all those years and throw it out the window. It was time to let go, he thought.

The string flew away, almost in slow motion, almost appearing to defy gravity, falling over the bridge and onto the parking lot, where no one noticed but him; no one knew the immense weight of personal history that he had just gotten rid of. It was incredible that something he had kept for so many years could disappear in a second. He felt bittersweet relief, but also a strange sense that he had done something illegal, like throwing a dead body over the bridge.

Perhaps randomly, at that moment Diógenes also remembered a Heidegger quote that his brother once read to him when they were both lying on their bunk beds with their dark green comforters and the dark mahogany blinds of their room shut: "If I take death into my life and acknowledge it, and face it squarely, I free myself from the anxiety of death, and the pettiness of life—and only then will I be able to free myself."

The first time Diógenes realized he had left himself under that over-pass was probably three months later, when the novelty of his new town had already passed, and when the cold winter of his new country was starting to assail him. He was walking to the library that he had taken to as refuge. As the light started getting dimmer and he walked amid the thick snow, he smelled smoke from chimneys in a distant warmth and his stomach sank: he realized that he was still sitting there at that diner.

Sometimes we have these dreams of our long-gone childhood home, in which we suddenly think we remember that we left our pet—a dog, a cat, a goldfish—abandoned for many years, that we haven't returned to our room to feed it. That was the feeling Diógenes had when he first heard from himself, still sitting in that diner. (Let's just call that Diógenes "diógenes," in lower case, for the sake of clarity.)

Contrary to what you might think, after the initial shock, he was not particularly surprised, but instead somewhat oddly comforted. It made a lot of sense to leave himself behind, with that piece of string, not really having been left, as if the string still connected him to him. Yet, on the other hand, Diógenes felt uneasy. diógenes's presence served in a way as a reminder of his perceived failures to constantly change.

To him, the matter was settled anyway. He could not go back to live in that diner's booth. He would not fulfill the cynical mold of the Greek Diogenes. As a result, he tried not to concern himself too much with diógenes.

Years went by, and diógenes remained sitting in that '70s-style orange and ocher interior with large geometric ornaments on the walls, Formica tables and vinyl-upholstered and cushiony booths, just there, in his average everydayness, sometimes reading a book from his youth, sometimes watching the news or a soap opera on a TV in a corner of the restaurant. Diógenes remembered hearing once that they always designed these places with bright colors like orange and yellow in order to stimulate customers and encourage them not to linger in the restaurant, supposedly to keep things moving and make more money. In any case it was kind of ironic that diógenes had sat in that particular restaurant for so many years, outlasting legions of customers, waitresses, and managers.

A decade went by. He would, of course, forget for periods of time that diógenes was sitting in that diner. Every now and then it provided some kind of, let's say, existential reassurance. But at the same time he started becoming increasingly aware that he, Diógenes, was starting to look different from diógenes. diógenes was still a teenager: slim, nervous, and somewhat shy, full of hopes and vague expectations, a kind of Dorian Gray of orange diners.

Diógenes didn't feel that they were the same person anymore. Rather, they appeared to be competing for the same identity. In such a situation, Diógenes was in a much more challenging position, always trying to change for the better, without really knowing what, exactly, "better" was supposed to mean. While, in contrast, diógenes lived just to be there, fulfilling his existence by breathing in his own immobility, with the sole purpose of being aware of his own living entity.

In fact, part of the problem was that Diógenes had long ago given up attaching importance to that kind of quest for a "true" self. He married, moved to yet another country, too busy already to think too much about that teenager, who, nonetheless, would make himself be remembered every now and then. Perhaps also out of frustration, Diógenes eventually stopped using his first name and instead began using his middle name, Emiliano. More decades went by. Emiliano went grayer, balder, gained weight. As for diógenes, he continued sending messages to Emiliano every now and then, but they were more spaced out over the years. They usually came whenever Emiliano experienced strong smells or arrangements of light that suddenly led to a small opening in his mind in which he would see diógenes, always smiling, waving at him.

It was when Emiliano's brother passed away in an untimely accident that he received an urgent message from diógenes. It's not as if he never heard from him anymore, but this time around it was a strikingly clear message:

Now we are both the younger and the older brother.

Emiliano didn't quite need an explanation for that. He thought of it as irritating, condescending even. He had become more sedentary; his desire to explore the world had become extinct. He didn't feel that same urge to go around and explore the world anymore. Also, his brother's death made him more immutable in his feelings. He suddenly felt inauthentic, and all because of diógenes. When his father also passed away, Emiliano knew that he also had become like his father: more somber, quieter. He developed circulatory problems and started to wear non-elastic socks, often telling himself in the morning:

I grow old. . . I grow old . . .
I shall wear the bottoms of my trousers rolled.

Emiliano's relationship with diógenes became strained. He was now forty years older than diógenes, with illnesses, financial problems, low energy, and many of the worries that age brings. Emiliano didn't mind most of those things, but he knew that if he entertained further conversations with diógenes, the latter would ask him whether the use and tear on that mind and body had been productive, and he didn't feel like talking about that. In contrast, diógenes still seemed to be enjoying himself, sitting at that booth in the orange diner, using expressions and listening to music that fewer and fewer people understood today, looking at the office workers in their brown polyester suits with their mustaches (who, incredibly, didn't appear to have changed at all either), discussing the latest gossip from the office. Emiliano, now very seasoned, and probably with his most significant professional work behind him, had become permeated by dry thought and cold analysis. He regarded the exercise of personal introspection not only as a waste of energy and time, but something altogether irrelevant, something that only the feeble of mind would concern themselves with. And yet it bothered Emiliano that diógenes, who once felt only like a projection of his, had now started to appear as the real person onto which Emiliano was only a vague projection. He never said it, but in his own introverted style, he started to block diógenes from his thoughts.

Then, one day, as he was sitting waiting for a bus amidst a snowy day, standing under a heat lamp, Emiliano knew something had happened to diógenes. He had a sinking feeling, this time accompanied with an ominous feeling, exactly like the one he first felt as a child when he let go of the string and thought it was gone for good. Of all the philosophical thoughts that have ever been written, in some book out of those millions of philosophical treatises written down the ages, there has to be at least one that expresses the thought that the reason why eventful things happen when we are most unprepared is because we are, in reality, always unprepared.

He couldn't bring himself back to his country right away, but he eventually did. It was the very first time he had been back. After the airport,

Emiliano asked the cab driver to take him over the overpass. He stumbled clumsily while giving directions: he hadn't spoken his mother tongue in many years. He was also shocked to learn that he had forgotten the names of most of the streets.

It took them a while to find their way: the city was now completely unrecognizable from when Emiliano had left nearly forty years before. The roads had changed dramatically, overpopulated with street vendors, trash everywhere, half the parking lot occupied now by a new building that was like a low-class nightclub. What he remembered as new and impressive modern buildings were now in ruins. The diner was still there, but had clearly been abandoned for many decades. The windows were broken and gray with the dust of many years; the orange and ocher ornaments on the walls were discolored and decayed and piled to the side, as were the cushiony orange booth seats, all in a pile near a dumpster. There was no one there.

Emiliano had the vague sensation that he had been fooled, that he was somehow the victim of a practical joke. But he wasn't sure who to blame. There may not have been a culprit other than himself, even if it was the self that he used to be.

The following day he boarded the plane, this time certain that he was leaving for good. If he was conflicted about that fact, his attitude certainly wouldn't betray it.

After liftoff, he fell into the usual stupor you experience as the plane reaches thirty-six thousand feet. In that dream-like state, he imagined himself in a race with diógenes. diógenes was a tortoise, and Diógenes, or perhaps Emiliano, was Achilles, forever trying to outrun the slow-moving animal, trying to reach half the road, and half of half of that road, with all the velocity of the world descending into an infinitesimal cosmos of fractions and unreachable measurements, where the faster he traversed space, the more it appeared to translate into greater stillness, a present succession of dead ends, while the smiling diógenes, the modest tortoise, moved ever so slowly toward the finish line at the increasingly visible horizon, demarcated by a long, bright, blue string.

EDUARDO HALFON

Eduardo Halfon was born in Guatemala in 1971. When he was ten, his family moved to the United States, where he attended school in Southern Florida. He studied industrial engineering at North Carolina State University, and taught literature at Universidad Francisco Marroquín in Guatemala for eight years.

Halfon has written ten novels. His first novel to be translated into English is *El boxeador polaco* (2008), published as *The Polish Boxer* (2012). In 2007 he was named one of the best young Latin American writers by the Hay Festival of Bogotá, and won the José María de Pereda Prize for the Short Novel in Santander, Spain, for *La pirueta* (2010). He lives in Nebraska, but frequently travels to Guatemala.

In an interview with Joshua Barnes, Halfon shared that he "never felt that I belonged anywhere—not in Guatemala, not in the United States, not in Spain. I don't know why that is, but it's my reality. . . . I can pretend to be where I'm at: I'm very American if I'm in the U.S., and I'm very Guatemalan if I'm in Guatemala. . . . Yet I'm not really there." This ability to belong everywhere yet nowhere is a recurring theme in Halfon's writing.

Bamboo

I was drinking café de olla from a rusty blue pewter cup. Doña Tomasa had placed a kettle of the same blue pewter on the shack's sandy ground. There were no tables or chairs. The palm fronds on the roof were already black and frayed. The mild breeze stunk of rancid fish. But the café de olla was strong and sweet and helped to wake me up a bit, to animate my legs, which had gone numb after two hours of driving to the port of Iztapa, on the Pacific coast. My back was wet, my forehead sticky and sweaty. The heat seemed to increase the fetidness in the air. A scrawny dog was sniffing around on the ground, in search of leftovers or crumbs that might have fallen on the sand. Two barefoot and shirtless kids were trying to catch a gecko that was chirping above, hidden among the palm fronds. It wasn't yet eight o'clock in the morning.

Here you go, said Doña Tomasa as she handed me a tortilla with pork cracklings and chiltepe, wrapped in newspaper. She leaned on one of the shack's columns, wiping her plump hands on her apron, pushing her feet in and out of the warm volcanic sand. She had salt-and-pepper hair, weathered skin, and a slightly cross-eyed gaze. She asked me where I was from. I finished chewing what I had in my mouth and, with my tongue still slightly stunned by the chiltepe, told her I was Guatemalan, just like her. She smiled pleasantly, perhaps suspiciously, perhaps thinking the same thing I was thinking, and turned her eyes back to the cloudless sky. I don't know why it's always hard to convince people, to convince myself even, that I'm Guatemalan. I suppose they expect someone darker and squatter, more like them, and who speaks a more tropical Spanish. It's not like I ever miss an opportunity to distance myself from Guatemala, both literally and literarily. I was raised abroad. I spend long periods of time away. I write and describe things from the outside. As if I were a perpetual migrant. I blow smoke on my Guatemalan origins until they become opaque and unclear.

I don't feel nostalgia, or loyalty, or patriotism—in spite of the fact that, as my Polish grandfather liked to say, the first song I learned to sing when I was two years old was the Guatemalan national anthem.

I finished the tortilla and the café de olla. After collecting the check, Doña Tomasa gave me directions to a lot where I might park my car. There's a sign, she said. Ask for Don Tulio, she added, and walked off without saying goodbye, dragging her bare feet as if they were weights and muttering something bitter, perhaps a little tune.

I lit a cigarette and decided to stroll for a bit on the Iztapa highway before returning to my car. I passed a cashew and mango vendor, a deserted gas station, a group of bronzed men who stopped talking when I walked by them and looked at me sideways, out of resentment or maybe modesty. The ground was a layer of papers and wrappers and dried leaves and plastic bags and discarded green almonds, crushed and rotten. A pig squealed ceaselessly in the distance. I continued walking, slowly, unconcerned, and watched a mulata on the other side of the highway, too fat for the black-and-white striped bikini she had on and too big-assed for her heels. Suddenly my foot felt wet. Because I'd been distracted by the mulata, I'd stepped in a red puddle. I stopped. I turned to the left and looked inside a dark and narrow warehouse and realized the ground was littered with sharks. Small sharks. Medium sharks. Blue sharks. Gray sharks. Brown sharks. Even a couple of hammerheads. They were all floating in a briny mud of viscera and blood and even more sharks. The smell was practically unbearable. A girl was kneeling among them. Her face shimmered from the water or perhaps sweat. Her hands were buried inside a long slash on the shark's white belly, as she pulled out organs and entrails. In the back of the place, another girl was spraying down the ground with the weak stream from a hose. It was the fishermen's cooperative, according to a badly painted sign on a wall. Every morning, I imagined, all of the fishermen in Iztapa would take their catch there, and those two girls would clean, butcher, and sell it. I noticed that most of the sharks did not have fins. I remembered reading somewhere about the international black market for fins. They called it finning. I'd have to be careful later, I thought, in the sea. It looked like it was a day for sharks.

I tossed the cigarette butt and quickly returned to my car, almost as if I were fleeing from something. When I drove away I realized that I'd already begun to forget the image of the sharks. I understood that an image, any image, inevitably begins to lose its clarity and strength, even its coherence. I felt an impulse to stop the car in the middle of town and look for a notebook and pencil to write it down, to make a record of it, to share it through words. But words aren't sharks. Or perhaps they are. Cicero said that if a man could climb to heaven and contemplate everything that there is in the universe, the admiration he'd feel for all that beauty would dwindle if he didn't have someone with whom to share it, someone to tell it to.

After a couple of kilometers on a dirt road, I finally found the sign that Doña Tomasa had told me about. The lot was owned by an indigenous family. Their house was made from pieces of sheet metal, bricks, broken tiles, cinder blocks with rusted steel bars exposed. There was a plot of corn and beans, a few sad and lifeless palm trees. Chickens ran free. A white goat chewed on the bark of a guava tree while tied to that very same guava tree with a wire. Under a canopy, three young women sat on the floor and cleaned cornhusks while they listened to an evangelist preaching on a portable radio.

An old man, tanned and taciturn and still sinewy in spite of his years, approached me. Don Tulio? At your service, he said without looking at me. I told him I had been sent by Doña Tomasa, the woman from the shack. Right, he said, scratching his neck. A five- or six-year-old boy came over and took refuge behind one of the old man's legs. Is he your son? I asked, and Don Tulio whispered that yes, he was the youngest. When I stretched out my hand, the boy lowered his eyes and blushed at having to perform such an adult gesture. I opened the trunk and started to pull out my things when, as if emerging from an abyss, as if choked by something— perhaps the dryness or the humidity or the now merciless sun—I heard a guttural cry. I stood still. I heard more cries. In the distance, behind the house, I managed to see an older woman who I assumed was Don Tulio's mother, or perhaps his wife, helping a fat and seminude young man who wobbled drunkenly and stumbled to the ground, then kept on with his inebriated screams and headed straight for us. He was struggling to come in our direction. Whatever he wanted had to do with us. The woman, fighting with all her might, was determined to stop him. I averted my gaze, out of respect, or shame, or cowardice. No one else seemed very worried.

Don Tulio told me it would be twenty quetzals to park all day. I plucked a bill from my wallet and paid him while listening to the young man's moans. Don Tulio asked if I knew how to get to the beach or if I needed his son to accompany me. I was going to say thanks, that I didn't know how to get there, when suddenly the young man screamed something incomprehensible to me, but which sounded crude and painful, and Don Tulio immediately rushed off. Now strewn on the ground, the young man convulsed like an epileptic. The old man and woman were finally able to drag him away and pull him up behind the house, out of sight.

His howling, although softer and more distant, could still be heard. I asked the little boy what was going on, who the young man was, if he was sick or drunk or something worse. Kneeling, playing with an earthworm, he ignored me. Leaving my things on the ground, I slowly, cautiously, started toward the back of the house.

The young man was in a bamboo cage, thrown on a muddy floor, wet with water or perhaps urine. I could hear the buzzing of the flies around him. This one turned out badly, whispered Don Tulio when he saw me beside him, but I couldn't figure out if he meant morally or physically, if he was referring to a perverse behavior or an alcoholic tendency, a nervous condition or mental retardation. I didn't want to ask. I silently watched the young man through the thick bamboo bars. His pants were wet and semi-open. His chin was white with spit, his chest saturated with tiny fistulas and sores, his bare feet covered in mud and muck, and his eyes were red, weepy, almost closed. I considered that, for a poor indigenous family, the only option was to separate him from the world, to keep him away from the world by building a bamboo cage. I thought that while I could take a free day and drive two hours from the capitol to a beach on the Pacific simply to go for a swim, this young man was a prisoner of something, of some kind of evil, perhaps alcohol, perhaps dementia, perhaps poverty, perhaps something even bigger and more profound. I wiped the sweat from my forehead and eyes. Maybe because of the bright light that was coming in from the side, the cage suddenly seemed sublime to me. Its craftsmanship. Its shape and fortitude. I went near and grabbed two of the bamboo bars. I wanted to feel the bamboo in my hands, the warmth of the bamboo in my hands, the reality of the bamboo in my hands, and in that way not feel my own indifference, nor the indifference of an entire country. The young man writhed in the puddle, stirring up the swarm of flies. Now his moans were docile, resigned, like an animal that's been mortally wounded. I let go of the two bamboo bars, turned around, and went to the sea.

Roberto G. Fernández was born in Sagua la Grande, Cuba, in 1951 and moved to Florida at the age of ten. He is currently a professor of Hispanic literature at Florida State University.

Fernández has published novels and short stories in both English and Spanish. His two English-language novels, *Raining Backwards* (1988) and *Holy Radishes!* (1995), are both well-received satires of the Cuban American experience. Of his work, Fernández says, "The inspiration for my writings is derived from the aim to leave the constancy of the mythical land where we came from, an image that disappears little by little with the passing of the older generations and the integration of those that were born in the United States."

In his 2001 short story "Encrucijada" ("Crossroads"), Fernández focuses on an immigrant's return to her homeland and the ensuing familial complications.

Encrucijada

For Ambrosio from Bayamo

I had decided to go up the northern route to connect with Vía Blanca instead of driving to Santa Clara and hooking up with the central highway there. I'd been reading about the heroics of 1895 the week before, and I was enthusiastic about the idea of going through the towns of Quintín Banderas, Martí, and Máximo Gómez, following the route I had laid out. But the first town I ran into was Encrucijada. Because I'm a man who believes in symbols and premonitions, the sign at the edge of town terrified me. Luckily, it's a small town, so I breathed deeply and pressed the accelerator to the floor.

I was on my way to the airport to pick up Mercy's aunt, who was arriving at nine in the morning. I'd left at six the day before to have enough time in case of any setbacks. I am very cautious. To entertain myself along the way, I'd started to count royal palms. It's a prodigious tree, truly generous. Palm berries for hogs, hearts of palm for salads, fronds to make roofs for huts, bark for walls, and wood for pens . . . What I like most about the royal palm is that slenderness and elegance, which always reminds me of Mercy. In fact, the national currency should be called the palma. How sweet that would sound: How much is that goat? 150 palmas and 23 centavos.

When my mind starts to wander during a long trip, it's surprising what I can come up with. Of course, there are certain circumstances that lend themselves to this. For example, my idea for laundromats was the result of a drop of sweat that fell in my eye. It occurred to me right away that with the heat and how much we sweat in this country, if they installed automatic laundromats as you enter and leave each town, everyone would arrive at their destination smelling clean and not sweaty. It would be a pleasure to embrace each other and cordiality would reign.

I was about to go off on my third digression when I remembered the reason for my trip: Mercedes, which is Mercy's aunt's name. Even though it's been thirty-five years since they've seen each other, they're very close. They're namesakes, and that's how it is. Mercy was ten years old when they said goodbye. This is what I know: Mercedes is the only sister to Matilde, Mercy's mother. They had an uninterrupted correspondence for thirty-three years, a mystical number. That first Saturday when Mercy did not receive the monthly letter, she spent the day disturbed, depressed. The next day, she got up late. She didn't go to work, which is very rare for her. She is very dutiful; she's been named an exemplary worker three times. She made her coffee in silence and did not even greet the mockingbird that comes to the window every morning to hear her sing. I felt that listlessness in her as if it were happening to me. The truth is, I'm pretty aloof, except when it comes to Mercy. From that afternoon in which I first saw her buying sesame seeds at Pepe Gabilondo and Migdalia la Conga's kiosk, I fell under such a passionate spell that I've never experienced a moment when I might have looked at another woman. That first morning without a letter, in the early hours, Mercy began to sob in silence. She would stifle her moans in the pillow so that I wouldn't hear her. I threw an arm around her, pretending I was still sleeping. I did it that way so I could comfort her without her having to explain her anguish to me. That went on for innumerable sleepless nights until that dawn when she couldn't take it anymore, and she got up moaning and sobbing. She begged me not to make fun of her, but she had a presentiment that something had happened to her aunt; in spite of the years and the distance that separated them, they were still tied together by a special love. That love was inexplicable to me. I'm one of those for whom it's "out of sight, out of mind." But perhaps blood calls like drums.

There were many months of unease without any news from Mercedes. One afternoon in May, we received a letter with a return address from Consuelo Esparza from Anoka, Minnesota. The correspondent, a Mexican woman, wrote to say that Mercedes had arrived there two years ago after she'd been evicted from a senior home in Macon, Georgia, where, from what she understood, Mercedes had been living until they threw her out because she did not have the resources to pay. She went on to say that she had found our address in Mercedes's purse and imagined that we were family. She added that Mercedes had been admitted to Transitions Gardens of Rest, where she, Consuelo, worked on the cleaning crew, after her pension had been transferred over. Consuelo told us that Mercedes could not write because her hands shook too much, and that she had dared to write us a few lines even though Mercedes had never asked her to.

"And where is that place?" I remember Mercy asking, anguished.

"Judging by the latitude, it's a town buried in snow," I answered.

I should confess that if she'd been that worried about an uncle instead of an aunt, I think I might have been jealous. And God only knows what crazy ideas I might have gotten and what misfortunes they might have provoked. When it comes to Mercy, Othello learned everything from me.

The epistolary relationship between Consuelo Esparza and Mercy blossomed. In her last letter, the Mexican woman wrote: "All the Latinos who work in Transitions Gardens have raised enough funds to send Mercedes for a visit."

I arrived at the airport hours ahead of time, but I didn't approach until they announced the flight's arrival. People gathered, looking for familiar faces, and you could hear the rhythmic smacking of kisses and hugs. I wouldn't have to go through all that drama, which I considered pretty tasteless. I was exempt. I didn't know the old woman. The multitudes eventually dispersed, carrying the many trophies that had arrived for them from abroad.

I couldn't find the old woman anywhere. I was convinced the trip had been in vain, and I lamented not having realized it when I passed through all those towns with the names of heroes. I was more than certain that I'd wasted time, money, and time off work when a figure appeared wearing a blue hat, walking with a cane and with a white rose pinned to the center of her chest. She walked slowly while escorted by a flight attendant. I approached and read the sign that hung from her neck: "*Hello, my name is*: María de las Mercedes del Risco Castellanos. *Home*: Transitions Gardens of Rest, Anoka, Minnesota. *Final destination*: San Antonio de las Vueltas, Cuba. *Responsible party*: Mercedes Ramos del Risco. *Relationship*: Niece." Mercedes had arrived with a shipping label, as if she were merchandise. I identified myself to the flight attendant and spoke to the old woman for the first time.

"I am Mercy's husband. It's so good to finally meet you. Mercy couldn't come. She's getting everything ready for your arrival. She is so very happy."

"Oh, yes," Mercedes responded as she stared at the escalator as if it were humanity's most recent achievement.

Her interest in the escalator surprised me. She asked me how many steps it would be if it wasn't moving.

"Approximately seventy-seven steps," I responded. She appeared to not care too much about my calculations. This bothered me. I have a very good eye.

"And does it snow much in this country?" she asked.

I smiled at her for the first time. And I decided to go along with her.

"Yes, quite a bit. We celebrated the Winter Olympics here last year. But I suppose it must snow quite a bit in Anoka, as well . . . "

"Anoka?" She looked at me sunnily. "What's that, a bug?"

I laughed, thinking that I was starting to like this playful old woman. We walked slowly towards the car, and I helped her get in. As soon as she was settled, she looked around and asked what kind of car it was.

"It's a Citroën," I answered with satisfaction.

"Papá drives a Chandler. A Chandler Six with a green top and a Pikes Peak engine. That is something to see!"

In spite of being irritated by the disdain with which she referred to my Citroën, which I cared for as if it were a precious jewel, I offered her a cup of café con leche. Mercy had made sure I brought a thermos of it. She brought the cup to her lips, savored it, and remained quiet until we were past Cuatro Caminos.

"Autumn here must be dangerous," asserted Mercedes.

"What makes you say that?" I asked, surprised.

"Because when those palm trees lose their fronds in the middle of fall, a lot of people must get hurt. What color do they turn?"

I had also noticed those very same trees on my way to airport. And I don't know why I didn't respond, but instead changed the subject.

"Mercy is waiting for you. She's preparing some guinea fowl; you're going to lick your fingers. It's probably been a long time since you've had guinea fowl."

"So the hotel manager is named Mercy? What a coincidence! When I was young, I was also called Mercy."

"No, no, no. You're not going to a hotel. You're staying with us. Mercy is your niece, your sister Matilde's daughter."

"Matilde never had any children," she responded sharply.

"Matilde was Mercy's mother!"

I had raised my voice at her. I don't like to be contradicted.

"You must be talking about another Matilde. That is certainly not my Matilde. Matilde del Risco Castellanos never had a family. Felipe, her husband, died two days after the wedding. His death was a real tragedy: so young, so full of life . . . He looked like Clark Gable. They'd gone to Mayajigua for their honeymoon, and Felipe had boasted that he was an equestrian. There was thunder, lightning flashed, and the horse went wild because of the racket. Felipe never saw the low branch on the locust tree that decapitated him. Eventually the horse calmed down and galloped towards the lovers' cabins with Felipe's decapitated body still upon it. When my sister saw it, she was speechless. She didn't speak for an entire year. Matilde has been in mourning ever since. She never noticed another man. She's dedicated her entire life to making paradise plum sweets in the form of little horses."

I'd never heard of any Felipe. Neither Matilde nor Mercy had ever spoken of this Felipe. Mercy's father was Arturito, and if he'd ever resembled anyone, it was Sancho Panza.

"If you don't believe me," Mercedes continued, "we can call Matilde tomorrow, or we can go up to the beach to see her. We'll find her where she always is, picking paradise plums for her sweets."

"Your sister died ten years ago." This time I contained myself and did not raise my voice.

"You are crazy!" Mercedes said, smiling.

I kept my eyes on the road and tried to come up with a topic of conversation that would distance us from the headless horseman. But nothing came to mind. I'm not a great conversationalist. Words are not my thing. An hour of silence went by before Mercedes restarted our dialogue.

"And you, are you the hotel chauffeur?"

"Yes," I said, to not contradict her.

"These vinyl seats get very warm. They stick to your skin. Papá's Chandler has leather seats. If you want, we can stop by to see it, and maybe Papá will even let you drive it. I was surprised that they did not go to pick me up at the airport. When I didn't see the Chandler, I imagined that he had come to pick me up in the convertible. He knows how much I like to feel the wind in my hair."

Mercedes stuck her head out the window and kept it there for a long time. I thought that another car might come in the opposite direction and decapitate her. Mercy would never forgive me.

I tried to talk to her so that she would pull her head back in.

"I read that in Anoka they make tree syrup. Do you know what kind?"

Mercedes responded, but I couldn't hear her because of the rush of wind. I asked her the same question again, and she pulled her head back inside the Citroën.

"I don't know what you're talking about. The air here can make you feel drunk."

"I was saying that in Anoka, the town where you live, they make a tree syrup."

"I don't know what Anoka is, nor what tree you're talking about."

I turned my focus again to the highway, and we maintained silence until we entered Camajuaní. Then Mercedes brought me out of my self-absorption.

"Isn't there a town around here called Encrucijada?"

Why did she have to mention that place? My hairs stood on end.

"Yes, there was a town with that name here during the colonial period, but it doesn't exist anymore. The sea washed it away."

Mercedes accepted my false explanation.

"We're almost there," I hurried to tell her so that she would not think too much about my explanation and realize that it was impossible for the sea to have washed away Encrucijada. "You're going to meet your grand-nieces, Yameylysis and Tamysleisis."

"Those names sound like viruses," said Mercedes.

I almost stopped the Citroën to scream at her to get out of the car and finish the trip on foot, but I contained myself. I had named those girls.

"We're ten minutes from home," I said, indignant.

Mercedes did not respond, and instead began to sing a song.

> *Once I turn the four corners*
> *I run into a convent.*
> *It's a convent full of nuns*
> *all dressed in black,*
> *each with a candle in her hand*
> *looking like a funeral.*

"Mercy is dying to see you. And the girls are thrilled about your visit." I was trying to ease the tension.

Mercedes did not show a flicker of emotion and went back to talking about her father's Chandler.

"The Pikes Peak is the most powerful engine there is. What kind of engine does your car have?"

"I don't know exactly. It's a French motor."

"The Pikes is a real marvel. It can change speeds without any difficulty, go down hills with total ease, stop without skidding, and master any situation it's presented with on the highway. It's no wonder that Papá says it's a car made to ride on the boulevards, because of its style, and to climb the Turquino, because of its power."

Suddenly her brain put on the brakes.

"Where are we going?" she asked.

"Where?"

"You should know. That's why you're the chauffeur."

"I told you, I am Mercy's husband. She's your niece."

"My niece?"

"Mercy is your sister Matilde's daughter."

"Don't be so stubborn. Matilde never had a family. She found misfortune on her honeymoon."

"Yes. She did have a family. With Arturito, her husband."

"I'm telling you, Matilde never knew a man other than Felipe. You must be thinking of another guest at your hotel, *with another visitor.*"

I wanted to turn around and take her back to the airport and add a note to the sign that continued to hang around her neck, scribbling in large letters: DAMAGED GOODS. But I stopped myself. I went around the town twice before I drove home. I used every second to explain again and again who Mercy was. But Mercedes didn't want to understand.

"She's your niece," I said, one last time, almost out of breath.

Mercedes stuck her head out the window. By the time I saw the house, with its large porch and the two custard apple trees flanking the entrance, the girls were already running in our direction. The Citroën's noise had alerted them. I stopped, and the girls and their friends formed a circle. They surrounded the car and drummed on the hood and the trunk. When they finished with that welcoming dance, when they finally calmed down, I told the oldest to take the whole tribe back to the house, that her mother wanted to be alone with her aunt. My daughters are very obedient.

María de las Mercedes got out of the car without help, using her cane, and leaned on the vehicle. Mercy approached her and covered her in kisses. Mercedes was completely stunned, unable to understand. She looked disconcerted. I don't know why it didn't occur to me to stay there, at Mercy's side, for when Mercedes explained that Mercy didn't exist, that she was a product of the chauffeur's imagination. But it didn't turn out like that. I had started to walk away, towards the highway. I was contemplating a single palm tree. I don't know exactly what happened between the two of them, but I can tell you with certainty how many rings there will be on the trunk of that palm the day they decide to cut it down to widen the road.

Suddenly, I felt an irrational envy about Mercedes's father's Chandler. Where could that car be, so powerful that it humiliated mine? How many cylinders did it have? Would the old lady know where it had ended up? Or did they bury it with her father, like a pharaoh? I had to figure out a way to get the secret out of her. I was ready to go and interrupt Mercy and her aunt and ask her about the fate of that car when I was suddenly terrified. It was reflected on my temples, my veins were popping. Could there be a connection between the Chandler and oblivion? Would I later affirm that I had never married, never had my daughters? Would I end up denying Mercy, whom I loved more than anything in my life? I was pretty sure the day Mercedes had forgotten her niece, she'd begun to remember the Chandler. I went back home, but they were no longer talking. Mercedes was sitting in a chair, rocking as if she'd always been there, while the girls sat enchanted under their aunt's spell, listening to stories about the Chandler and the numbers from the Chinese lottery.

I went inside and looked for Mercy. She was in the kitchen making lemonade for her aunt. I closed my eyes and reviewed the image of my wife: her ample breasts, the curves of her hips, her strong thighs, her delicate feet, her smile . . . I sighed with relief. The Chandler's spell had not touched me yet.

"What's wrong with you?" asked Mercy as she dried her tears.

"Nothing, it's just that I love you very much," I answered.

"Aunt Mercedes doesn't remember very well who I am. I showed her the room that I prepared for her with such care, and she told me that I own a very pretty boarding house that gets a lot of light."

I didn't say anything to Mercy, I didn't comfort her with the lie that everything would be all right the next day, or make her confront the truth that she already expected. Mercy continued talking.

"Go out into the yard and butcher the biggest guinea fowl we have, the one with the broken wing. I'm going to make a soup."

I made my way to the chicken coop. There was the guinea fowl, with its broken wing, pecking at an earthworm. For no reason that I can discern, I called out to it: "Felipe, come here."

There was no resistance when I grabbed it to twist its neck.

QUESTIONS FOR DISCUSSION

M. EVELINA GALANG "Letting Go to America"

1. Why does Milagros believe that her deceased husband wants her to move on?

2. Why does Milagros finally accept her husband's dream of going to America?

3. Why does Milagros advise her daughters, "You better learn now, you can never love this much. You must learn to live independent of each other"? (9)

4. Why does Milagros make a shrine to her husband?

5. Why does Milagros believe her husband laughs when she feels she is being pushed toward another man?

6. What causes Milagros to change her mind about the possibility of leaving?

DANIEL ALARCÓN "Absence"

1. Why does Wari wander around New York "to forget everything"? (15)

2. Why doesn't Wari bring any brushes, paints, or pencils with him to New York?

3. When Leah tells Wari about Fredy and his Chinese wife, why does Wari want to say that "you can never know anyone completely"? (21)

4. As Wari prepares to leave his family, what is it that he feels "ready" for? (24)

5. What does the narrator mean when he says, "The grandiose illusion of the exile is that they are all back home, your enemies and your friends, voyeurs all, watching you"? (26)

6. Why does Wari tell Ellen that it "is good" that she sees violence in his paintings? (27)

POROCHISTA KHAKPOUR "Mother the Big"

1. Why does Mother the Big describe her new surroundings in America as "a fake place"? (36)

2. Why does Mother the Big repeatedly try to kill herself? And why do the attempts always fail?

3. Why does Moe tell Michael about his grandmother's first husband, the Butcher?

4. Once she returns, why does Mother the Big say she is "quite happy here in hell"? (51)

5. Is Michael's life in America a failure?

6. Does Mother the Big prevail over Michael at the end of the story?

ALEKSANDAR HEMON "The Bees, Part 1"

1. When the narrator's father begins to write, why does he write about bees?

2. Why does the narrator devote time to discussing "the conditions of his [father's] truth production"? (67)

3. Why is the narrator's father "oblivious" to Nada's wretchedness? (70)

4. What does the father mean when he says to the narrator, "You've become American"? (72)

5. Why does the narrator say that "it is easy to imagine" what the message of his grandfather's story might have been? (72)

6. What does the narrator mean when he tells his father "that Americans understand honey even less than Canadians do"? (73)

MEENA ALEXANDER "Grandmother's Garden"

1. After the house has been sold, why does the narrator say, "Perhaps now I can start to speak of it"? (75)

2. Why does Amma not answer the narrator's question, "Why did Grandmother have to die?" (78)

3. What does the narrator mean when she says that "beautiful things summon ruin" before describing her grandmother? (79)

4. While reading the Tagore play with her grandfather, why does the narrator think she is like the "girl with two heads . . . never knowing which way to look"? (89)

5. Why does the narrator say that the migrant becomes "hostage" to something in her soul? (93)

6. At the end of the story, why does the narrator ask, "Where else could you be?" (93)

JUNOT DÍAZ "Otravida, Otravez"

1. Why does Yasmin always feel better after reading Virta's letters to Ramón? Why does she add that she does not think this "says good things" about her? (102)

2. Why do Yasmin and Ana Iris choose the locations they do— the McDonald's, a bookstore, and the university—for the first photographs she sends home?

3. Why does Yasmin believe that "bread is stronger than blood"? (106)

4. What does Ramón mean when he say that women don't know "how to let go"? (108)

5. Why does Yasmin want to tell Ana Iris that Virta is writing again?

6. At the end of the story, why does Yasmin not open the latest letter from Virta, and instead give it to Ramón still sealed?

SEFI ATTA "Wal-Mart Has Plantains"

1. What are the criteria by which the narrator chooses friends in Mississippi?

2. Why does the narrator begin to research MBA possibilities, after stating she couldn't return to school?

3. Why are Rolari's parents not alarmed when she tells them of her ailments?

4. Why does Rolari say to her mother that "if you look after me, at least you won't need a work permit"? (127)

5. While the narrator is playing with Rolari after the fight with Sanwo, why does she want to cry?

6. Why is the narrator so keen to work and not to stay at home?

LARA VAPNYAR "Fischer vs. Spassky"

1. Why does Sergey want his son to perceive the act of cutting newspaper to use as toilet paper as a "courageous anti-Soviet act"? (136)

2. Why does Marina prefer to read random scraps of the newspaper? Why, when she reads them, does she realize that she doesn't "really mind the Soviet Union so much"? (137)

3. Why does Sergey choose to base the decision of his family's potential emigration on the outcome of a chess match?

4. Why does Marina decide she does not want to emigrate, and why does she hide her true feelings from her husband?

5. Why does Marina come to hate Fischer "with all her heart"? (139)

6. Why does Marina defend Fischer after his death? Why do her feelings toward him change?

REESE OKYONG KWON "The Stations of the Sun"

1. Why does the narrator say that moving to America "turned the six Sung brothers' blood to water"? (145)

2. Why does Annabel's mother tell her she went out in the car with the top down because she "wanted to see"? (146)

3. Why is it only after the death of her mother that Annabel ventures out into the sun?

4. Why does Annabel drive to the desert and lie in the sun for "a day and a night"? (149)

5. Why does Annabel want to keep her burn scars?

6. Why does Annabel tell different stories about her scars to different men?

LAILA LALAMI "Echo"

1. When Perry delivers the out-of-print book to Mona, why does she believe that his gaze and the gaze of others "was never neutral or dispassionate"? (160)

2. Why does the identification of the missing activist intrigue Mona much more than it intrigues her sister?

3. What does Mona mean when she refers to "an intimate quarrel with her sister"? (163)

4. When she sees herself in the windowpane, why does it seem "as if her likeness were coming to her from another era"? (164)

5. Why does Mona finally tell her sister the truth, that she has lost her job?

6. Why does telling her sister the truth about her job remind Mona that every life, including her own, is "tethered to that of others, to all the living and all the dead"? (164)

CAROLINA DE ROBERTIS "No Subject"

1. Why does the father want to retire back to Uruguay even though he views those who stayed there as "poor old fools"? (168)

2. Why does the father describe rage as "a source of comfort and distraction"? (170)

3. Why does the father remember his young daughter looking at him as though he offered "a map of reality"? (171)

4. Why does the father decide to open the e-mail from his daughter after all?

5. After the father thinks about the possible meanings of his daughter's message, why does he conclude, "She has only shown me a picture. Nothing more"? (172)

6. Why doesn't Angela include a subject in her e-mail?

YIYUN LI "The Science of Flight"

1. What does it mean that Zichen has become "accustomed to who she was in other people's eyes"? (182)

2. Why might Zichen think that holding hands with John is a betrayal of Margaret?

3. Why, every year, does Zichen cry in the car after drinking with her coworkers?

4. Why does Zichen feel "that in all stories she must be left out"? (188)

5. Why does Zichen see her life as a "life of flight"? (188)

6. Why is Zichen reluctant to tell the truth about her past?

EDWIDGE DANTICAT "Hot-Air Balloons"

1. What does Polly mean in ascribing to her parents "ambivalent parenting"? (193)

2. After Clio asks Sherlon what he wants her to do, why does Clio imagine numerous alternative fates for Polly?

3. Why does Clio's mother not allow her to stop to aid the injured dog?

4. Why does Clio withhold the knowledge of Polly's whereabouts from Sherlon?

5. Why does Clio go to visit Polly after the phone call from Sherlon?

6. Why do Polly and Clio kiss before they part?

EMMA RUBY-SACHS "Home Safe"

1. Why does Ahmed reveal his cancer diagnosis so lightly at the opening of the story? Why is the narrator's response to the news so different from Ahmed's?

2. Why does Vermont appeal to the narrator but repel Ahmed?

3. When faced with a threat to his homeland, why does Ahmed react so differently than the narrator?

4. Why does Ahmed feel so strongly that after migration the narrator is "literally disappeared, erased, nothing is left"? (207)

5. What does the narrator mean when she says, "Maybe the memory of home is too far away to inspire anything but bare reason"? (208)

6. What is the meaning of the story's title, "Home Safe"?

LAWRENCE LA FOUNTAIN-STOKES
"SJU-ATL-DTW (San Juan-Atlanta-Detroit")

1. Why does Mickey tell Charles that he didn't know how to drive the first two years he was in Detriot?

2. Why might Mickey feel he is "unable to keep up with the demands of being here and there at the same time"? (212)

3. Why does Mickey present Detroit as home when in fact he lives in Ann Arbor?

4. Why does the narrator compare Puerto Rico to the case of an elderly woman dazed by medication?

5. Why does Mickey point out the negative aspects of Puerto Rico to the Native American scholar?

6. Why does Mickey think his life "resembles that of a boxer"? (215)

PABLO HELGUERA "Diógenes"

1. Why does Diógenes believe that to pursue his quest for authenticity it is "paramount for him to leave his country"? (221)

2. Why, when being driven to the airport, does Diógenes envy those who are "unaware of themselves, happy to be unquestioning victims of the circumstances of their uncomplicated lives"? (224)

3. Why does the narrator assign the lower-case version of Diógenes's name to the one who stays, rather than the one who changes?

4. Why does Diógenes feel that he and diógenes appear to be "competing for the same identity"? (226)

5. Why does Emiliano think that diógenes begins to appear "as the real person"? (227)

6. Why does Diógenes recall the blue string long after he has abandoned it?

EDUARDO HALFON "Bamboo"

1. Why does the narrator struggle to convince himself and other people that he is Guatemalan, and then say he never misses "an opportunity to distance [himself] from Guatemala, both literally and literarily"? (231)

2. Why does the narrator describe himself as a "perpetual migrant"? (231)

3. What does the narrator mean when he thinks, "It looked like it was a day for sharks"? (232)

4. Why does the narrator seek out the young man behind the house?

5. Why does the narrator want to feel the bamboo in his hands?

6. Why does the narrator finally turn and head to the sea?

ROBERTO G. FERNÁNDEZ "Encrucijada"

1. Why is the narrator terrified by the sign at the edge of Encrucijada?

2. Why does Mercy become depressed and anxious when she doesn't receive the regular letters from her aunt?

3. When Mercy cries in the early morning hours, why does the narrator want to "comfort her without her having to explain her anguish" to him? (238)

4. Why does the narrator think that "perhaps blood calls like drums," even though such a connection is "inexplicable" to him? (238)

5. Why does Mercedes's memory of her sister's honeymoon upset the narrator?

6. Why does the narrator feel that "words are not my thing"? (241)

ACKNOWLEDGMENTS

All possible care has been taken to trace ownership and secure permission for each selection in this anthology. The Great Books Foundation wishes to thank the following authors, publishers, and representatives for permission to reproduce copyrighted material:

Letting Go to America, by M. Evelina Galang. Copyright © 2013 by M. Evelina Galang. Reproduced by permission of the author.

Absence, from WAR BY CANDLELIGHT, by Daniel Alarcón. Copyright © 2013 by Daniel Alarcón. Reproduced by permission of the author.

Mother the Big, by Porochista Khakpour. Copyright © 2013 by Porochista Khakpour. Reproduced by permission of the author.

The Bees, Part 1, from LOVE AND OBSTACLES, by Aleksandar Hemon. Copyright © 2009 by Aleksandar Hemon. Reproduced by permission of Riverhead Books, an imprint of Penguin Group (USA), LLC.

Grandmother's Garden, by Meena Alexander. Copyright © 2013 by Meena Alexander. Reproduced by permission of the author.

Otravida, Otravez, from THIS IS HOW YOU LOSE HER, by Junot Díaz. Copyright © 2012 by Junot Díaz. Reproduced by permission of Riverhead Books, an imprint of Penguin Group (USA), LLC.

Wal-Mart Has Plantains, by Sefi Atta. Previously published in the *Crab Orchard Review*. Copyright © 2004 by Sefi Atta. Reproduced by permission of the author.

Fischer vs. Spassky, by Lara Vapnyar. Previously published in the *New Yorker*. Copyright © 2012 by Lara Vapnyar. Reproduced by permission of the author.

The Stations of the Sun, by Reese Okyong Kwon. First published in the *Kenyon Review*. Copyright © 2011 by Reese Okyong Kwon. Reproduced by permission of the author.

COVER (from left to right)